So Much Aid, So Little Development

So Much Aid, So Little Development

Stories from Pakistan

Samia Waheed Altaf

Woodrow Wilson Center Press
Washington, D.C.

The Johns Hopkins University Press
Baltimore

EDITORIAL OFFICES

Woodrow Wilson Center Press
One Woodrow Wilson Plaza
1300 Pennsylvania Avenue, N.W.
Washington, D.C. 20004-3027
Telephone: 202-691-4029
www.wilsoncenter.org/press

ORDER FROM

The Johns Hopkins University Press
Hampden Station
P.O. Box 50370
Baltimore, Maryland 21211
Telephone: 1-800-537-5487
www.press.jhu.edu/books/

Library of Congress Cataloging-in-Publication Data

Altaf, Samia Waheed.
    So much aid, so little development : stories from Pakistan / Samia Waheed Altaf.
        p. cm.
    Includes bibliographical references and index.
    ISBN 978-1-4214-0137-9
    1. Economic assistance—Pakistan.   2. Pakistan—Economic conditions.   I. Title.
    HC440.5.A48 2011
    338.91095491—dc22

                                                                                    2010053430

**Woodrow Wilson
International
Center
for Scholars**

The Woodrow Wilson International Center for Scholars is the national, living U.S. memorial honoring President Woodrow Wilson. In providing an essential link between the worlds of ideas and public policy, the Center addresses current and emerging challenges confronting the United States and the world. The Center promotes policy-relevant research and dialogue to increase understanding and enhance the capabilities and knowledge of leaders, citizens, and institutions worldwide. Created by an Act of Congress in 1968, the Center is a nonpartisan institution headquartered in Washington, D.C., and supported by both public and private funds.

Conclusions or opinions expressed in Center publications and programs are those of the authors and speakers and do not necessarily reflect the views of the Center's staff, fellows, trustees, or advisory groups, or any individuals or organizations that provide financial support to the Center.

The Center is the publisher of *The Wilson Quarterly* and home of Woodrow Wilson Center Press and *dialogue* television and radio. For more information about the Center's activities and publications, including the monthly newsletter *Centerpoint,* please visit us on the web at www.wilsoncenter.org.

For Anjum

Contents

Preface   xi

Acknowledgments   xv

Introduction: Why This Story Needs to Be Told   1

1 Meeting Lucymemsahib and Starting Our Project   14

2 The Organization of Our Project   24

3 The Pakistan Nursing Council: A Dead End   33

4 The Allama Iqbal Open University's Bureau of University
  Extensions and Special Programs   45

5 The Women's Division: A Brief Encounter of the Worst Kind   56

6 The Population Welfare Division: To Be or Not to Be . . .   64

7 Regional Training Institutes and Other Such Things   81

8 A Day in the Life of a Provincial Health Department   99

9 The UNICEF and UNDP Workshop and the Sindh
  SAP Proposal   122

10 The Punjab Proposal and the Firing of the Learned Dr.
   Sahiba: . . . And That's the Way It Is . . .   142

11 The Immunization Program in the North-West Frontier
   Province   154

12 Bank's World: Witches' Oil and Lizards' Tails   178

13 Packed, Sealed, and Delivered: Our Project Is Finished—
    in More Ways Than One   187

Epilogue: The Beat Goes On . . .   195

Index   199

Preface

This book is about one participant's understanding of why international development projects fail in Pakistan—and also, by analogy, why they fail in other developing countries. The book is in the form of a set of interleaved vignettes within a larger story about the people, places, and organizations and the hopes, frustrations, and ambitions that I encountered during my journey through the life of one development project in Pakistan, the Social Action Program. The book examines the project on many levels—policy, implementation, governance, training, and monitoring—and explores the myriad causes, both large and small, that undermine the most elaborate plans and the best intentions. Anyone who has worked on or been affected by a development project has seen this in living color, from bureaucratic absurdity, questionable starting points, and inadequate frameworks at the highest levels to the unintended consequences of one man's attitude, one expert's assumptions, or one person's bad day at the smallest scale.

At one level, this book is about the "how" and "why" of foreign assistance—how and why it succeeds or fails in developing countries. It is about the growing dependence of developing countries on international agencies like the World Bank and bilateral donors like the U.S. Agency for International Development, and about the forces that are set in motion when large amounts of money flow into the coffers of countries whose decisionmakers may not consider themselves accountable to their people.

On another level, the book is an inside look at the bureaucracies, of both donors and recipients, that together "deliver" a development project. The interactions of these agencies are moderated by the very human demands and dreams—a tight schedule here, a foreign trip there—that go into the making or unmaking of a project. The book runs the gamut, from the major bilateral and multilateral donor institutions and the Government of Pakistan's administrative agencies to the many small and specialized organizations associated with the social sectors in Pakistan.

The book can also be read as a story about women in Pakistan. It attempts to portray their vulnerabilities in a society that, despite its rhetoric of inclusion and "women in development," refuses to accept them as equals. Those who are professionals in their own right are forced to use the positions of male relatives to maintain their own jobs or simply function effectively. Those who choose not to accept this subordination, or who lack such male support, expose themselves and their families to hostility and discrimination that come in subtle and not-so-subtle ways, from intimidation to sexual harassment. The status of women in the development process remains perilous. Every day they face many hurdles, and they must juggle their roles as mothers, wives, and daughters while trying to live and work effectively in an environment that relegates them to a secondary position.

In the end, this is a book about people. It consists of day-by-day, individual stories, which hopefully coalesce to reveal a larger landscape. It is about both the ordinary people in whose name development is orchestrated and the privileged ones doing the orchestration. The main character in the book is a Canadian woman who epitomizes for me the typical consultant brought in by any donor agency. I have called her "Lucymemsahib," based on the character in Paul Scott's *Staying On,* the epilogue to the Raj Quartet, his series of four wonderful novels set in British India. As in Scott's world, foreigners' and natives' perceptions of each other and of themselves are constantly changing—sometimes in response to the interactions of the rulers and the ruled, and sometimes in reaction to small and large events controlled by neither—and in turn they influence unfolding outcomes in unexpected ways.

Finally, the book is also my story: the story of a woman born and raised in Pakistan, who has experienced the torments, tortures, and hypocrisies of a schizophrenic country perpetually on the path to self-destruction while demons from its uncertain future and its fractured past continue to haunt its present—a country that has lost generations of men and women to ignorance and deprivation, and continues to lose more; a sad country that is still so beautiful and so rich in history; a country with towering mountains, scorching deserts, clear lakes, glorious birds, magnificent flowers, brilliant sunshine, inspiring legends, fabulous poetry, haunting music, and delicious food. Above all, the book seeks to portray Pakistan's wonderful people, so warm and hospitable, resilient and optimistic, who cooperate with us as we "do development," who continue to hope for the best and expect the worst from international assistance, technical consultants, and expert advice from development-bearing authorities—and who, when all is said and done, somehow survive and go on.

The characters, events, and physical locations that appear in this book are all true to life, though their names have been changed, for obvious reasons. Although I call this a story, it is a portrayal of the people and institutions involved in and the events triggered by the process of putting together a specific development project in Pakistan. I hope that this portrait provides new insights into the human complexity involved in issues of development, not only in Pakistan but also in many other countries.

> Aa gayee aap ko Maseeha'ii,
> Marnay waalon ko marhaba kahiyay. . . .
>
> (Applaud those who die,
> They are the ones who give you the opportunity to be the Messiah. . . .)
>
> —Faiz Ahmad Faiz

Acknowledgments

I owe an enormous debt to the many people who have contributed to this book, among them all the dear Pakistani men and women who welcomed me into their lives and helped me understand aspects of health care service delivery that I could never learn from books, and also my professional colleagues, who forced me to think of alternatives when I disagreed with them. I am grateful to my parents, Waheed and Saleema, who gave me enormous love and showed me that one could dare and do anything.

Akbar Noman was the first to suggest that I write these stories down; Aly Ercelawn read an early draft and encouraged me to keep going. The Fellowship Fund for Pakistan supported the completion of the book, and the Woodrow Wilson International Center for Scholars provided a stimulating environment in which to do so and wonderful colleagues who helped shape my arguments. For their good cheer and encouragement, I thank my colleagues in the Center's Asia Program, Sooyee Choi, Robert Hathaway, Michael Kugelman, Sue Levenstein, and Mark Mohr. I am also grateful to my interns at the Center, Neil Kumar and Lam Huynh. I benefitted enormously from John Sewell's critical reading of this manuscript and from discussions with William Milam. George Seay was the first to read this manuscript. I remain grateful for his encouragement and am sorry he was not able to see this book in print.

I am also grateful to the editorial staff at the Woodrow Wilson Center Press, including Joseph Brinley and Yamile Kahn, and to the copyeditor, Alfred Imhoff, for their invaluable help in bringing this book together.

My family has lived with this book for many years, my children for all their lives, and has contributed to it in many ways. Kabir's love for stories about children and about the adventures of Lucymemsahib sowed the seeds of the book. Hasan, who makes a cameo appearance as a baby, brought a poetic sensibility and a nuanced understanding of South Asian culture to give the book its final editorial polish. To Anjum, my partner in crimes of head and heart, I owe more than I can say, for taking care of home and hearth and of our children while I traveled, and for his critical reading of the manuscript at every stage. I dedicate this book to him.

So Much Aid, So Little Development

Introduction:
Why This Story Needs to Be Told

Developing countries have been receiving aid and assistance for many years, but it is now clear that, in most, the social sectors have failed to respond sufficiently to the strategic interventions of the past. People involved with the development sector know how foreign aid is theoretically supposed to work, but they are equally familiar with the sense of failure and frustration they encounter a couple years down the line, when a project does not work out the way it was meant to. Then the blame game begins, with managers charged with corruption and mismanagement, locals blaming international experts, and political instability becoming, in some countries, the most convenient scapegoat. The upshot of all of this, however, is that it is no longer possible to deny that there is a serious problem in the structure of foreign aid.

During the past few decades, international criticism of this failure has been growing more insistent. In 1996, Howard French wrote in *The New York Times* that "three decades of foreign development assistance in the third world has failed to lift the poorest of the poor in Africa and Asia much beyond where they have always been."[1] Even the World Bank itself has recognized the need for change; in 1997, its president, James Wolfensohn, recommended sweeping changes within the institution, with "the intent . . . to signal a more fundamental shift in the approach to development."[2]

The chorus of criticism is particularly loud, and particularly critical, in the case of Pakistan, especially as the country has become a key partner in

1. Howard French, "Donors of Foreign Aid Have Second Thoughts," *New York Times,* April 7, 1996.
2. Richard W. Stevenson, "World Bank Chief Asks Slimmer Staffs and Better Lending," *The New York Times,* February 21, 1997.

the war against terror while simultaneously sliding into instability and religious fundamentalism. It is clearly understood that one of the causes of Pakistan's perennial instability is its lack of social services, and money has been poured in to improve these (between 1960 and 1998, the country received $58 billion, in 1995 dollars, of foreign development assistance), but the fact remains that development programs in Pakistan have yielded extremely disappointing results.[3] The money has not produced improvements in service delivery for the people of Pakistan, nor has it created goodwill for those doing the giving, such as the American taxpayer. With more money now being diverted now to Pakistan, as in the U.S. Kerry-Lugar-Berman legislation, which authorizes $7.5 billion in economic assistance over five years, there is understandable anxiety among U.S. policymakers: What if this assistance also fails?[4]

Depending on one's perspective, there are many possible explanations for the failures of social-sector development in the past. The economist William Easterly, for one, has called it a case of "growth without development," citing reasons of political economy.[5] Ruth Levine of the Center for Global Development, a Washington-based policy think tank, has argued that the operational aspects of the programs might be the cause; testifying before Congress in March 2006, she said that "independent impact evaluation is crucial for ensuring that the billions of dollars spent on development actually helps poor people."[6] In a comprehensive analysis of the Government of Pakistan's and World Bank's overall development policy during the 1990s, Nancy Birdsall and others determined that poor program design and implementation were the culprits.[7]

I have worked for almost three decades in public health and program

3. William Easterly, *The Political Economy of Growth without Development: A Case Study of Pakistan,* Development Research Group Report (Washington, D.C.: World Bank, 2001), 2.

4. Nancy Birdsall, Wren Elhai, and Molly Kinder, *Beyond Short-Term Thinking: How to Spend Billions Well in Pakistan, for Them and for Us* (Washington, D.C.: Center for Global Development, 2010), http://www.cgdev.org/content/publications/detail/1424399.

5. Easterly, *Political Economy.*

6. Ruth E. Levine, Director of Programs and Senior Fellow, Center for Global Development, "Testimony to the Senate Committee on Foreign Relations," March 28, 2006.

7. Nancy Birdsall, Adeel Malik, and Milan Vaishnav, "Poverty and the Social Sectors: The World Bank in Pakistan 1990–2003, prepared for World Bank's Operations Evaluation Department," Center for Global Development, Washington, D.C., June 1, 2005, and revised August 29, 2005.

development in the United States and in Pakistan, most recently with the Pakistan Mission of the U.S. Agency for International Development, and I have seen firsthand the continued failure of donor-supported health and population programs in Pakistan. My own understanding of this situation is that program designs are based on limited conceptual frameworks that reflect a woefully inadequate knowledge of local realities, and thus are inappropriate in the context of national constraints. We are, as of now, continuing to implement these outdated, failed models. To be able to improve program design for the future, we first need to understand the contextual complexities.

This book is an effort in that direction. It examines the larger context within which the health services delivery programs are meant to function. It tries to explain how the health and population sectors in Pakistan have arrived at their present state, why very large infusions of assistance have had a minimal impact on the relevant indicators, and how available resources might be better used. It describes the institutional weaknesses that are impediments to successful implementation. It does this by following the program design process for the Social Action Program, a comprehensive social-sector development project undertaken by the Government of Pakistan. It describes the hurdles and pitfalls encountered during this process, in the hope that we can overcome these impediments and begin to design service delivery programs that are contextually appropriate, technically sound, and fiscally sustainable.

The Social Action Program

The Social Action Program (SAP), a major social-sector development program initiated during the 1990s and implemented from 1993 to 2003, was the Government of Pakistan's and the World Bank's primary policy vehicle for service improvement. It was a multiyear and multidisciplinary program, whose primary objectives were to increase access to social services—including primary education, with a particular focus on girls; primary health; family planning; the rural water supply; and sanitation—and to improve their coverage and quality. It proposed to upgrade the existing service delivery system for primary health care through basic health units and rural health centers, and to recruit and train community health workers. Similar human resource targets were set to improve nutrition, family planning, and the supply of potable water. Immunization coverage in the provinces of

Balochistan and Sindh was to be increased by focusing support on the national Expanded Program of Immunization. The SAP cost the Government of Pakistan close to $8 billion, of which $450 million was in loans.[8]

Problems with the SAP were apparent early on. Writing in the national Pakistani newspaper *Dawn* in 1994, a year after the start of the program, Shahid Kardar noted that "any unbiased assessment of SAP-1 [the first phase of the program] will have to concede failure in achieving any of the key objectives of SAP."[9] Even on moral grounds, Kardar felt there was no justification to continue the program beyond its first phase, which ended in 1998. After the fact, the World Bank itself ranked the program's performance mostly as unsatisfactory,[10] and in its approach to the Ninth Five-Year Plan, the Government of Pakistan too acknowledged that in spite of the generous funding, the SAP had been unable to provide "a consistent policy framework for the autonomy of public institutions and facilitation of private institutions, or made much headway in community participation."[11] The SAP fell short of achieving even its first-level targets, and it is now considered largely a failure.

Basic Questions

This postproject hand-wringing is by now familiar. It has happened repeatedly over the years with respect to numerous programs all over the developing world, and it will continue to happen unless there is a fundamental change in development strategy—a paradigm shift. To that end, before going forward, it is important to back up and ask a few basic questions, which really add up to one question: Why?

Why do good ideas continue to turn into practical disasters? Why does the service delivery system fail to deliver in spite of expensive improvements? Why has this situation persisted for so many years?

8. Nancy Birdsall and Molly Kinder, *The U.S. Aid 'Surge' to Pakistan: Repeating a Failed Experiment? Lessons for U.S. Policymakers from the World Bank's Social-Sector Lending in the 1990s,* CGD Working Paper 205 (Washington, D.C.: Center for Global Development, 2010), 3. http://www.cgdev.org/content/publications/detail/1423965.

9. Shahid Kardar, *Dawn,* April 20, 1994.

10. World Bank, "Implementation Completion and Results Report," Report 26216, 2003, 6.

11. Planning Commission, Government of Pakistan, *Ninth Five-Year Plan* (Islamabad: Planning Commission, 1998).

Program evaluation reports routinely document poor results, yet agree that the program's objectives have been met. Whose objectives?

Programs are reviewed and approved only after they fulfill the national sector's needs and satisfy the donor agency's internal requirements, but they are completely out of context with the reality of the situations they intend to address. Somehow, the Web sites of donor agencies are still full of "success stories." Success from which perspective?

The problem is larger than it appears on the surface. As development experts like to say, it's the nature of the beast.

The Development "Beast"

The literature attempting to pin down the nature of the development "beast" is extensive, and its conclusions are numerous. Developing countries are an amalgam of outmoded, decayed institutions; they have poor human resources; they are mired in political instability, subject to push and pull factors outside their control; and they sit on extremely shaky foreign reserves. These concerns become overriding at the policymaking level. In the case of the Government of Pakistan's motivation for the SAP, Shahid Kardar wrote in *Dawn* that "this apparent impropriety is invariably driven by the urgent need to raise foreign exchange for the national kitty."[12]

The role of international loan-giving agencies, both multilateral and bilateral, has also been analyzed from various perspectives. It is clear that their policy staffs are under pressure to "give" loans or grants—otherwise they would be out of business. A certain commitment or infrastructure investment by the national government is a prerequisite to obtaining a loan or grant, and lending agencies do not and cannot enforce this commitment; it is enough that some minimum criteria are met, usually on paper or promised verbally, and some tangible results are agreed upon. Agencies must give, governments must receive, money is given, and the project is on. The history of Pakistan's health and population sector, and its education sector, is full of such lopsided programs, long before and long after the SAP.

To satisfy the donor's demand for results, the Pakistani government builds service delivery outlets, such as health centers, that usually exist only on paper; if a few do exist physically, they remain empty and unused. Equipment bought with donor funds, which no one knows how to oper-

12. Shahid Kardar, *Dawn,* April 20, 1994.

ate (or there is no electricity or fuel to run it), stands idle and rots in warehouses or is vandalized piece by piece, or occasionally sold, by some particularly enterprising person, in the market. Although the training of large numbers of technical staff members also falls under the same grant, these health centers never have the people they need. The training of health workers or schoolteachers—"capacity building"—is one of donors' favorite activities, because it quickly utilizes impressive sums of money and produces "results," in the shape of skilled manpower. Most of the time, these trained health workers or teachers remain unused and are largely unusable.

The education sector is in the same straits as the health sector. "Ghost" primary schools exist only on paper, yet they have impressive enrollment figures and continue to receive funding and get counted in project results. In 1998, more than fifty thousand such schools were discovered in Punjab alone.[13] The United States is once again increasing its aid to Pakistan, with $1.5 billion of the Enhanced Partnership with Pakistan Act earmarked for education, but if problems of program design and larger systemic issues are not addressed, this money cannot be expected to have results any different from all that has gone before.[14]

Donor funding "builds" human and capital "capacity," but there is no concomitant building of institutional capacity to absorb the trained manpower, to store and use the supplies and equipment, or to streamline or improve the administrative and governance systems involved in managing those assets. The human and capital capacity, therefore, is poorly utilized.

Other factors also contribute to this problem. The maintenance costs of facilities and equipment, staff salaries, the procurement of supplies, and day-to-day operational costs are the responsibility of the government, but the government does not take this responsibility seriously. In their rush to spend money and "do something," international donors rarely insist on this point. No grant or loan is ever tied to the government doing its part, and project directors and their contractors go off to Washington or London to look for more funding for the next cycle or the next project. Thus is the beast fed.

13. "Pakistan Army Seeks Out Phantom Schools," BBC News, March 23, 1998, http://news.bbc.co.uk/2/hi/despatches/68762.stm.

14. Bryan Gibel, "U.S. Aid to Pakistan: The Kerry-Lugar Bill," *Frontline/World*, PBS, http://www.pbs.org/frontlineworld/stories/pakistan901/aid.html.

The Human Factor

Project completion reports rarely capture the specific contextual details in which the development programs were designed and the critical decisions were made. One does not get an understanding of the day-to-day events or the motivations, incentives, and disincentives of the people involved in shaping these projects.

In a country like Pakistan, the officials who make these far-reaching decisions are usually political appointees who know that their shelf life is extremely short. For these officials, donor-funded projects offer opportunities, financial and otherwise, for personal enhancement and benefit—an official vehicle, an salary add-on, or a paid foreign trip. So, knowing that the next ten staff members in line will always be ready to comply, these officials do whatever they are asked. There is little time to think and analyze, and very little chance or motivation to ask any difficult questions. The officials in the government's management structure are nontechnical people, so they sign onto whatever the "technical experts" place before them—they are, after all, the experts.

These technical experts, who are responsible for designing the programs, work for the development agencies, either as permanent staff members or as consultants hired for specific tasks. Usually, they are narrowly trained technicians from Europe or the United States with very little understanding of the developing country's social conditions and institutions. This lack of understanding is one thing; but on a personal level, they bring something more lethal: that certain arrogance that comes with being an "expert." They represent the donor agencies, they are in a position to make decisions that involve millions of dollars, and they command exorbitantly high salaries. In addition, they are almost always foreign nationals and are usually white, which in a country like Pakistan creates an automatic aura of superiority.

These experts pick up on this very quickly, and being human, they exploit it to the maximum. They do not entertain ideas divergent from their own. Also, they are only in the country for a short period of time, and so they must focus on the immediate, time-bound task they have signed up to complete. Their interest is in delivering a product. Moreover, because the development problem is usually formulated as a technical one, rather than as an institutional or a social problem, the country's social context is immaterial. To take the SAP as an example, Nancy Birdsall writes that "the fact that the SAP consistently fell short of its objectives is easy to understand. The SAP was based on an incomplete understanding of Pakistan's social and political context."[15]

Representatives of most donor agencies, when they come to developing countries, live and move in isolated cocoons meant to mimic as closely as possible the environment of their homes in Washington or London or Geneva: "Living and working comfortably in the Washington area and venturing forth in luxury, with first-class flights and hotels, [they] are out of touch with both the realities and the causes of poverty in the Third World."[16] Whatever context they bring to their designs is usually that of their own country. For instance, writing about the Orangi Pilot Project, Arif Hasan, one of the leading development experts in Pakistan, says that "donors manage to impose their own cultures on government agencies."[17] Neither donor culture nor government culture is above reproach, but the disjunction between the two and the imposition of one on the other creates more problems.

Failure by Design

I was puzzled when I read and heard the concerns regarding the poor outcomes and ineffectiveness of the SAP, and I remain puzzled when very smart and experienced people express surprise at this outcome or similar ones in other circumstances. What puzzles me is not the outcomes but the element of surprise—not the programs' failures, but the surprise with which those failures are greeted. I still find it difficult to understand why such smart people—representatives of the World Bank and the donor agencies, experienced contractors, local government officials, technical experts, anyone who has spent any time in this business—do not see that their programs are doomed from the start to fail.

This was certainly the case with the SAP. Grandiose, unrealistic, and fuzzy objectives were put in, without any clear implementation strategies or commitment for associated infrastructure support, right under the noses

---

15. Birdsall and Kinder, *The U.S. Aid 'Surge' to Pakistan,* 28.

16. Michael Irwin, former head of the World Bank Health Department, quoted by Bruce Rich, "World Bank/IMF: 50 Years Is Enough," in *Fifty Years Is Enough,* edited by K. Danaher (Boston: South End Press, 1994), 5.

17. Arif Hasan, "Financing the Sanitation Programme of the Orangi Pilot Project—Research and Training Institute in Pakistan," *Environment and Urbanization* 20 (October 2008): 339–60.

of the donor agencies. There was little focus on critical management issues, such as governance.[18] Strategies likely to facilitate, if not encourage, corruption were accepted. Very little consideration was given to the most critical factor, human resources and their management. Other important implementation constraints were brushed aside, and those who raised them removed themselves or were removed by others from the project. What happened to the SAP was exactly what should have happened. Failure should not have been a surprise; it was an integral part of the project design.

Inside the Black Box

Perhaps, however, the technical experts, the representatives of the international donor agencies, their contractors and local partners, and national government officials really do not know what actually happens with development projects. It is as if no one were to look inside the black box after a plane crash. But to understand and prevent further project failures, it is necessary to look inside the aid-and-development black box.

Even at the earliest stages of designing the SAP, it was clear that the policymakers were oblivious, deliberately or otherwise, to what the exercise was about. Putting together the SAP proposal involved designing a large-scale services delivery system in three related yet distinct government ministries, with major and complicated issues such as financing, regulation and quality assurance, and monitoring. It required producing the appropriate manpower for service delivery in health, education, and water and sanitation, and addressing the issues in the utilization and management of this manpower. These issues never made it onto the agenda. The program developers and policymakers, both local and international, were focused on immediate, operational objectives—that is, those activities that were liable to be funded and that would help disburse funding quickly—and on their own contractual agreements, work plans, deadlines, and careers.

---

18. In 2007, the Asian Development Bank, evaluating the past ten years of social-sector development in the country, mentioned this issue, saying that "the lesson [of the SAP] was that social-sector development was not the result of a financing gap, but an inability to convert resources into services efficiently"—i.e., a management problem. Operations Evaluation Department, "Country Assistance Program Evaluation for Pakistan," Asian Development Bank, Manila, May 2007, 57–58.

Those of us involved in the SAP had the vague feeling that we were "doing something" to respond to the crisis in the social sector. All of us did our jobs, whatever piecework was assigned to us, honestly and to the best of our abilities. We prepared the Government of Pakistan's Proposal for the SAP; the proposal was funded; and on its basis the government launched the SAP for development of its social sectors. We did our job, knowing full well that we were just muddling through. In the end, everyone involved was left to hope that "some" good would come out of the muddle, but what comes out is what goes in, and this muddle is now before us in the shape of the SAP's failure.

There are as many realities as there are histories. One is the arranged-for-the-occasion reality put up for the consumption of the guests. Another truer and larger reality is what the Spanish philosopher Miguel de Unamuno calls "intrahistoria"—the largely submerged and unrecorded realities of common people, their sayings and their doings and the motivations behind them, the descriptions of places never visited by tourists.[19] Through this intrahistoria, I try to show the intricate yet poorly-thought-out and mostly chaotic process of program design—the muddle. The delight is always in the details, and thus this book is an attempt to capture the details of the muddle of the SAP, to look inside the black box.

Why was the process chaotic? Why was the SAP poorly designed? If the money was not spent on programs, where did it go? I do not pretend to have the answers to these questions. (Maybe, as one of the government of Pakistan officials merrily told me when I worried that the money for health and education would be wasted, it was to be used to make the bomb.)

So is this, then, a true story? On the publication of *Heart of Darkness,* Joseph Conrad was asked the same question. He answered that it was the truth stretched by his imagination and his own experiences.

My Involvement

I was involved in the SAP as a technical expert for the health and population sectors, working for the Government of Pakistan's administrative committees responsible for managing the proposal preparation and designing

19. On Unamuno's concept of "intrahistoria," see, e.g., Paul R. Olson, *The Great Chiasmus: Word and Flesh in the Novels of Unamuno* (West Lafayette, Ind.: Purdue University Press, 2003).

the program; these were the Federal SAP Committee and the provincial SAP committees of Sindh and Punjab. I worked as an external consultant, and my particular task was to propose incentives to attract more women to work within the rural health delivery system. My salary was paid, at various stages from November 1991 through March 1992, by the Canadian International Development Agency (CIDA), UNICEF, and the United Nations Development Program, as part of the technical assistance these agencies provided to the Government of Pakistan.

As part of my diagnostic work for the SAP, I traveled extensively within Pakistan, visiting pertinent institutions (rural health centers, district hospitals, and training institutes for midlevel workers) and meeting the people (nurses, midwives, lady health visitors, medical officers, and many others) who were the actual implementers. These wonderful people had insights into the working of the health and population programs that, unfortunately, never made it into the SAP. They did, however, add to my existing knowledge of the nuts and bolts of Pakistan's institutions and their internal links, from the federal level down to the most remote service delivery outlet.

During this exercise, and during my more recent work in Pakistan, including an assignment as senior adviser to the U.S. Agency for International Development's (USAID's) Health Office, I saw the dynamics of the international agencies as well, and how all these work—or don't work—together to make development programs succeed or fail. For behind the labels of World Bank, UNICEF, USAID, CIDA, and so on are people, with their particular mindsets, their own hopes and fears, their own immediate and at times petty interests. These incentives and disincentives are equally important as other systemic factors in examining the end product.

This account is also colored by my own perspective, or perspectives. As a Muslim woman, a physician, and a Pakistani, I have a native understanding of the institutions in Pakistan, and I am familiar with the confusing and complicated details of the country's health delivery system. I also understand the external and the internal dynamics of the issues critical to the development of the country's social sectors. The role of, pressures on, and motivations of Pakistani women are close to me. I speak the local languages and understand their cultures, so Pakistanis are comfortable with me. At the same time, having lived, studied, and worked in the United States, I have specific technical skills and a theoretical understanding of large, comprehensive service delivery systems with which to interpret specific local realities and constraints. I can speak the language of the international experts as well, so I form a bridge between these two groups.

This places me in a unique, at times disorienting, position—in a no man's land between the cultures of developed and developing countries, at times belonging to neither, and at times part of both. I find this state of "perpetual otherness," so well described by Salman Rushdie, to be vastly amusing and extremely advantageous to my work in developing countries. It is from this position that I present to you, building piece by piece, this strange and familiar puzzle of how and why aid does not work.

Methodology

Purists looking for a research methodology will probably not find one here. Though I do not lay claim to exceptional expertise in the social science disciplines, I have tried to develop a people-centered, holistic framework of analysis, derived from these disciplines—anthropology, psychology, economics, and sociology—and combined with the evaluative skills used in clinical medicine and, of course, personal intuition and instinct.

In applying the clinical assessment model within this larger framework, I approach "sick" public health programs or service delivery systems as a clinician would a patient, and I assess my "patient" to arrive at a "diagnosis" of its sickness. It is only based on a diagnosis that a prescription can be proposed. For a treatment to be successful, it must be implemented in the context of the lived reality of the patient. For health services delivery systems to be successful, the "treatment," the program, must be implemented in the lived reality of institutions and people.

The adoption of this framework follows from the observation, gained from twenty years of involvement with development programs, that well-meaning, committed, and technically competent individuals often get it wrong because they rush to write prescriptions without carefully reaching a diagnosis. In *The End of Poverty,* Jeffrey Sachs proposes something similar, using the clinical assessment model to analyze the failures of the model of economic development.[20]

My hypothesis is that if the prescription for treatment is based on a correct diagnosis and consistent with the constraints imposed by the context, the patient will have a better prognosis for improvement. I hope that the analysis presented here will help in examining the failures of development

---

20. Jeffrey Sachs, *The End of Poverty: Economic Possibilities for Our Time* (New York: Penguin Press, 2005).

programs in Pakistan and will yield new insights for reforming these kinds of programs, both in Pakistan and elsewhere.

In the end, this book wrote itself. The main characters in the SAP—Pakistani institutions and their people—insisted on walking onto these pages and having their say, so here they are.

This Book

This book is a detailed, day-by-day account of the process of preparing the SAP proposal. It is in the form of interconnected vignettes, organized in thirteen chapters. Each chapter describes a particular institution that, directly or indirectly, has something to do with health workers and the health delivery system in Pakistan, from the local training institutions to the international donor agencies such as the World Bank.

For example, chapter 3, on the Nursing Council, describes the decay of a critical institution that is responsible for the regulation and certification of female health workers; and chapter 5, on the Women's Division, describes the workings of the administrative/policy unit supposedly working for women, and in reality suffering from the malaise and arrogance of policy-makers. Chapter 8, "A Day in the Life of a Provincial Health Department," describes the push and pull factors, mostly imposed by the immediate need to allocate and use donor money, on the major administrative unit responsible for health services in the province. Chapter 10, on the firing of the learned Dr. Sahiba, describes the corruption and nepotism that are perpetrated in the broad light of day. And chapter 12 illustrates how program implementation and design are done within the standardized framework common to donor agencies. Finally, the epilogue, "The Beat Goes On," describes how the process has still, as of 2010, not changed. It is my hope that the following vignettes will better illuminate the issues facing development today.

One

Meeting Lucymemsahib and
Starting Our Project

I have arrived at Nadia, the rather ostentatious coffee shop in Islamabad's Holiday Inn (now the Marriott, which suffered a devastating terrorist attack in 2007), for a briefing with our project's supporting agency, the Women in Development (WID) Section of the Canadian International Development Agency (CIDA). I am the local consultant. Here I am to be introduced to Lucymemsahib, the project's external consultant and technical expert, who has arrived the night before from Toronto, and to the team from CIDA, the agency that is funding and managing our consulting services. The CIDA grant is a "tied" grant, as are most grants for international technical assistance, and thus it stipulates that a consultant from the grant-giving country must be hired as the lead technical expert. This is how Lucymemsahib, a Canadian national, gets piggybacked onto me to work on the project—or, more correctly, I onto her.

We are at times in each other's way, at times at tangents. We are unsure of who is actually in charge. She is battling jet lag and diarrhea or just simple disorientation at being exposed to an unfamiliar culture. Later, she will be seduced by the exotica of it all—the shopping, the courteous locals, and the government officials who make her feel special because she is an external consultant, a foreigner with a presumably big pay package. Once she understands this, she quickly gets into the mode of an expert and becomes more difficult. I am frustrated by the general flow of things, by having to humor her along, and by being forced to develop a program that seems badly designed in the first place to complete the assignment on a short deadline.

The CIDA officer for WID, who will introduce us to the federal Social Action Program (SAP) adviser in the Planning and Development Ministry, is a tall, big-boned, pleasant-looking woman made bigger by an almost full-term pregnancy, and she seems to be full of it in more than one way. She is dressed in a beige tusser-silk trouser-suit with a pashmina thrown over her left shoulder. The pashmina is turquoise-blue, chosen as if particularly to complement the color of her eyes.

Her Pakistani counterpart, the assistant WID specialist, is a graceful, slender woman with close-cropped hair and a trendy *shalwar-kameez,* the baggy trousers and long tunic that make up the traditional dress of Pakistani women. She is wearing her *shalwar-kameez* without a *dupatta,* the long scarf that completes the ensemble (even today, it is considered brave to not wear a *dupatta*), and is smoking a cigarette with awesome nonchalance, the smoke curling out from the corners of her freshly painted bright red lips. She makes me think of Marlene Dietrich, drinking black coffee in a shady café on the Mediterranean, perhaps with Humphrey Bogart in tow. Her demeanor tells you that she is a modern, Western-educated woman and is most likely the wife of some high-ranking government official. She exudes a quiet confidence and total support for her boss.

Up the Learning Curve
with the International Consultant

Then there is Lucymemsahib. I take one look at her struggling with her omelet and am seized with a panic that alternates with exasperation. I have worked long enough with international consultants to know that Lucymemsahib will need a lot of time and energy to be brought to some level of basic understanding of what Pakistan's health and population sectors are all about, and of the role of female workers in them. I do not look forward to the task before me. I shall have to take care of all the required business, as well as of her—and of her ego.

The first impression she gives is one of a gray limpness. Her hair is limp, her hands—one of which she offers to shake—are limp, and her clothes are limp. All evoke indeterminate shades of gray, from the crumpled scarf around her neck to her sturdy walking shoes. With her neck huddled in her shoulders, she looks out of sorts. She has a stomachache. Her bag has been misplaced by the airline, so she is understandably anxious. This is her first trip to a developing country, not counting a holiday trip to Mexico. And she is not sure if she should have brought a chador with her or not. The chador, which became famous after the Iranian Revolution in 1979, is a long cloak worn by women when in public spaces. It covers the hair and much of the upper body; in Pakistan, it would be considered a marker of supermodesty and piety. Where do you get one of these things, anyway? Could she, maybe, borrow one from me? Being relieved on that account, she halfheartedly goes back to tackling her omelet.

This has turned into a strange meeting. The boss lady from CIDA is in a pregnancy-induced euphoria. She had learned yesterday at her obstetrical exam that her cervix was dilated 3 centimeters, though the membranes were intact. She has been thrown off-kilter because this is her thirty-second week of pregnancy and she had planned to travel to Canada to have the baby. She is not sure if she can travel now. What if she went into labor on the plane? It is not likely to happen, because her doctor says so, because the membranes were intact—but . . . she looks at me for confirmation. I think of something wise to say: She really must arrange for an early flight out of Islamabad. She digs into a huge plate of fried fish—at this time of the morning!—making mental calculations. And, oh God! She had completely forgotten! Her husband! He is not even here. He is in Bangkok. Should she wait for him or fly out alone? She looks around the table for ideas, and all pitch in with sympathetic murmurings.

The WID coordinator has been quietly smoking all the while, making clucking noises and nodding her head from time to time as her boss speaks. Lucymemsahib is still struggling with the omelet, muttering under her breath, "I don't even know why I am here." The omelet, which was supposed to be Spanish (our love for all things foreign!), is apparently lacking, for she has eaten very little. She looks around the table with her fork poised. The boss lady pushes away her plate, and Lucymemsahib, with an "if you do not want it, can I have your fish?" digs her fork into it, reaching across the table with an agility that belies the first impression of extreme lethargy.

The WID officer briefs us on the project. She has done her homework and knows her stuff. She has also managed to get the federal SAP adviser to meet with us, despite his extremely busy schedule. Lucymemsahib, occupied by her fish, looks gratefully at me as I take notes. Can she get all the information from me later? She has left her papers and things in the room. This, as we can see, is a bad morning for her, so I reassure her.

Our assignment is to study the regulations and incentives for recruitment and service in basic health services in rural areas and make recommendations for revisions to attract more suitable staff, especially women, to these positions. This issue is a major component of the ten-point program proposed in the World Bank's *Country Strategy Interim Report 1992,* which was prepared to identify crucial areas needing attention in developing and implementing the SAP for Pakistan.[1]

The 1992 report and the World Bank Country Assistance Strategy of 1994 stressed social-sector development as a priority. The *Interim Report* identified the underutilization of the extensive network of health facilities in the rural areas as a crucial factor in the poor performance of the health services delivery system. It was felt that services at rural health facilities were underutilized because appropriately trained manpower—and, especially, womanpower—was deficient. The government also recognized that even those few women who were trained and willing to work found it difficult to do so effectively, due partly to cultural and social factors. Along with these underlying factors, however, systemic problems also contributed to the underutilization of health facilities. This problem was especially acute in the provinces of Balochistan and Sindh, which were considered relatively less developed than Punjab and the North-West Frontier Province. The Government of Pakistan, recognizing this problem and its effects, wanted to analyze the factors that would attract and induce women to work in rural areas. The proposed changes would be implemented as part of human resource development within the SAP, which, in total, eventually cost $8 billion ($450 million in loans) and took ten years (1993–2003) to implement.

Can Lucymemsahib and I handle this work? Of course! Lucymemsahib is an experienced nurse who has been involved with women's issues for more than twenty years in Ottawa. Her strength lies in getting women in abusive relationships to walk away from the abuse, get vocational training, find jobs, and be rehabilitated in a new life. She had risen to be the director of her own agency and now trained master trainers in other social service agencies. Along the way, she had also rid herself of her own husband. He was a liability, she tells us candidly. Women do not realize that they do not need husbands, she says in between mouthfuls of fried fish. Yet she is still anxious—even after the briefing. "I don't even know what this is all about," she says for the third time. Surely she has some background information about her task? Otherwise, why would she even be here? Her answer is an interesting story.

One of Lucymemsahib's girlfriends, while a student at McGill University, for a time dated a fellow student, an Aga Khani from East Africa who

---

1. "The Country Assistance Strategy of 1992" was an attachment to the following report: World Bank, *Fordwah Eastern Sadiquia (South) Irrigation and Drainage Project,* Report No. P-5749-PAK (Washington, D.C.: World Bank, 1992).

had been born and raised in Karachi. Both enjoyed downhill skiing and South Asian restaurants. This young man, a graduate student in the Department of Statistics, had worked for a while as a consultant to the Aga Khan University in Karachi. His uncle was part of the top management at the Aga Khan Hospital during the mid-1980s, when the university was setting up its Primary Health Care Program, for which McGill University's Department of Epidemiology had provided technical assistance. He could not get over the fun he had then—the wonderful weather, the trip up north to Hunza and Gilgit at the base of the Karakorams, and the warm hospitality offered by the local people in the government as well as in the community. His girlfriend had joined him for a week's holiday in Pakistan, and she had come back raving about the country.

Earlier in the year, the CIDA office in Islamabad, where he had many friends, had asked if he would consult for a project for which a Canadian was needed. He would have loved to, but there was a major ski meet in Utah during this period and he had already signed up. Yet he was reluctant to let his friends down, so he was looking for someone to replace him, and his girlfriend gave him Lucymemsahib's number. Would Lucymemsahib like to go?

"Well, why not?" asks Lucymemsahib, looking at all of us around the table as she continues to nibble on the fish. She had never been to this part of the world, although she did not care much for skiing. She was sure, however, that there might be other interesting things to do. And then this project has to do with women, a subject close to her heart. So here she is. The whole thing happened very quickly, so she didn't even have time to do find out anything about Pakistan. She was told she'd be briefed here.

"Besides, the CIDA office told me the local consultant would be responsible for the technical aspects of the work. Is that you?" she asks me trustingly, briefly interrupting the trajectory of the fish impaled on her fork. She seems to revive somewhat when she sees all of us nodding. She didn't even know where Pakistan was until she'd bought her ticket, she tells us. She had thought it was somewhere in India. . . .

"Don't worry. A lot of foreigners make the same mistake," the WID assistant tells her soothingly.

Lucymemsahib looks reassured. She wonders if her clothes are going to be appropriate. Oops! Speaking of clothes, she had better check to see if her bag has been found. "This was really too much fish, wasn't it? Does the coffee shop serve these large portions, or had you ordered for two?" she asks with a wink to the pregnant lady, a bit more color in her face as she goes off in pursuit of her bags. We set out soon afterward, this contingent of assorted and colorful females, for the orientation meeting with the federal SAP adviser at the Civil Secretariat, the offices of the federal government.

Appointment in Islamabad: Meeting the Federal SAP Adviser

The Civil Secretariat, the federal government's administrative offices, is at the end of the tree-lined, two-way Constitution Avenue, which runs like a conveyor belt connecting the government buildings to one another. In present-day Islamabad, this area of the city has been upgraded, with the roads widened and underpasses built to accommodate the increased traffic. It is kept manicured and has been landscaped to a perfection found only in picture postcards. Even at this time, in 1991, it is Spartan and clean—there are no pushcart vendors, shoppers, pedestrians, schoolchildren, or any of the other indicators of ordinary life in Pakistan. It is eerily quiet on this Monday morning. Only a few vehicles are on the road, and most of them are plying their way to the same Civil Secretariat—someone petitioning for a transfer from one dead-end job to another—or to the American Embassy, in the adjoining Diplomatic Enclave (these being the days when private vehicles could drive right up to the embassy's parking lot), bringing desperate occupants to the incessant though fruitless search for entry visas to the United States.

Islamabad is a contrived city, and looks it. Having been created as the federal capital during the 1960s, and planned on a grid with relatively modern buildings, it lacks the organic flavor and lopsided historical development of other, older cities. There are none of the architectural features that reveal a colorful history of growth and decay, or the invasions of different ethnic and cultural groups, or the chaotic lives of inhabitants—as, for example, in Lahore. But even though the city is new and its buildings are modern, the institutions they house remain as old and outmoded as ever.

There is much activity in the corridor as we step out of the elevator on the sixth floor of the P Building (the buildings in the Civil Secretariat complex are named alphabetically), the seat of the federal Planning and Development Ministry. Office assistants, assistants to assistants, peons, stenographers, cleaners, and other assorted males of similar nature are hurrying back and forth. Most are empty-handed, while some look intensely worried, with files clutched desperately to their skinny chests. In one door and out another they go, as if on a merry-go-round. One glides past us, balancing at shoulder level, on one hand, a tea service laid out on a silver tray. There is the mouth-watering aroma of warm samosas in the air. Seeing four "begums," two of them kosher "goree-memsahibs" ("begum" is a title of respect roughly equivalent to "madam"; "memsahib," a term left over from the British Raj, was originally reserved for Englishwomen, but now "goree," or white, is added for specificity, for the Raj is gone and "memsahibs" can be brown, too), the men stop to stare unabashed, scratching themselves here and there.

"We need to see the chief," says the boss to the skinny man who is in the outer office of the SAP Secretariat, a room that has freshly painted red flowerpots by the door but is otherwise quite dusty and grungy. "We are from CIDA." He looks blankly at her. She towers over him. "We have an appointment."

He flips the pages of a dog-eared appointment book and says, "I am sorry, Madam, but he cannot see you. He is in meeting with the 'Wud' Bank."

"But we had an appointment."

"Yes, I know. But this is the 'Wud' Bank, Madam," he says, and adds— no doubt for extra emphasis, puffing out his chest ever so slightly, as if this were his personal achievement—"from Washington," and "in Amreeka," just in case she might be unaware of the whereabouts of Washington.

While this business is being sorted out, Lucymemsahib has slumped into a chair, and by the way her chin is resting on her chest, I suspect she has decided to use the opportunity to grab a quick snooze. Jet lag and all that. The boss lady, drawing herself up to her full length—and breadth—whips out a visiting card and sends the assistant in with a look that means business. He scuttles off, and sure enough, she is soon called in.

As we wait, out comes the "Wud Bank" of which the little assistant had spoken with such awe. It consists of one incredibly tall and incredibly good-looking young man in his mid-twenties. He is fashionably tanned, with baby-blue eyes, and wearing an immaculate tan suit. Definitely Italian. The suit, I mean. Maybe the man, too. He takes the chair next to mine, and we introduce ourselves. He too, it turns out, is working on the SAP, but in a roundabout way. He is a graduate student at American University in Washington, and is interning at the World Bank for the summer and ended up here through the friend of a friend. He doesn't know much about the SAP, he adds hastily and a bit apologetically. He is studying anthropology, which can contribute to the SAP, he has been told. He has actually just walked into the job, for everyone is taken up with the SAP, aren't they?

"It must be pretty big, this SAP," he says. He seems to be in a chatty mood, for he proceeds to tell me more about himself. He is an avid hiker, and has already "done" the Pyrenees and the Alps. "But the Karakorams are something else, aren't they?" His dream is to one day "do" Everest. He tells me he likes Pakistan, because of its hospitable people and exquisite cuisine, and especially Islamabad, which is so green. He hopes to get up north to the mountains, and wonders if it would be more interesting to go by road via the Karakoram Highway or take the plane for an "aerial view." He leans back in the chair, crossing one long leg over the other, refusing gently the offer of a cigarette from the WID officer, who has been smoking constantly, much to the amazement of the population of peons hovering in the corridor and in the doorways. I half-suspect that some have been invited over just to see this wonder—a memsahib (a brown one) smoking away in public.

"And what do you do?" the "Wud Bank" asks conversationally. I tell him.

"Oh good! What wonderful luck! Now you can tell me about this SAP thing that has everyone so worked up and is worrying me so much." He smiles sweetly at me, displaying a set of blindingly brilliant, even teeth.

I smile sweetly back at him, wondering if he would have asked my opinion of his teeth this quickly if they had been worrying him and I had been a dentist. He looks at me for a minute and then, flicking an imaginary speck of dust off his immaculate lapel, smiles even more sweetly. We are quiet now. The WID officer continues to smoke, the peons continue to gawk, and I think I am not off to a good start.

At last, we are also invited in to meet the chief, a man with a balding head, short neck, and weighty jowls made heavier by his high position. We have five minutes to ask any specific questions before the chief goes back to his meeting with "the Wud Bank," more of whose representatives are on the way, in addition to the hunk in the fancy suit, who has calmly strolled in with us.

"Do we have any questions?" the chief asks, looking encouragingly and automatically at Lucymemsahib. But she is still suffering and out of it.

"You are the team leader. You ask the questions," she says to me, with a hint of flattery in her voice. Team leader? What team? What leader? There are only two of us on this project. "Still, it is better to have one person ultimately responsible. It works better that way." She turns to the CIDA ladies with the same agility she had demonstrated earlier with the fish. "You don't have any objections, do you?" What objection could they have?

So I turn to the chief. I want to know of the government's and his vision and his expectations for this project. I want to know the extent of assistance we can expect from his office in wading through the information here and in the provincial offices. There is a certain desperation in my voice. I feel as if I am not doing this quite right. How can you discuss in five minutes issues that have been neglected for five decades?

The chief lets me blabber on, and then tells us, with portentous gravity, about the "national importance" of the SAP, about this wonderful opportunity for Pakistan to finally, once and for all, "pull up" its social sectors, about the "importance of women in our society." And he tells us about his satisfaction at the prospect of all the international agencies being aligned to give all the help we need, and about his government's desire to see this done as soon as possible. He toots the horn of the exemplary "political will" demonstrated by Nawaz Sharif's government, which is so exemplary and so willful that the SAP chief expects to get from us, at the end of three weeks, a set of recommendations that will fulfill all these expectations.[2]

Recommendations in three weeks! But what about the review of the situation? Surely his government is interested in finding out why the health workers do not appear at their posts, and why rural health facilities continue to be underutilized? Surely the issues merit at least some critical analysis? How could we justify any recommendations without this backup? How would isolated recommendations regarding health workers make sense if the other related factors were also not dealt with? And my fellow consultant has only recently learned that Pakistan is a country!

Lucymemsahib is calm. She is daintily sipping green tea.

"Yes, yes, that is all very well," the federal SAP adviser says, waving an impatient hand. "We need the recommendations first, for the Consortium meets in April and the 'project' has to be ready. There will be time enough for all that later. . . ."[3]

> And indeed there will be time . . .
> And time yet for a hundred indecisions,
> And for a hundred visions and revisions.
>
> —T. S. Eliot, "The Love Song of J. Alfred Prufrock"

2. The SAP was initiated during the first term of Prime Minister Nawaz Sharif, from 1990 to 1993. Sharif's second term began in 1997, but a military coup led by General Pervez Musharraf in 1999 put him out of power, and Musharraf's military government implemented the second half of the SAP.

3. The International Aid Consortium was made up of the Asian Development Bank, the U.K. Department for International Development, the Government of the Netherlands, and the World Bank; during Phase II of the SAP, the European Union also became a partner.

"This is like writing a prescription without reaching a diagnosis, an exercise that is not effective in the long run—and not very ethical either," I demur, using a clinical analogy.

The chief looks mildly exasperated. "Who is talking about prescriptions?" he says with a darkening of his brow. "We just want the recommendations." He ends this sentence definitively. There is to be no more discussion of this.

The boss lady gives me a reproving look that makes me feel like a misbehaving kindergartner who has been called into the principal's office. As if on cue, half a dozen assistants appear with documents to be signed and verbal messages to be whispered into the master's ear, and our meeting is over. As we leave, I turn around at the door to see the World Bank hunk cozily ensconced on the red satin sofa. He lifts his cup to me in a half salute, smiling sweetly, his teeth a flash of brilliance in a field of equally brilliant tan.

Two

The Organization of Our Project

Later that night, after our first meeting at the Planning and Development Ministry, Lucymemsahib and I are sitting in our hotel's coffee shop, Nadia, trying to determine how to tackle this project. Lucymemsahib has had a refreshing nap, and I have put my young children to sleep upstairs. The baby is a year old, and the older boy is four and just beginning to read, so he enjoys listening to stories. I have read him *Cinderella* for the nth time, and thinking of our meeting that morning, I wish some fairy godmother would come down to rescue the Government of Pakistan and fix the health and education delivery systems with a wave of her magic wand, for it does not look like the Prince Charming of the morning will be able to pull it off.

My children are traveling with me, for it is difficult to leave them alone at home. Lucymemsahib thinks I will find their presence distracting. I tell her I have no other option, that it will be more distracting if I leave them alone at home with even a reasonably intelligent nanny. There is no easy way out for working mothers of young children—this is also true of some of the women we are trying to help.

In the early 1990s, Nadia was the only gathering place in a five-star hotel catering to Islamabad's international community and government elite, and also the only late-night spot in the city (Serena was a later addition), and so as Lucymemsahib and I sit there it is bustling, the noise many decibels above the acceptable limit. It has a festive air in spite of the blue haze of cigarette smoke and the lateness of the hour. This is the place to see and be seen.

Members of the National Assembly—Islamabad being the seat of the federal government—members of the provincial assemblies, and their assorted hangers-on, with an air of self-importance extending at least three feet on either side, walk in and out. Most wear *shalwar-kameezes,* some of cotton and others of shimmering material; others are bundled in voluminous woolen chadors, which are quite the fashion these days and come in men's sizes. Some have their slick hair set stylishly, or whatever passes for that in their scheme of things, with dark, carefully trimmed moustaches that they smooth every now and then. Others are bald and gray—and paunchy. All cough deeply. All speak loudly and in expressive Punjabi and fling their chadors over their shoulders with wild abandon, wheeling and dealing (or pretending to) or watching the wheelings and dealings around them, while an Anglo-Indian (as the Christian minority in Pakistan is called) band surrounds the grand piano in the far corner singing hopeful tunes from the 1960s. Nawaz Sharif, a son of Punjabi soil, was then prime minister, after Benazir Bhutto's government had been thrown out on charges of corruption and mismanagement. Shahbaz Sharif, Nawaz's dynamic brother, was chief minister of Punjab, and so this was their time and their territory. For now, and maybe forever, they thought, they were the top dogs, and if nothing else, they were going to act like them.

A group of Japanese business and government officials just off the plane from Tokyo came into Nadia half an hour ago, and its members wait while their rooms are being prepared. The Japanese government provided, on a turnkey basis, technical and financial assistance to the Pakistan Institute of Medical Sciences to build its Children's Hospital, and this group is here in connection with that work. These small, neat men and women wait patiently with a gentle, Zen-like stillness—or maybe just jet lag. One young man, with luminous skin, a sensitive mouth, and hair like the finest black silk falling over his hooded eyes, I would see again a few days later in a lingerie shop in Jinnah Super Market, longingly fingering a big black lace bra. Tonight he looks dazed after an obviously long flight, smiling as the band belts out Sinatra's "Strangers in the Night."

There are also a few famous television personalities here in Nadia. Amer Hasan (one of those famous brothers) and his pretty young wife, who are in the middle of making a movie, are being schmoozed in one corner. He is big, broad, and heavy, beginning to grow jowly but still with that grand wave in his thick salt-and-pepper hair, and she is petite and prim in pink, and they are generously allowing the public at large to get a load of them. Kaleem, a close friend of mine and at the time the extremely accommodating head of the Duty Free Shops, is at their table and seems to be familiar with them. One could say with a reasonable degree of certainty that he has helped the Hasans secure the latest model of a high-technology microwave oven or some hard-to-come-by Corning Ware bowl or a set of fancy golf clubs. These things were in short supply in Pakistan at the time because of import restrictions, and thus could only be obtained through the system of government-sponsored import arrangements managed through the Duty Free Shops. These arrangements gave the government access to foreign exchange—because these items could only be purchased with foreign currency—and likewise gave the public, or those with foreign exchange, access to "foreign things." On seeing me, Kaleem comes over to say hello and magnanimously offers to introduce me to the much-sought-after stars, who are of course surrounded three deep by fans.

Outside Nadia, under the vast chandelier in the hotel's bright lobby, luggage is being moved here and there, and elevator doors are swishing open and closed. People are milling around, while the staff hovers, bright-eyed and cheery, greeting all with "Good evening, Sir/Madam, can we help you?" And the waiters in their crumpled suits, neckties askew, carry trays back and forth, serving meals that are most likely worth their whole month's salary with a scowly sulkiness that I find intimidating.

"Do you think I could order? I am starving," asks Lucymemsahib, bright-eyed at one-thirty in the morning. She can. Nadia operates twenty-four hours a day. And so, over more fried fish (!), we decide what to do.

Female Peripheral Health Workers

First, we list all the categories of female peripheral health workers in Pakistan by their title and cross-list them with the facilities in which they are placed and the departments for which they work. Before giving our list here, however, it is best to clarify what is meant by "peripheral health workers."

According to the Primary Health Care Model of health delivery systems for developing countries, which Pakistan was trying to implement at the time, access to primary or immediate health services, including contraceptive services, should be available within the community. The persons who provide these primary or first-level health services are called peripheral health workers. They provide services directly in the community, in people's homes, or they are placed in rural health centers that are generically called peripheral health facilities.

The work done in these centers was considered to be mostly preventive, and thus "simple," so it could be done by a "simple" person—that is, someone with a minimal amount of training, considerably less than that provided to medical graduates, who are the first contacts in urban areas and represent the Western model of service delivery. This cadre of "peripheral health workers" became the backbone of the new health services delivery system for rural areas. Interestingly enough, these workers were also trained to and expected to provide curative health services. They are the de facto doctors in rural areas.

In 1991, the following groups of women came under the heading of "peripheral health workers" (some years later, the government created another category of female health workers, called lady health workers, who obviously are not part of our story here):

- *Community health workers,* who were trained to provide family-planning services. They were given basic training by any nongovernmental organization that could secure funding from donors.
- *Multipurpose health workers,* who were similar to community health workers, except for their name, a semantic difference due to the fact that their training funds came from a different donor or grant.
- *Traditional birth attendants,* who were older women, mostly illiterate, trained to provide antenatal care and deliver babies. They were trained over the past three decades by health departments or nongovernmental organizations funded by the World Health Organization (WHO) and UNICEF. They worked (or not) wherever they could, on their own steam.
- *Female medical technicians,* who were trained in medical technician schools by the Health Department, using a University of Hawaii curriculum, during the 1980s. This project was financed by the U.S. Agency for International Development. No one knows the whereabouts of the medical technicians trained under this program, though one runs into them sometimes in rural areas, where they can be found working as minidoctors.
- *Nurses,* who were trained in major hospitals all over the country, worked in hospitals, and sometimes were placed in peripheral facilities.
- *Midwives,* who were trained under an international grant, managed by WHO, UNICEF, and the Canadian International Development Agency, mostly in urban centers. There were no special outlets for placement. They worked as individual providers anywhere they could make money.
- *Paramedics,* who could be trained by anyone. There were no special outlets, and no one knows what they did.
- *Health educators,* who were similar to paramedics.

- *Family welfare workers,* who were trained in regional training institutes set up under the Population Welfare Division (now the Ministry of Population Welfare), and were required to work in family welfare centers, the service delivery outlets of the Ministry of Population Welfare.
- *Lady health visitors,* who were trained in the schools of public health under the provincial health departments and worked in these departments' service delivery outlets.
- *Expanded Program on Immunization (EPI) workers,* who were trained as vaccinators using a standard curriculum designed by international experts, with training conducted by special staff, and were also paid under an international grant managed by WHO and UNICEF. Programmatically, these women worked exclusively for the EPI.
- *Control of diarrheal disease workers,* who worked for the Control of Diarrheal Disease Program, another internationally funded vertical program like the EPI.
- *Malaria control workers,* who were in another vertical program, the Malaria Control Program, and who were trained and worked in the same way as control of diarrheal disease workers.
- *Workers for the World Food Program,* who were part of another vertical program like the EPI.
- *Tuberculosis control workers,* who were part of yet another vertical program, the Tuberculosis Control Program.

Who are these women? Where are they placed? What is their job description? How is their work regulated? How are they supervised and monitored? How are they recruited? What problems do they encounter during their work? What is their service structure, and what are their career paths?

If the truth be told, no one knows, and frankly no one cares.

Regarding Pakistani paramedical personnel, WHO says:

In Pakistan this important category of heath personnel is very loosely organized. It lacks clear classification and standardization of nomenclature, training requirement and job description. The main reason is that there is no controlling agency or organization that can work towards standardization and upgrading of this important component of this important health personnel. Paramedical personnel in Pakistan are not required to be registered or licensed by any organization. Efforts are now under way to establish a Pakistan Paramedical Council to act as a regulatory and registration agency and to upgrade training requirements. It is difficult to get an estimate of the numbers of paramedics in the country because of the absence of any national or provincial registration system. There is a consensus, however, that the existing ratio to doctors is approximately 1:2. In addition to a large number of informal training programs, usually in large hospitals, there are 30 recognized government training institutes, mostly run by provincial governments. The annual period of training is 1–2 years after matriculation. These institutes usually lack qualified faculty and have a relatively low intake and low output.[1]

The same description could have been applied to almost all peripheral health workers in 1991. All of them were fairly similar—in socioeconomic profile, education level, training, background, and expectations—just the labels and the sources of funding were different. They were part of the health sector's manpower, trained under one vertical program or the next—immunization, tuberculosis, maternal health, and so on. Their funding came from the World Bank, the Asian Development Bank, the U.S. Agency for International Development, the Canadian International Development Agency, and the U.K. Department for International Development, among other agencies, as part of "capacity building" for service delivery.

The funding was usually managed through an international contractor or nongovernmental organization, which then formed partnerships with local organizations, for example, nongovernmental organizations or government facilities such as schools of public health or regional training institutes. The workers' training consisted of general health-related skills, some preventive health knowledge, and curative skills that were mostly pharmaceutically based, such as information about malaria tablets or oral rehydration for diarrhea. Some learned to treat minor cuts and boils, along with other curative skills that, however rudimentary, they continued to use to their own advantage. These workers were, and still are, expected to serve in the rural health systems of the nation's four provinces, which have well-defined outlets for service delivery. This rarely happens.

During training, participants are offered stipends, usually much more than their daily earnings, in addition to room and board—a perk of which many can only dream. Partly for this reason, there is great demand for both initial

1. Regional Health Systems Observatory, World Health Organization, *Health Systems Profile: Pakistan.* Chapter 7: Human Resources (Cairo: WHO Regional Office for the Eastern Mediterranean, World Health Organization, perp. 39, 2004), 87–88.

training and refresher courses. Once the training is over, by which point the grant has been fully utilized, these trained workers are on their own.

Theoretically, trained manpower increases capacity. In reality, it has had very little impact on service delivery in rural areas, because this capacity building—the training of peripheral health workers—has been piecemeal and out of sync with institutional realities. Simultaneous and matching capacity for these workers, to utilize their skills and training, is not built into the institutions—there is no room or space or purpose for them within the system—no jobs, no salaries. The program "does well" for the duration of the training, usually a week or three to six months, and for the duration of the loan or grant, usually two to three years, but then the funding is exhausted and it is back to square one.

The funding agencies, which are aware of this problem, argue that the utilization of trained manpower is the responsibility of the provincial governments. The donors hope and the provincial governments agree, on paper, that they will build institutional capacity in time to utilize these workers. But these promises are never kept, and this does not happen. By the time the agreements are made, however, the gears of the machine have been set in motion, and the piecemeal training for "capacity building" gets going once again.

This process has been repeated during the past three decades; the latest efforts that I have seen firsthand were funded by the U.K. Department for International Development and the U.S. Agency for International Development. There is no discussion on the reasons that these programs fail to "build capacity," and therefore it seems that the process will simply repeat into the future.

Because the provincial government agencies that are responsible for these workers—the Health and Population Welfare ministries—are unable to employ them, they prefer not to be "hassled" by them. The government's best hope is that most of these women will leave for jobs in the Middle East, get married, or do anything else. The "smart" ones, whatever their training program, go into "private practice," where they act as minidoctors and prescribe medicines, mostly aspirin and basic antibiotics. For these "smart" ones, it is in private practice that even the most rudimentary obstetrical skills picked up in training become of vast personal benefit. Because there are no regulations—and no way to enforce any regulations that might make it onto the books—trained workers can easily get away with this practice. And so they limp along for a while, until they get married, fall by the wayside, go to the Middle East, or are called up for retraining under a new grant for a new program—and thus get a new, even if temporary, lease on their professional life.

Though it seems improbable to Lucymemsahib, the truth is, in a country where there is no accountability and no way of enforcing whatever rules and regulations might exist, it is extremely easy for even minimally trained health workers to set up their own shops. The consumer has no way of knowing which of these "doctors" are trained and which are not. And all this happens with the tacit approval of the local health authorities, who turn a deliberate blind eye. This negligent behavior is commonly justified with the belief that these women are providing at least some service to people who would otherwise have none.

"How do you know this?" asks Lucymemsahib, a bit suspiciously, I think. I tell her that she has to either trust me or spend the time to find out for herself. She decides to trust me, for as she says with a laugh, I am, after all, the team leader. I tell her that if she says that again, I shall strangle her.

The Next Steps

As we ponder all this, it is clear that we face a formidable task. This job is made more complicated by the fact that there are no job descriptions available and that any documentation will be difficult to come by. Clearly, all this work cannot be completed in three weeks. "So should we study all these types of health workers?" I ask Lucymemsahib.

She looks helplessly at me in the middle of a bite of her interminable fish dish. "This is a very long list, is it not?" she asks, peering over her plate. "What is a family welfare worker, and how is she different from a lady health visitor, and why is one a 'lady' while others are not? They are women too, aren't they?"

Good questions, indeed.

Because there is a time constraint, we decide to concentrate on the cadres of workers who fulfill these criteria:

- The workforce is exclusively female.
- The workers have their own independent and categorical institutions for training.
- These institutions are under the administrative control of the provincial government.
- A specific curriculum is used during training, which is focused on the group and is structured.

- Students must sit for and pass a certifying examination, which is organized and conducted by the Pakistan Nursing Council.
- The graduates are eventually certified and registered by the Pakistan Nursing Council.
- They have a place in the government's service delivery system, and there is an established career path on which they progress in their respective fields. That is, somewhere in the system, there is a record for these workers. There is some longevity to the workforce, there is some system of evaluation, and there are methods of recruitment.

Only three cadres of workers fulfilled all these criteria: nurses, lady health visitors, and family welfare workers.

"I think, if we can even make sense of these job categories in the given time, it will be an achievement," I say.

"OK by me," says Lucymemsahib, as she digs into her sliced grapefruit, "whatever you say. You are the team leader."

I give up.

We decide that given Lucymemsahib's unfamiliarity with the environment, we should visit all the institutions connected with the production of these cadres of workers. At the same time, we will get a chance to talk with people who are part of these institutions and get the relevant documents from each place. We will do this review at both the federal and provincial levels. Because we are now in Islamabad, where the federal offices are located, we decide to begin here and then move to the provinces—first the North-West Frontier Province, then Punjab, Balochistan, and Sindh. The final week will have to be spent back in Islamabad, wrapping things up.

Because it is the certifying and regulatory body for all female peripheral health workers, our first stop will be the Pakistan Nursing Council.

Three

The Pakistan Nursing Council: A Dead End

For our meeting with the director of the Pakistan Nursing Council (PNC), we arrive on time at a neat, though small, two-room office tucked away in one corner of the campus of the National Institutes of Health. The table in the center of the first room is covered with a flowered plastic tablecloth, as if for a picnic; on it rest a pencil holder, some writing materials, and a telephone. A rather ornate chair with red velvet cushions is on one side of the table, and on the wall above and behind the chair is the standard 8 × 10–inch framed photograph of Mohammed Ali Jinnah wearing a severe *sherwani,* the long, high-collared coat worn by nobles of Northern India, and a Central Asian cap, which, because he took to wearing it in his most patriotic phase, came to be known as the Jinnah cap. There are four straight-backed chairs, a bit dusty and rickety, on the other side of the table. The other room has an identical table—this one set with an elaborate tea service—and rickety chairs, but no red-cushioned chair or Jinnah portrait.

A sleepy little person sitting on a stool by the door, wearing a stained *shalwar-kameez,* mumbles something while rubbing his eyes, which have sleep deposits, or perhaps are infected.

"She's what?" I hear my companion, Lucymemsahib, ask in a panic-stricken tone. Because I am a little behind, I have not heard what he has said. "Dead! Oh my God, do you hear that?" she says to me. "The director of the PNC is dead." She stands still for a minute, as if paying her respects. "How did she die?" she asks the little fellow.

He looks a bit offended. What did he say again? "Late. Mrs. S." Ah, Mrs. S will be late, is what he meant.

Lucymemsahib had been confused by the way Urdu, Pakistan's national language, is translated into English. The peon had used the word as an ad-

33

jective, but lacking a verb. Lucymemsahib had understood it as another kind
of adjective entirely. Though English is the country's official language, the
majority of the population, which is illiterate to start with, is unable to use
it. Even those who can use English, when forced to, do so in local pidgin
fashion. Yet, in a surrealistic way, this inadvertent slip of the tongue is quite
symbolic. The PNC, as far as the changing needs of the health delivery system are concerned, might as well be dead. We tell the little man that we shall
wait. He offers to bring us tea, pointing us toward what I call the tearoom.
We decline and decide to wait in the office of Mrs. S, the director.

Mrs. S arrives an hour later, quite flustered. She is a shy-looking, slightly
built woman in her fifties, wearing a flowery *shalwar-kameez,* her head covered by a starched *dupatta* from which her raven-black hair peeps through.
Dyed, no doubt. She looks a bit startled at my sari, wrinkling her nose delicately in what I interpret as disapproval while adjusting the *dupatta* on her
head with an elaborate gesture.

"You are not a Pakistani?" she asks, pretending nonchalance. I tell her
that I am. In a phase of intense nationalistic fever, Pakistanis, trying again
to distinguish themselves from Indians, adopted the *shalwar-kameez* as the
acceptable national dress for women. The sari was rejected as "Indian," and
sari-wearing Pakistani women were considered insufficiently patriotic.

Mrs. S, apologizing for the delay, says that she had been called away unexpectedly.

"Must have been something important," I say conversationally, for she
is quite out of sorts. I wonder if my sari-clad persona is contributing to it.
Actually no, as it turns out. Another member of the World Bank's delegation was visiting, and she was called away to meet them "right away."

"Couldn't you tell him that you had an earlier meeting and have them
wait?" asks Lucymemsahib, who has found the wait in this stuffy little windowless office a bit tiresome, partly because it throws us off our schedule.

"How can you do that?" Mrs. S asks her innocently. "They are the World
Bank."

And now, what can she do for us? We tell her the purpose of our visit.

The PNC is the federal government institution concerned with all policies pertaining to nursing and related professions in the country. This includes the recruitment, training, examination, placement, promotions, certification, and registration of nurses and related professionals, such as
family welfare workers and lady health visitors. It is a semiautonomous
body ruled by a Board of Governors, which consists of the provincial sec-

retaries of health, the principals of all the medical colleges, and the nursing directors of all the four provinces, plus the designated staff from the National Institutes of Health. Strangely, the provincial health directorates, the agencies responsible for implementing the rural health services, are not represented. The board consists entirely of people representing the urban health services. Yet the PNC certifies and registers lady health visitors and family welfare workers, both cadres trained to work exclusively in the rural health system.

The Pakistan Nursing Council was formed after the Partition of India in 1947. (Official recognition of the profession, however, had more to do with the establishment of the separate Armed Forces Nursing Service, which is completely outside the Civil Service Structure and is not under civilian control. Armed forces nurses are generally better off, professionally, than their civilian counterparts.) The PNC regulates all nursing schools in the country, both the military schools and the sixty civilian nursing schools. All of them use the same basic "nursing curriculum" that has been in use since the beginning of nursing services in the Indian subcontinent, in the nineteenth century. Pakistan inherited the curriculum—along with some nurses—at the time of Partition, as part of the overall inherited health system.

"We use the same curriculum that was used to train British nurses during World War II," Mrs. S tells us proudly.

"Surely it has been updated since then," says Lucymemsahib jokingly.

"No."

"You really mean it has never been updated since then? Why not?" asks Lucymemsahib, quite aghast.

"There was no need to," replies Mrs. S. "Only recently, after all this Alma-Ata business, there is pressure to change it," she adds, sounding as if this is completely unnecessary.

Briefly, the Alma-Ata business she refers to was the International Primary Health Care Conference held in the city of Alma-Ata, then in the USSR and now part of Kazakhstan, in 1978. This conference, which was considered a watershed event for the design of health delivery systems in developing countries, declared that services based on the Western model of health care were inappropriate for these countries. Because most of the health problems in developing countries, such as poor sanitation and malnutrition, were believed to be environmental, it was decided that they should be tackled by improving the environment. Any remaining medical needs could be addressed by using minimally trained local health workers;

these would be inexpensive and available on the spot, as opposed to skilled health services, which are usually available only in urban areas and are beyond the financial reach of the majority of the population.

The wisdom or folly of this policy, and the story of its selective, lopsided implementation, is for another time. Most developing countries, including Pakistan, signed on to the resulting Alma-Ata Declaration and promised to reorient their programs according to the Primary Health Care Model introduced at the conference.

Because there was no discussion of the constraints on and challenges to its implementation, Pakistan translated this model as it saw fit. The Ministry of Health directed its provincial departments and all related health services institutions to reflect a "primary health care orientation" in their programs.

Mrs. S continues: "We are now going to stress much more community medicine and family planning in the nursing curriculum. Nurses will be doing all this along with their regular work."

"Why?" asks Lucymemsahib. "Nursing is, as its name says, nursing. And equally important. What hospital can function without good nurses?"

"That is true. But it is in the declaration. We have to do community medicine."

"But what about nursing?" insists Lucymemsahib, clearly not happy with nurses in this community medicine business.

"What particular aspects of community medicine?" I ask, knowing full well the many colors and constructions of this much-abused term.

"Oh, just some things to do with the community," offers the director nonchalantly.

After completing a twenty-four-month curriculum, including a practicum rotation in a tertiary care hospital, nurses take the examination administered by the PNC. Once they pass, they are certified and registered by the PNC. This means, theoretically, that there are standards that can be monitored.

"But it does not matter," our good Mrs. S says, shattering this hope, "whether they are certified or not. A lot of organizations hire nurses without any certification and registration. Especially the private hospitals and clinics. And because these institutions pay a lot more money than government service does, the nurses prefer to work for them rather than for the government. Many do not even wait to complete the training program."

"Do these organizations then train these people themselves?" asks Lucymemsahib.

"Oh no, there is no need to train them. They can work." At least Mrs. S is honest.

"What do you mean, there is no need?"

"Well, they do know the work."

"What work do they do?" Lucymemsahib is genuinely confused.

"Nursing work," responds our hostess calmly, adjusting some papers on her desk.

"But nursing is a skilled profession. A nurse, to be effective, has to perform certain tasks that are technical, and many times critical." Lucymemsahib looks at me, her face flushed and eyes shining in indignation. She is a registered nurse, in Canada, where nursing is a highly skilled, well-organized, and respected profession.

"Ah, but you see there is no rule which says that you are not allowed to work as a nurse without certification," Mrs. S explains patiently. "And practically speaking, even if there were, there is no way we can reprimand them. There is no way to enforce this rule."

"Can you not change the rules and put in regulations?" Lucymemsahib turns again to Mrs. S.

"What rules?" asks the lady mildly.

"The rules regarding the employment of people who are not properly qualified to do the job."

"No, no, rules should not be changed, for this would lead to a lowering of standards, and it is very important to maintain high standards." Mrs. S's voice rises with emotion. For all her life, she tells us, she has fought to adhere to standards "against all odds."

"What standards are you talking about?" Lucymemsahib is getting into the spirit of things. Her voice is also rising.

"The standards of nursing, the noblest profession in the world. It must have the highest standards in the world." Mrs. S's voice cracks on the high note.

And, just as suddenly, both ladies stop talking, out of breath, their faces red.

The Highest Standards in the World

Lucymemsahib's worry is justified. All you need to do is to visit any facility in Pakistan, rural or urban, to see exactly what is going on. "Nurses," whose only claim to the title is their little starched uniform, are blundering through people's lives. I once saw a nine-year-old die after a routine appendectomy, because the nurse did not know that she needed to give him a test dose before administering the penicillin, to check for an allergic reaction. A hypertensive man had a stroke because the nurse monitoring his blood pressure did not think she had to alert the doctor when it became dangerously high. There are nurses who do not know how to read a thermometer, let alone anything more complicated.

At the same time, some "nurses" have thriving "private practices" of their own, in towns and villages where they are called doctors. They write prescriptions, dispense medicines, perform abortions, fix ingrown toenails, suture wounds, and excise boils; treating "fevers" is old hat. One enterprising young lady was doing outpatient cataract removals in a small town just 50 miles from where we sat. Her name would come up again and again whenever the subject of private medical care or palatial houses—the two go hand in hand in Pakistan, as in other countries—came under discussion. She had done well enough to build a mansion within two years of the beginning of her "practice," complete with a marble foyer and imported toilets, which, though completely unusable because of the lack of an adequate water supply, were nevertheless the cause of much envy and a validation of her success in life.

"Why do employers hire unregistered nurses when they know that these women might not be adequately trained?" My good friend Lucymemsahib is persistent.

"Because there is an acute shortage of nurses in the country, and no clinician can work without nurses," replies Mrs. S. That, too, is a fact consistently documented. "To date, nineteen thousand nurses have been registered with the PNC, and given the population, this is an extremely poor ratio of nurses to population. This means we have one nurse for about six thousand people.[1] On top of this, we think that easily half these nineteen thousand are out of the country, and the other half are trying their best to get out too. As you can see, there are just not enough nurses to meet the demand. That is why even untrained girls are hired. That is why we need to train more nurses." Mrs. S ends on a high note with, "Do you know, in Islamabad, Lahore, and Karachi, a nurse can get five to six job offers in the private sector?"

1. Regional Health Systems Observatory, World Health Organization, *Health Systems Profile: Pakistan* (Cairo: WHO Regional Office for the Eastern Mediterranean, World Health Organization, 2004), 89.

(According to the World Health Organization, by 2004 the number of registered nurses in Pakistan had risen to 44,520, but there is no way to know how many of these are actually in the country and how many are employed. This particular health indicator may have improved, but the improvement is slight and exists mostly on paper.[2])

"This situation exists only in urban areas, does it not?" I ask, for Pakistan is certainly more than three large cities; almost 70 percent of its population is rural, and rural/urban disparities are a major hurdle in developing standard programs or uniform employment salaries, benefits, and the like.

"Of course. What need is there for nurses in rural areas where there are no hospitals? As it is, we do not have enough nurses for urban areas," says Mrs. S.

"Why do you then not increase the output? Surely in a country where there is a shortage of jobs, this should be a very attractive option for women." Lucymemsahib is being logical and applying the law of supply and demand. But this is Pakistan, and there are yet another ten layers of the problem.

"This is easier said than done," Mrs. S replies, pursing her lips. "It is not easy to attract girls and women to go into the nursing profession, especially if they come from good families."

"What on Earth do you mean?" Lucymemsahib is horrified. "Is it because of poor salaries? Is the pay that low?"

"Oh no. Pay has nothing to do with it," replies Mrs. S. "Girls prefer to go into teaching, although that has still lower pay. It's just that nursing is not considered a . . . a . . . decent profession."

Lucymemsahib looks like she is going to have a heart attack. She stares at us, from one to the other, her mouth opening and closing. She looks like a fish gasping for breath. "But you are a nurse, aren't you?" she asks the director, once she gets her breath back.

"Oh no, no, I am not." Mrs. S is quick to correct her. She is from the federal bureaucracy, a civil servant. At that time, no nurse had ever risen to be the director of the PNC.

The Vanishing Nurses

The institution of nursing in Pakistan is a strange hybrid. It is built on the foundations of the health and medical system created by the British in In-

---

2. Ibid.

dia in the nineteenth century to serve the colonial and local elite. Initially, nurses came from Britain as part of the administrative management cadre.

Later, especially during World War II, nursing programs were set up in the local hospitals, based on the existing British model. This was a problem. Educated women from middle-class households who, at that time, had some schooling, were reluctant to go into professions. Those that required close contact with people, especially unrelated males, were particularly unattractive.

At the same time, Christian religious missions had been well established in India since the late eighteenth century, and they had their own hospitals and schools. The mission hospitals were associated with the Church, which took care of abandoned infants and children, most of whom were the offspring of English men (often soldiers) and local women. These Anglo-Indians, like the "mestizos" of Latin America, were mostly the products of nonmarital unions and were shunned by society, and were therefore prime candidates for conversion to Christianity and for less desirable jobs. Almost all Anglo-Indians on the subcontinent are Christians. At first, most of those who went into nursing were Anglo-Indian Christian girls. From the beginning, nursing in Pakistan suffered from a double handicap, and it is still seen as an "inferior" profession.

"You have mentioned that nurses leave the country at the first opportunity. Is that a major problem?" I restart the conversation on a topic that seems safe.

"Oh, yes! It is a terrible loss." Mrs. S's voice has genuine feeling. "Our own country desperately needs the manpower. But what can we do?"

"All governments can stop the qualified personnel from leaving the country," says Lucymemsahib. "The government can mandate this." Poor Lucymemsahib! For the life of her, she cannot understand why it is so difficult for a government to control the exodus of its trained womanpower, especially because the training is financed either by the taxpayers or by other government-funded programs, as in the case of nurses and doctors.

"All government servants who wish to leave the country need to obtain a No Objection Certificate from the government, and then they can go wherever they like," Mrs. S tells us. "Most of the time, people are granted this certificate. But it can be withheld in case of essential personnel."

"Aha!" Lucymemsahib pounces on this opening. "Then the government can refuse to give this document to people who it thinks are needed in the country. And it is clear that nurses, being in short supply, are essential personnel."

"But why do it?" Mrs. S asks, patiently and sincerely. "As it is, there are not enough jobs in the country to absorb all the qualified nurses. They go, for they too have families to take care of." She looks to me for understanding. "They work for some years on short-term contracts, and after they have made enough money to build a house, or educate a brother, or collect a dowry for themselves or for a daughter, they come back again." And then Mrs. S adds, after a brief pause: "In fact, it is better to let them go; otherwise, they create trouble for us."

Later on, we shall meet another senior government official in the Provincial Health Department of Punjab who also voices exactly the same feeling. His office created training programs for peripheral health workers within the context of the Family Health Project in order to overcome the shortage of qualified personnel. He too hoped that once they were trained and ready to work, the "qualified personnel" would all go off to the Middle East. Government officials share a common vocabulary, and he will use Mrs. S's exact words: He did not want these workers to "create trouble."

International assistance pays for the training of personnel but does not concern itself with their employment or salaries. This is a major and unresolved problem in all the peripheral health programs in Pakistan. The aid organizations assume that trained manpower is an asset to the country, produced to help the government, and they expect the local health systems to absorb it. In reality, the local governments do not have the capacity to deploy, pay, and utilize the new trained workforce. Senior government officials are then left to hope that trained personnel, who can be demanding and vocal, will just go away. Their exodus runs contrary to the objectives of the programs, but it relieves the government of blame for not utilizing them.

Though well aware of this situation, policymakers and development experts agree that skilled manpower is essential to improving services, and they continue to design the same kinds of training programs. The programs bring in large amounts of funds, and the government feels under pressure to run them. Technical experts feel the same pressure.

As the same officer who wished away his workers to the Middle East would say in relation to my comments on the subject, "What can we say, Dr. Sahiba? These World Bank people, they are very fond of trainings. We have to comply if we are to get any money."

Pakistan has been the recipient of donor assistance for such programs many times, but international technical experts do not try to figure out how the workers produced by the programs might be used—their utilization is the host government's responsibility. In unstable regimes, program administrators, who are often political appointees with little accountability and slim hope for long tenure in their jobs, have neither much interest in doing this nor any idea of how it might be accomplished, or their hands are tied because programs developed outside the country bind funding to specific activities. It does not matter if those activities are of little use and ultimately waste money and effort.

Most program evaluations, which usually are conducted in house by the donor organizations, rate these training programs as successes because there is a tangible product that can be measured. The host country is also happy, because the programs bring in a great deal of money. And the local managers are happy because they reap personal benefits—a special remuneration, a project vehicle, a trip to the donor country, participation in an extended study tour, and so on. Finally, the lending agencies like the World Bank and the grant-giving agencies like the U.S. Agency for International Development and the UK Department for International Development are happy because they are able to disburse funds in time for the next budget request.

Lucymemsahib sees some advantage even in this bizarre situation: "Once these nurses come back, they are more experienced and thus more valuable, so they can be hired at that time. At least the government will have the trained manpower it can use."

"Oh no, no." Mrs. S almost recoils from this suggestion. "Now they cannot be hired at all. The government has placed a ban on the reemployment of returning nurses. Any nurse who has worked outside the country in her private capacity cannot work for the government again." She sounds as if these women have been somehow eternally tainted.

"But why? Why not? They are more experienced. . . ." Lucymemsahib is understandably bewildered.

"Because," and here Mrs. S seems personally hurt, "they have rejected us in the first place. Now why should we accept them?"

Actually, this ban is not based on sentimentality alone. According to the government's service rules, anyone over the age of thirty-five years cannot join the government service in any branch—because, so the explanation goes, a government employee can retire with full benefits after twenty years of service, and older people would be more likely to leave the service as soon as they became eligible, taking their experience with them and drawing full benefits. Most nurses, when they return after spending some years out of the country, are close to or beyond the age of thirty-five, and are thus automatically ineligible for employment in the government system.

Not enough nurses. Not enough jobs. Nurses working as "doctors." Trained nurses being encouraged to go out of the country. Untrained and uncertified "nurses" working in private hospitals. What a strange and paradoxical situation. Yet there is no discussion on the central issues that lead us to this place time and time again and are critical to the success or failure of any project. And new ones are developed all the time, because there is pressure from the international community to include more women, supposedly to meet the human resource shortage.

Lucymemsahib shakes her head. "This," she says, pointing to the Social Action Program terms of reference, "makes no sense at all."

Mrs. S is starting to look restless. She signals to the little peon for tea and snacks. In a government office, the tea break can become a project unto itself.

"The problem with women," Mrs. S volunteers conversationally, again adjusting the *dupatta* delicately on her hair as the tea is being laid out, "is that they all want to get married." Quite a problem, and one the world over. "So eventually they must leave the profession to take care of their husbands and children."

We decide to let this pass and raise another possible solution for this "problem with women": training male nurses. As the primary wage earners, men would not be compelled to leave once they got married, and they could tend to male patients, making it easier to attract women to work with female patients.

"Not a good idea," according to Mrs. S. And why not? "Because men are very unreliable. As students, they will agitate the girls," she continues, oblivious to the effect of her remark on her audience. "If they are in classes together, they will induce them to strike on petty matters."

"But the girls are under no obligation to do their bidding," Lucymemsahib says.

"Yes, but the poor girls have no choice but to follow the boys. It is natural for them to do so. By themselves, girls never cause any problems. They quietly do what they are told or get married and go away."

Ah! Nature! How we are forever slaves of nature, our cruel master. . . .

"Look at what is happening in Liaquat National Hospital, all because of these boys! So much headache these boys are causing us." She strikes her forehead with the palm of her right hand in the traditional gesture of frus-

tration, causing the *dupatta* to flop off her hair so that it must hastily be re-
trieved before she can go on. "And the girls are not listening to us, either.
They are naturally listening to the boys, stupid things!" She shakes her
dupatta-clad head in indignation at the stupidity of the girls in general.

The Liaquat National Hospital in Karachi is one of the few institutions
in the country that recruits and trains a certain percentage of male nurses.
About a third of each entering class is male. During the weeks before our
visit to Mrs. S, the nursing students at Liaquat had gone on strike demanding better living conditions for students, which could, of course, be blamed
on the presence of male students in the mix. Girls on their own would not
agitate for such a thing. Lucymemsahib looks at Mrs. S as if she is from another planet. Thankfully, by now the tea is ready, and we fall to it with gusto,
while the Quaid continues to smile his enigmatic smile, high up on the
wall.[3] Mrs. S, very generously, has her attendant run out for some mint chutney to go with the samosas, which are really out of this world.

---

3. "The Quaid" is short for the Quaid-i-Azam (the Great Leader), an epithet for Mohammed Ali Jinnah.

Four

The Allama Iqbal Open University's Bureau of University Extensions and Special Programs

As part of official policy, peripheral health workers are recruited from rural areas so that they can continue to live and work in their own communities. The basic requirement for enrollment in most of the training programs for peripheral health workers is a high school matriculation certificate, which one earns after ten years of schooling. Because the literacy rates for women in Pakistan are low in general, and worse in rural areas, finding eligible candidates is a major problem: There are simply not enough women who qualify to make up a substantial recruitment pool.

The Allama Iqbal Open University (AIOU), through its Bureau of University Extensions and Special Programs, offers an adult education program to help address this situation and improve the recruitment pool. Education services are also part of the Social Action Program (SAP), so we decide it is important to see how the AIOU functions, whether this educational aspect can be improved under the SAP, and if the AIOU's managers have ideas that can be made part of the SAP proposal.

Part of the nonformal education system in Pakistan, the AIOU was founded in 1974 as the People's Open University and was renamed in 1977. It is the foremost institution in the country for reducing adult illiteracy and providing an educational opportunity for those who cannot afford to attend regular academic institutions. It provides nonformal learning and distance education, ranging from minimum literacy all the way to the award of baccalaureate, master's, MPhil, and PhD degrees, to students all over the country. A student enrolled at the AIOU is taught with printed course books, media programs, and tutorials; completes the assignments according to a predetermined schedule; and takes a final examination administered by the university.[1]

In 1990, the AIOU had just started its adult education program through its Bureau of University Extensions and Special Programs. These programs enrolled young people who had dropped out after a only few years of schooling and gave them formal instruction for a period of six months to two years, with the objective that they would eventually qualify to take the matriculation examination given by the provincial education boards and receive a high school matriculation certificate. This made them eligible to participate in general vocational training programs and already-established health programs, such as the lady health visitors' program, or other programs that were to be established within this new social-sector development effort —the SAP.

Meeting Mrs. A

Today we are scheduled to meet Mrs. A, the director of special programs in adult education. The Bureau of University Extensions and Special Programs is housed in a neat, barracks-like building on the AIOU campus in Islamabad. We go through many corridors and take many right-angle turns to finally emerge in Mrs. A's office, a huge rectangular room with a huge desk in the center, almost obscuring the lady behind it. The status of a government official being proportionate to the size of her desk, one can safely place Mrs. A quite high in the administrative hierarchy.

Mrs. A is a fine-featured, petite woman in her early fifties. She is dressed in a sunflower-yellow *shalwar-kameez,* very cheery, matching the color of the flowers outside her window. She, too, eyes my sari-clad form a trifle suspiciously. Her hair is short and stylishly cut, and her eyebrows are penciled in brown. Both her hair and her dress are styled in a way that was fashionable during the 1960s—the shirt tight, longish, form-fitting; the hair elaborately back-combed—and she looks slightly dated. Her office, on the other hand, is contemporary, with modern furniture, a cluttered desk, and papers and files all over the place. There are many file cabinets of different sizes, some with half-open drawers showing neat rows of brown files. There are also many piles of papers, some dusty, placed untidily on the windowsill or spilling onto the floor.

1. Allama Iqbal Open University, "Teaching Methodology," http://aiou.edu.pk/TeachingMethodology.asp.

Mrs. A tells us about the program. Since it started in the 1980s, many thousands of people have been enrolled, half of them women. The program has been quite well accepted in academic circles as well, and the bureau has opened regional offices in different universities in all four provinces. It is from these provincial headquarters that classroom teaching is organized for the remote rural areas. When no physical facilities are available for classroom instruction, teaching can be broadcast on the radio and television.

Mrs. A's dedication to the program has shown results. It is thanks to her that there has been not only an expansion but also a measurable improvement in the quality of recruits—the women who join the health delivery system to work in the rural areas. One of her staff assistants tells me later that Mrs. A comes from a very wealthy and influential family. Her husband is a senior official in the government, and one of her brothers is high up in the army, meaning that she is well connected in the armed forces as well as the bureaucracy. In Pakistan, this means that she has all bases covered. And she has no need to be doing this "job," her assistant continues, implying that Mrs. A's incentive to work is not an economic one. It is purely her dedication and interest in the women's "cause." I, for one, am very glad that Mrs. A does this job, whatever her incentive, for she seems to be using her influence to promote the greater good. It is not easy to get social programs, especially in a "nontangible" area like education for women, to have a high priority with policymakers, who are usually men.

"It's not that they mean ill will," says Mrs. A, when someone comments on this tendency of the policymakers, "it's just that they do not see any advantage in educating women. It only creates more problems."

She goes on to tell us more about the program.

The curriculum is developed by the bureau with assistance from foreign experts, who help with the content and the teaching methodology. Before its implementation in the classroom, the curriculum has to be approved by the provincial education boards of each province, because it is these boards that set and administer the certifying examinations. At the end of two years, after the defined curriculum has been covered, the students sit for their province's certification examination. Though the skills that are measured in these exams are not particularly different, the provinces are under no obligation to set a standardized exam.

The teaching is didactic. Students, separated by gender in groups of ten to twenty, are taught, preferably in a classroom. For rural areas, there are two teaching cycles each year. The first cycle begins in November and the second in March, so as not to clash with the planting and harvesting seasons, when all able-bodied men and women are needed in the fields. The teaching modules, which are developed by experts, are used by an intermediate–level person called the field supervisor who "goes in the field to do the teaching." By "field," Mrs. A means a place way out of the main cities.

At times, the program is fortunate enough to have a foreign expert involved in direct classroom teaching—as they have for the current session. Mrs. R, a Dutch consultant whom we shall meet later, has been in the country for the past three months, and has been actively involved in classroom teaching in areas around Islamabad and in the North-West Frontier Province.

Who are the teachers, and what are their qualifications? Who are the students? What are the results of the examinations? Where are the women who have gone through the program? How do they compare with their peers in regular school settings? Is there a difference in the costs of the program in different provinces? How do the graduates of this program compare with those from more traditional schools when training as health workers? Mrs. A cannot answer these questions for us because her office is not required to keep this information; we should be able to get it from the provincial boards of education. Her office is concerned only with the development of the curriculum and the administration of the teaching program. She, however, seems to feel that the program is doing well.

"How do you know you are doing well? Do you have any figures of how well your students do on the exams as compared with students from other universities?" asks Lucymemsahib.

"No, we do not have the results," replies Mrs. A. "As I said earlier, all the results are with the Board of Education. But we do know that we are doing extremely well; otherwise, why would there be a demand for so many centers from universities in the different provinces?" she adds candidly and, I presume, innocently.

There were many other questions in my mind besides these, which I didn't even get to voice, for two reasons. The first was because Mrs. A looked so earnest and so happy—so convinced that the program was doing well that one didn't have the heart to learn anything different. At times, human beings need good news. The second was that, at that very moment, we were joined by Mrs. R, the Dutch consultant who was working with the bureau during this period. She had, as a special favor, set the afternoon aside to meet us and give us a demonstration of her responsibilities in the adult education project.

Mrs. R's Pedagogic Strategy

Mrs. R is tall, loose-limbed, and angular, with thin stringy hair bleached pale blond. Her face is long and thin, the complexion burned and skin thickened by the sunshine to which she was exposed during many months out in the field in Indonesia and Bangladesh, where she had gone for the first part of her consulting assignment. She is wearing a poorly tailored, colorless, and crumpled *shalwar-kameez,* though in the contemporary style. With her cheery demeanor and unkempt look, sensible rubber-soled boots, and obvious determination, she could easily pass for a modern-day missionary. She radiates the same commitment and sense of purpose, the same disregard for the elements, the same ability to plod on regardless, the same aura of infinite patience.

Mrs. R is a health education expert and has worked in the Netherlands for many years teaching high school children about reproductive health issues and protection against sexually transmitted diseases. She is an expert in the proper and effective use of the condom. She comes to the AIOU as part of a grant from the Government of the Netherlands to develop the Health Education Program for pregnancy prevention. The program emphasizes the proper use of the condom as part of preventive practice. She will help develop a training curriculum, as well as teach the curriculum to community health workers.

Mrs. R has proposed using in Pakistan the preventive health curriculum she has used in other countries, including the Netherlands. We wonder if the curricular content shouldn't be more specific to the local environment.

"What difference does the content make, when you are learning to read and write?" says Mrs. R, by way of explanation. As she puts it, her girls will have a "head start" on other community health workers. And God knows, this country needs trained people as quickly as possible.

There is evidence against her point of view. Curricular content is critical to the acceptance of a teaching program, especially one for adult education. In a country like Pakistan, teaching contraceptive practices to young, unmarried women carries a social stigma, and families are quite liable to withdraw their girls altogether from such a program. Disregarding this issue entirely seems risky. "Does this not have implications for the overall adult literacy program?" I ask Mrs. A.

"This has all been sorted out with the relevant authorities," responds Mrs. A, looking me straight in the eye. It seems there was an issue of the grant running out if one waited for rewrites and approvals, and so here we are. Also, Mrs. R does not have too much time for Pakistan. She has to go first to India and then on to Nepal, countries that are also under this regional grant, to fulfill a similar training assignment. She is determined to finish her task here. She is excited. She is enthusiastic.

Mrs. R tells us about her work. She shows us half a dozen laminated plastic sheets: the health education curriculum that she has been using for the past ten years, apparently with great success. "I have easily trained half the population of high school children in the Netherlands on the proper use of condoms," she says with obvious pride.

As we talk some more about the curriculum content—which is clearly for a Western, more sophisticated, and more liberal audience, but which Mrs. R thinks should not be a problem to teach to unsophisticated Pakistani rural women—tea begins to arrive. I say begins, for the arrival of tea in a senior government official's office is no small matter. It is an event—a performance that reflects on the officer. A bearer—a tall, well-built Pathan in a flowing *shalwar* and a huge *pagri,* the cloth turban worn by men in rural areas—comes in carrying china and silverware on a huge silver tray with ornate handles. He is followed by another bearer with the tea service on another huge, expertly balanced tray, which he carries on one hand at shoulder level as he holds a folded, starched white tablecloth in the other. This bearer number two is followed by yet another one, a smaller version, a peon, who brings in a tray full of accompaniments for the tea: samosas, warm and fragrant, and piping hot jalebis—that twisted, curved, sugary, deep-fried and cholesterol-laden thing of batter that is loved by and has probably contributed to the deaths of many South Asians on both sides of the border. The trio begins to move around the table with well-practiced, as if choreographed, movements, covering the table with the tablecloth and laying the whole production out before us.

While this slow and silent dance is going on, Mrs. R, encouraged by our interest and warming to her subject, offers to give a demonstration. Please do, we say, little suspecting what is in store. And I must admit that in spite of my worldliness and many years spent working in clinics treating sexually transmitted diseases in San Francisco and Washington, I am taken aback when Mrs. R reaches into the depths of a large and stained canvas bag lying by her side and pulls out an oversize replica of an erect penis, made of clear plastic, complete with a pair of clear, perfectly spherical scrota. She plunks it in the center of the starched white tablecloth, among the cups and saucers, the jalebis, and the steaming samosas.

"This," she announces with a dramatic flourish of her hand, like a magician pulling a rabbit out of a hat (one can almost hear the drumroll), "is the cornerstone of my pedagogic strategy."

My, my, and oh my! Silence and holding of breath as all stare ahead, trying not to look at this contraption, and our silent tea-men go on with their elegant performance. The tea is at last laid out, the samosas and the jalebis sitting in fancy crystal dishes on either side of this huge penis that seems to be straining heavenward.

All kinds of images and thoughts go through my mind as, for some inexplicable reason, I worry about our tea-men seeing all this. I find myself wishing them away. Inadvertently, I catch the eye of one of them and see the scene from his perspective—that of a conservative Muslim man, from the North-West Frontier Province (one can tell by the style of his clothes and the accent with which he speaks Urdu), the patriarch of his extended family, the one responsible for all the decisions. It is he who will decide whether to send his daughters to school or allow them to be trained as rural health workers. What he sees is half a dozen young educated women—begum sahibs, memsahibs, and two goree-memsahibs—all playing with indecent toys! See, this is what education does to women, I can almost hear him think. And then you insist that we educate our girls. . . . There is no way he is going to allow the women in his house to be associated with this . . . this immorality. How will he show his face to the Almighty on Judgment Day? Call it whatever you will, he calls it indecency—something that is frowned upon by the Quran and Sunnah and Hadith and his forefathers. Health education, indeed! No, sir. His daughters will not be thus exposed, and be an embarrassment to him and lose the chance of ever finding a decent man to marry them! Oh no. And while he is at it, he does not think much of our menfolk either, who have let us loose to do all . . . this.

I catch an admonishing glint in his eye, as if to say shame on you, you at least should know better! I cringe in my chair and try to hide from the spirit of my long-dead grandmother, Baiji, who, though from an educated family, very much subscribed to this point of view. Baiji had categorical views about what constituted acceptable activities for young unmarried women. This would definitely not have been approved. Such things were not meant for the eyes of unmarried girls; even for married ones, they were barely acceptable. If Baiji were to see this, she would beat her chest, invoking the end of the world. Hai, hai, she would say, . . . for shame. It is surely the end of the world, a time for the skies to fall, when young respectable women are talking about such things.

The enthusiastic Mrs. R, oblivious to the devastating effect of her model on the congregation, continues with her demonstration. She pulls out a bunch of colorful condoms and begins to unfurl them atop the plastic penis. Her "act" consists of teaching young people the correct way of using condoms. She concentrates on the condom because it is the only protection against both pregnancy and sexually transmitted diseases, and now the newly emerging HIV infections. She goes on to tell us how she has repeatedly and successfully used this training and demonstration module to teach thousands of Dutch high school children, both boys and girls, the correct use of condoms.

"If they can learn to use this well, public health problems will be greatly reduced. Which is not difficult, once you get the hang of it, but school kids are so impatient." She shakes her head indulgently. "Quite an ingenious little invention, don't you think?" she beams at me across the table while continuing her task. I am not sure whether she means the condom or the penis—the plastic model, that is. She continues with her demonstration as we watch mesmerized and speechless, silently and methodically consuming tea and samosas, which Mrs. A presses upon us, with the insistence of a gracious hostess.

"Try this with tamarind chutney. . . . Water?" The water would be for Lucymemsahib, who finds the chutney too spicy.

"How about Coca-Cola?" Coca-Cola it is.

I take another bite of my samosa, and crack! The plastic penis falls into two pieces. The lower half tilts toward the scrota. A half-opened blue condom clings to the rotund corona of the upper half.

"Blast!" Mrs. R is ticked. "See," she says, looking at Mrs. A, who tut-tuts in sympathy, "this has happened again."

Apparently, during class the week before, another one of her penises had cracked, also under the strain of an unfurled condom, sending a dozen already horrified young women scuttling home in great haste and in various stages of shock. A certain damsel, I was later told by one of the assistants, was so overcome that she burst into copious tears. Another went into a dead faint and had to be transported home in a tonga—a horse-drawn cart, an entirely unnecessary expense to the program. Now, most of the participants are too scared to come back to the class.

Mrs. R is very upset with the manufacturer of these models. This man, a plastic toy manufacturer from Lalukhet, in Karachi, had been given this contract, and paid in advance, as a favor to his brother. The brother was a small exporter of leather jackets whom Mrs. R had run into and befriended at a trade fair in Amsterdam. Having no money for a hotel, he was sleeping on his pile of leather jackets right there in the booth when Mrs. R stopped by. So she took pity on him (and the jackets) and brought him home.

Obviously, the manufacturer is using substandard material. Mrs. R thinks he has mixed sand in the plastic mixture, for she knows about these things, having dealt with the preparation of plastic models of the penis for many years. This, in spite of repeated assurances by the brother, who had assured Mrs. R on the Holy Book that this kind of thing will never happen.

"What will you do now?" I ask, half hoping that this will be end of *this*. . . .

"No problem," says the unflappable Mrs. R. She will not let the program suffer. She will just use the original model, specially made to her specifications in Finland. From the bag she pulls out another erect penis, with another rounded pair of scrota, this one made of thick, opaque Plexiglas. "Grade one airplane material," she calmly informs the cringing group, "able to withstand a shearing force of. . . ."

"How lucky for the program, that you have this," I am barely able to mumble. Why doesn't she just use this one and do away with the pathetic little substandard Pakistani model? She would have liked to, she says, but unfortunately cannot. There is a technical difficulty.

"As you can see," and she waves the thing like a handgun, pointing the tip toward me, "this one is of an uncircumcised penis."

And as her friend the resourceful brother of the plastic manufacturer had told her, an uncircumcised model, no matter how strong, will not be acceptable in a Muslim country. Also, she has repossessed it only today. It had been confiscated by the Customs Department on her arrival in Islamabad. They had suspected that it might be stuffed with contraband drugs—heroin. When she had protested, she was threatened with arrest, implying that she was smuggling heroin into the country.

"I am getting confused," says Lucymemsahib. "Why would anyone smuggle heroin into Pakistan? I thought it was smuggled out of it."

That is the general perception. But soon Mrs. R is going back to Amsterdam, and she had entered Pakistan from Bangkok. Ah! And here the group begins a quite knowledgeable discussion of the established and unestablished routes for the transportation of drugs, much to the enlightenment of those present. The Golden Triangle and the street value of unrefined heroin in Amsterdam and in Toronto are lobbed back and forth. Many stories of poppy cultivation in the Federally Administered Tribal Areas are exchanged, and there are supporters for all points of view.

So how was she able to get this thing back from Customs? This has got to be good, for bureaucracies come up with unimaginable hurdles. The unflappable Mrs. R had taken care of the whole nasty business there and then. She was able to show them very clearly that this thing was not stuffed with anything at all. It was just full of air.

How did she do that? We all want to know, forgetting the jalebis, the samosas, and our original objective.

"This thing," and she waves it around again, "can float."

"So?"

"Don't you see?" She looks around for signs of comprehension, which are nonexistent. "It is totally hollow. Here! Hold it." And she thrusts the obscene thing into my reluctant hands.

She had demonstrated this fact right at the Customs table after one of the little airport flunkies brought a half-filled bucket of water—and not very clean either, Mrs. R could tell, though she realized that was immaterial. Everyone, including the passengers from the incoming flights from Dubai and Manchester, had broken out of their lines to watch the plastic penis from Helsinki float in the muddy water. They watched mesmerized, while their children cried and pious Muslim women covered their faces with their veils, and hip young first-generation Brits—men with gelled hairdos and women in tight jeans, clutching red passports in hennaed hands—laughed.

But by then the snotty little Customs officer had made it a point of honor, and he confiscated the penis from Helsinki on the pretext of some dubious paperwork. Mrs. R, however, was experienced in these matters, too—as her friend the leather jacket exporter had briefed her, a bottle of Johnnie Walker Black Label comes in very handy at times such as these.

At this point in the story, the little peon comes to tell Mrs. A that a car has arrived to take her to a meeting at the Women's Division. Mrs. A traipses off, apologizing—she has only just learned of this important meeting with the World Bank and must go. The director of the Women's Division, who is hosting the meeting, is a very senior government official, and he does not like to be kept waiting. We continue with the tea, and Mrs. R continues to brandish the penis in the air, giving more details of the program, while the bearers continue to move in and out of the room, bringing warm milk, a glass of water, more jalebis. . . .

Some years later, soon after the 1994 Cairo Conference on Population, I read something in the international press that brought back in vivid detail the image of Mrs. R and her bag of assorted penises. This article described a contraceptive training program in Zimbabwe, where the staff members of a resourceful nongovernmental organization had carved wooden penises to use as demonstration models. These had become so popular that there was a serious discussion about transporting them for similar uses to other developing countries, while simultaneously creating an income-generating program for impoverished Zimbabwean villagers. I half suspect that Mrs. R is somewhere on that scene, and I wonder, vaguely, if some of the models might be circumcised.

Five

The Women's Division:
A Brief Encounter of the Worst Kind

Every five to ten years, a new buzzword or catchphrase emerges from the development world to convey the ethos of the time and provide a hook on which development programs can be hung. In sync with the United Nations Decade of Women (1975–85), the mantra for most donor agencies in the 1980s was "women in development." International donors, led by the World Bank, generously funded programs related to women. Not to be left behind, and to help manage programs and/or show its seriousness, the Government of Pakistan created a special administrative office at the federal level called the Women's Division, situated in the Ministry of Planning and Development. Originally set up in 1975, the division was upgraded to a ministry in 1989; Youth Affairs was combined with Women's Development from 1993 until 1997, and Social Welfare and Special Education from 1997 to 2004. The Ministry of Women Development in its current form dates from 2004.

The mandate of the ministry is "to make efforts for women's empowerment and gender equality," and to ensure that girls and women have equal opportunities with men and boys in all spheres of national life.[1] In reality, it is not clear how the ministry uses its position to define gender issues at the policy or operational levels, because it does not have formal institutional linkages with the body that actually makes development plans, the Planning Commission. Although the ministry participates in the interministerial dialogue during the discussion of five-year plans and has nominal input into the policy of each ministry, it can only give comments on annual policy doc-

1. Government of Pakistan, "About the Ministry of Women Development," http://www.mowd.gov.pk/about.html.

uments.[2] (The five-year development plans are made by the Planning Commission and are approved by the Pakistan National Economic Council, the country's highest economic decisionmaking body, which is chaired by the prime minister.)

The Ministry of Women Development does not have any implementation infrastructure; it liaises with other line departments through "coordination cells" in the provincial planning and development departments. This institutional infrastructure limits the ministry's ability to make a meaningful contribution to policy and programs for women's uplift. Even in the Social Action Program (SAP), the ministry played a marginal role and was not represented on the SAP's Implementation Oversight Committee.

The Women's Division was, nevertheless, expected to play a crucial role in the SAP. What that role would be, and how it would be played out, was left to the Women's Division to determine. Though all the ministries involved in the SAP—Health, Population Welfare, and Education—had their own notions of what the Women's Division should be doing, Lucymemsahib and I decided to find out what that role would be and requested a meeting with the division's director.

The office of the Women's Division is on the fourth floor of a (then-new) six-story building on Constitution Avenue in Islamabad, right next to the (now-closed) American Center and the fancy NAFDEC Cinema House, which was burned down by a rioting mob in the late 1990s. The mob had actually come to burn down the American Center, which was saved by timely intervention. However, at the time of our project, the American Center and the NAFDEC Cinema House were quite at the center of Islamabad's social and cultural life.

Mrs. X, the deputy director of the Women's Division, meets us by the elevator on the fourth floor. She seems to be in her mid-fifties, petite and pink, dressed in a most intricately embroidered peach-colored silk-chiffon sari. Her hair is made up neatly in an elaborate pompadour that starts from the top of her head, goes all over to the sides, and ends in a little French twist at the nape of her neck—very elegant, in a dated fashion. The whole lot is covered demurely by one flowing end of the peach silk-chiffon. Her nails are painted a peach pink, as are her lips. She wears dainty, high-heeled gold

2. S. Kazi, *National Machinery for the Integration of Women, Population and Development in Pakistan,* Labor and Population Team for Asia and the Pacific Working Paper 6 (Bangkok: International Labor Organization, 1991).

sandals, which show off her peach-colored toenails. Her appearance and mannerisms indicate that she belongs to the elite of Pakistani society and probably is the wife of a senior bureaucrat or a senior army officer—and that she is most probably a political appointee.

"The boss is waiting," she says in a breathy voice. When she points to the door of the boss's office, where the meeting is to be held, I am dazzled by the sparkle from her diamond rings.

The boss's office, beyond a sliding wooden door, is big. Big desk, big chairs, big plants, and big paintings on the wall, one a famous Jamil Naqsh of a seminude woman with pigeons. A big bay window, giving one a spectacular view of the Margala Hills, has the shade only partly drawn to allow the brilliant sunshine to stream in the room. The walls are lined with wood of a dark hue, most probably teak. Thick, deep red wall-to-wall carpeting muffles all sounds except that of the miniature waterfall placed on a marble corner table. One half expects a gentle "Bhairavi," the morning *raga,* to be playing in the background, the mood of an ornate and cultivated mellowness is so overpowering.

Right in the center of the room, behind the big desk, sits an imposing-looking man. Some would call him handsome. This is the boss, and by the look of blatant and bored arrogance on his face, you can tell he has a very healthy sense of his own importance. He seems to be in his late forties or maybe more, for that thick head of hair looks too evenly black to be natural, and the face, on closer inspection, is lined. Thick lips, thick face, thick voice, and thick waist too. He has a disdainful expression and looks impatiently at his watch as we enter. The watch is definitely diamond-studded, for it too sparkles mightily as it catches the sun's rays.

Lucymemsahib is two steps ahead of me, and without bothering to get up, he points her to a chair toward his right. After that, his conversation and his attention are directed totally toward her. The deputy and I seat ourselves wherever and are soon joined by a secretary or personal assistant, who is supposed to be taking notes of this meeting. This woman is such a contrast to the whole scene, young and colorless, wearing thick, tinted glasses and a faded, outmoded, shapeless *shalwar-kameez.* She too has her head covered, but by a drab, grayish *dupatta* that hides her hair completely—not a playful strand in sight. She sits with her head hunched between her shoulders, never raising her eyes from her notepad. Another woman, a junior officer but definitely higher in the pecking order (she is somewhat more colorful), is hovering around the boss with a file. He turns to her briefly and signs her paper, and she scuttles out with a distinct air of gratitude.

He makes small talk with Lucymemsahib, who commands his total attention. He is solicitous and vaguely flattering, extremely charming. He is talking of Montreal: What a wonderful city. Lovely restaurants, lovely bookstores, lovely streets, lovely women, . . . heh, heh. And then, is Lucymemsahib comfortable in Islamabad? Has she had a chance to see some of the sights, or is the Government of Pakistan working her too hard? Heh, heh.

I look at Lucymemsahib and am amazed at her immediate transformation. She looks as if she has been simply carried away by the atmosphere and by the attention from this "tall, dark, and handsome" senior government official. She is basking in it, soaking it in, carrying on the social chitchat. Matching each of his bon mots—heh, heh—with two of her own—heh, heh —she looks imperial. Tea and the interminable chicken patties are brought in on an elaborate silver tea service with fancy china.

"Wedgwood," the deputy leans over to whisper in my ear in that breathy voice. "Sir hates common china."

After the ubiquitous *shalwar-kameez*-clad peons, their heads swaddled in voluminous *pagris,* leave, I begin to get to the questions for the meeting. Lucymemsahib and I had worked long and late on these the night before. As the federal institution created for this special purpose, the Women's Division should be able to play a crucial role in the SAP. We had assumed that because the coordination of activities is a major bottleneck in implementing programs, the Women's Division might see itself as taking on this task. The director of the division would therefore have not only major input into the SAP but also the opportunity to make lasting improvements in program implementation. I wait anxiously for the last of the little ladies who have been flitting in and out all this time with one file or the other (they are never invited to tea) to flit out one final time so we can get down to business. At last, the big man dusts an imaginary crumb rather ostentatiously off his well-suited thigh, and turning again to Lucymemsahib, he asks what he can do for her.

Lucymemsahib, who is far away, still in highness mode, almost drops the Wedgwood cup she is still holding. The boss is looking directly at her with those deep, dark, mesmerizing eyes. She seems to have forgotten the original purpose of this "tea-ing and pattie-ing." She fumbles for a few seconds, says something, sits up straight, passes a hand over her hair, fumbles again, and fails. She puts the cup down, smooths her skirt, and looks around in panic. As she catches my eye, she calms down.

"This is Dr. So and So," she says, introducing me. "She is the team leader on this consultancy and will ask the questions." She sinks back into her chair as if exhausted.

This is the first time that the big man actually looks directly at me and acknowledges my presence. His deep, dark, mesmerizing eyes are pools of swirling irritation. After I have explained to him the purpose of our visit, he waves the rest of my half-finished sentence away with an imperious wave of a bejeweled and hairy hand. I must be brief, for he does not have much time.

I take a deep breath and begin again. "It is our understanding that the Women's Division was created to help with, and analyze, the issues related to women. . . ." I try to place the discussion in a context, but the boss interrupts.

"You understand nothing," he says. "That is not why the Women's Division was created." Period.

I am both stunned and frazzled by what seems like overt rudeness after blatant disregard. I feel like kicking his teeth in. So this is how it is going to be! I roll up my sleeves and put up my fists, ready for round two. I close my notebook and ask him to help us understand why the division was created and what its role is in women's development programs.

"That is not my job," he comes back—an uppercut. "If you are interested in finding out, you can read the PC-1." (A "PC-1" is the initial planning document prepared by the relevant departments for every public-sector project, to be reviewed and approved by the Planning Commission—hence "PC.")

I tell him that my understanding is based on the PC-1. "That is what I had read," I add lamely, conceding the round, preparing myself for the next one.

But now I am beginning to panic. I can detect a hysterical edge to my voice, for the boss is making motions as if this meeting is over. He is tidying up his desk, straightening the pencil stand. Wait a minute now, I feel like saying, we did not come here to drink tea and be treated in a frivolous manner. We are doing serious work here. I make another attempt.

"Can we get your views on what is the best possible way, given the constraints within your government, to improve the working conditions for women health workers?"

"Isn't that why you have been hired?" he says, with a bland look—a left hook. He is gaining points, but I do not give up easily.

"And we are doing exactly that!" I say. "And someone like you, who has been with the government for so many years, knows the constraints on implementation and the administrative problems that plague all development programs. You are in an excellent position to help us gain an understanding from the policy perspective," I finish, quite heroically I think, with a not-too-feeble left jab of my own. But realizing that I am fast losing ground and time, I look at Lucymemsahib for some support. She is dreamy-eyed, looking out the window at the brilliant green of the Margalla Hills.

Before the director can respond, the doors open with a muffled swish, and in comes another man of the same variety. Also "tall, dark, and handsome," well built, glowing with good health and good cheer, judging from his smile and jolly greeting. He is dressed in a smart charcoal-gray suit of fine wool. A trim moustache outlines gleaming white teeth, à la Clark Gable as that enchanting rogue, Rhett Butler, in the spectacular MGM film *Gone with the Wind.*

This is a fellow officer, from the famous—or infamous, and in any case now-defunct—District Management Group of the Civil Services of Pakistan, an elite group of government officials. These officers were responsible for the administration of the major government departments at the federal as well as provincial levels. Pervez Musharraf's Devolution Plan somewhat curtailed their powers, and they are no longer chiefs of their districts; that status has gone to the elected representatives, or nazims.

The visitor is obviously junior to the boss, as is evident from his demeanor and way of address. "Sir," he says in a deferential tone, as he walks around the table to shake hands with the boss, ignoring everyone else in the room, including Lucymemsahib, who looks quite indignant.

On the basis of the brief exchange between them, it seems that the visitor is here to confirm the final details of a hunting trip planned for the upcoming weekend. This is apparently a partridge shoot at our young hero's father's farm just outside Multan in Southern Punjab, with forays into the Cholistan Desert, the habitat for many endangered species of birds. In the early 1990s, *The New Yorker* published an article about the houbara bustard, an endangered bird found in this region, and how it is one of the favorites of the happy hunters from the Gulf countries.[3] I find myself worrying about its fate. The director and his visitor, however, after discussing the pros and cons of various weapons, start talking about "teetars," which are not the houbara bustard. They go on to discuss kebabs and some other stuff, which is spoken of in undertones, accompanied by much thigh slapping, subdued laughter, and a naughty wink or two. Everything is soon settled to both parties' satisfaction, and the young hero saunters out gracefully, giving us a grand view of his magnificent broad back and youthful stride. He throws a

3. See Mary-Anne Weaver, "Hunting with the Sheikhs," *The New Yorker,* December 14, 1992, 51 ff.

casual glance at Lucymemsahib and pauses briefly and magnanimously to allow half a dozen peons, who have been hovering around for just such a chance, to hold the doors for him.

The room finds it difficult to come back to normal after Rhett Butler is gone. Who gives a damn about the status of health workers in Pakistan's villages? One has instead been caught up in the drama and passion unfolding in the American—sorry, Punjabi—South. Development programs for improving the status of women, if ever they were close, are far from everyone's mind. The morning seems to have been lost somewhere between the Cholistan Desert and Tara.

"Coming back to our previous discussion," I say, clearing my throat ostentatiously, trying to retrieve the crumbs of the earlier conversation, "can you tell us how the Women's Division is collaborating or can collaborate with the Ministry of Health on this project?"

"Of course," says the director, without the earlier sharpness in his voice. It looks as if the prospect of the weekend festivities has put him in a good mood. "There are many collaborating strategies. All government departments work together. This gentleman who just left is the secretary for health of Punjab, and I assure you we have a very close working relationship." He smiles broadly at us, as if preparing to say goodbye, good wishes, and good luck.

"Can you cite some common problems that are an impediment, . . ." I begin again. Surely this man can contribute something substantial!

"The major problem regarding women's development," he decides to be generous and throws out something for us to chew, "is the problem of purdah in women. Unless that is done away with, no progress can be made." He stands up. "And now, if you will excuse me, I have to get to a meeting at the Secretariat, with the P&D [Planning and Development] Department." And he adds: "I am in fact meeting with the SAP adviser on this very issue. It is, as you can see, a very important project, and we are working day and night on it, with full collaboration between departments." He picks up the folded newspaper and his Ray-Bans, and pausing ever so briefly by Lucymemsahib's chair, says, "I shall be passing by your hotel, and would be happy to give you a ride back." He then strides out while the herd of scrawny peons, like honeybees around a hive, trip over each other to open the door, carry his paper, do something, anything, for the big man.

Lucymemsahib lifts herself from the chair like a swan preparing for flight and follows him out.

Oh, well! Might as well, I tell myself. Maybe we'll get a chance to chat a bit more in his car, and I can come back and meet with the deputy, who seems willing to help. The deputy, as if reading my thoughts, wants to give me references of some government documents that she thinks I would find useful, along with the telephone numbers of the provincial officers of the Women's Division in Lahore and Karachi. She detains me for some minutes to give this information and to tell me that the provincial staff can give me a better idea of the situation in the field, for it is the provinces that implement the programs.

I thank her and rush toward the elevator just as its doors close, and watch it go down and then get stalled on the ground floor. Because that is the only elevator in the building, I have to take the stairs four floors down. Dropping pens, scattering papers, tripping on my trailing *dupatta,* huffing and puffing, I emerge from the building in time to see the big black shiny Honda Accord, the car of those times, drive off with Lucymemsahib and the big man ensconced cozily in the back seat. I am left standing in its dust and exhaust fumes, clutching my notebook and what is left of my dignity.

Later that evening over coffee at Nadia, Lucymemsahib admonishes me for taking so long to come down to the car. What was I thinking of, lingering here and there? I must learn to be more efficient, especially when dealing with senior government officers who are incredibly busy.

That was also the last time she referred to me as the team leader.

Six

The Population Welfare Division:
To Be or Not to Be . . .

The Government of Pakistan's official attitude toward family or population planning has always been ambivalent, and the history of population welfare programs in Pakistan is one of a continuous existential angst. Still, as the nation's high population growth rates are considered a major and continuing obstacle for economic growth and development, the present government and all governments during the past fifty years have tried to "do something" about them.

Contending with High Population Growth

The Government of Pakistan began to confront the issue of high population growth in the 1960s, under the Second Five-Year Plan, when it asked the Ministry of Planning and Development to formulate a population policy and develop a program. The annual rate of growth was about 2.6 percent at the time.[1]

The first of these programs, started in 1965 and running through 1969, was called the Target-Oriented Approach. It was followed by the Continuous Motivation Strategy, which lasted from 1970 to 1975. The Contraceptive Inundation Strategy came next and remained in effect until 1980. All these programs worked under the same two assumptions, had the same objectives, and employed the same strategy. The first assumption was that high

1. Griffith Feeney and Iqbal Alam, "New Estimates and Projections of Population Growth in Pakistan," *Population and Development Review* 29, no. 3 (2003): 483–92; the citation here is on 485.

population growth rates were a result of the unavailability of contraceptive devices, and the second was that there was a demand for these devices by eligible couples.

These efforts, which were popularly known as family-planning programs, all followed a strictly supply-side strategy, paying no attention to issues of demand; their job was to develop mechanisms to distribute contraceptive devices to eligible couples. The contraceptives were paid for by donors and distributed through the health centers, from family-planning clinics, at specially organized family-planning camps, and with social marketing. Although population welfare and family-planning programs did not gain the notoriety in Pakistan that they did during the 1970s in India—where one even contributed to the downfall of Indira Gandhi's government—they were not particularly successful at the time in decreasing or even slowing the rate of population growth. This rate in fact peaked during the life of these programs, rising from 2.5 percent per annum between 1961 and 1965 to 3.2 percent per annum between 1986 and 1990.[2] In 2007, by comparison, the growth rate was 1.9 percent.[3]

In 1975, the percentage of married women using contraceptives was 5.2 —a rate in fact slightly less than that obtained by the National Impact Survey in 1968. The failure of the Inundation Strategy has been documented by N. M. Shah.[4] The programs, in general, did not make a significant impact on either fertility or the population growth rate in Pakistan throughout their two decades.[5] More recent statistics indicate an increase in contraceptive use, with the percentage of married women using contraceptives rising to 11.9 in 1990, to 27.6 in 2001, and to 29.6 in 2007.[6] However, although fertility rates

---

2. Griffith Feeney and Iqbal Alam, "Fertility, Population Growth, and Accuracy of Census Enumeration in Pakistan: 1961–1968," chap. 4 in *Population of Pakistan: An Analysis of 1998 Population and Housing Census,* ed. A. R. Kemal, Mohammad Irfan, and Naushin Mahmood (Islamabad: Pakistan Institute of Development Economics, 2003), 83.

3. National Institute of Population Studies and Macro International Inc., *Pakistan Demographic and Health Survey 2006–07* (Islamabad: National Institute of Population Studies and Macro International Inc., 2008), 2.

4. N. M. Shah, "Past and Current Contraceptive Use in Pakistan," *Studies in Family Planning* 10 (1979): 164.

5. Zeba A. Sathar, "Fertility in Pakistan: Past, Present and Future," paper presented at a workshop on prospects for fertility decline in high-fertility countries, sponsored by the Population Division, Department of Economic and Social Affairs, United Nations, New York, July 9–11, 2001.

6. Zeba A. Sathar, "Stagnation in Fertility Levels in Pakistan," *Asia-Pacific Population Journal* 22, no. 2 (2007): 118.

are on the decline, they are still high relative to other South Asian countries—that is, increased contraceptive prevalence is not the answer to the puzzle.[7]

After these early unsuccessful experiences, policymakers reached the conclusion that the issues in population growth and contraceptive usage were specific enough to require focused effort. The Primary Health Care Conference held in Alma-Ata in 1978 gave an added impetus to this idea and induced the government to develop the national Population Welfare Program as a "vertical" program, to be managed by a specially created administrative office, the Population Welfare Division (PWD) within the Ministry of Planning and Development.

Although the policy decisions were still being made by the Ministry of Planning and Development, the PWD had responsibility for implementing the program, including training, recruitment, oversight, and deployment of personnel as well as service delivery. At the same time, the government set up special training facilities called regional training institutes, funded by donors, to provide training in contraceptive delivery services to specific cadres of the program's workers. These specialized workers were called family welfare workers, and they were to deliver services through special outlets called family welfare centers. In 1991, the PWD was upgraded to an independent ministry.

Vertical Programs within the Public Health System

Thirteen years after Partition, in 1960, the government organized a formal system to provide health services in Pakistan's rural areas. Until that point, the health delivery system had consisted of civil hospitals and district council dispensaries. The Second Five-Year Plan (1960–65) proposed the development of 150 rural health centers in West Pakistan to provide services to the rural population.[8] After the 1978 Alma-Ata Declaration, and in support of the Primary Health Care Model, the government expanded this delivery system deeper into the rural areas. Starting in the 1980s, basic health units were set up beyond the rural health centers, one in every union council. (A union council is the smallest unit within Pakistan's administrative

7. John B. Casterline, Zeba A. Sathar, and Minhaj ul Haque, "Obstacles to Contraceptive Use in Pakistan: A Study in Punjab," *Studies in Family Planning* 32, no. 2 (2001): 95–100; the citation here is on 96.

8. Ministry of Health, *Pakistan Government Annual Report of Director-General of Health* (Islamabad: Ministry of Health, 1997–98).

framework.) The design driven by the Primary Health Care Model was limited to rural areas; the urban health system continues to expand and function on the "rejected" Western model.

The core concept of the primary health care service model—to offer community-based services through rural health facilities staffed by minimally trained community workers—was supported in Pakistan, as in other developing countries, by the establishment of vertical programs. These were single-purpose programs funded mostly by loans or grants and focused exclusively on arranging medical services, both preventive and curative, for a particular disease or demographic group.

Vertical programs can be effective initially, if implemented as they are intended: in a limited time frame, in targeted geographic areas, and with flexible donor funding. Eventually, however, the returns start to diminish.[9] In addition, vertical programs have their own inherent drawbacks—for example, a dual management and reporting system that fragments communication and care; competition for resources, including human resources; and problems of sustainability because of their dependence on donor funding.

Most vertical programs in Pakistan, including the Population Welfare Program, have suffered from these issues, and almost all of them have shown persistently disappointing results. In my observation, it is the lack of clarity regarding policy, administration, management, and financing, at all levels of the government, that causes much of the confusion. Soon after the Population Welfare Program was set up as a vertical program, a Cabinet-level decision in 1991 directed the Ministry of Health to filter population welfare activities (managed by the Ministry of Population Welfare) through the general health services delivery system (managed by the provincial ministries of health). Although this policy is in effect even today, it is still unclear, after two decades, how the services, administration, and roles of providers from two different ministries are to be integrated. In reality, each program office or program individual concentrates on jealously guarding his or her turf—and funding.

There has been a movement recently within international health policy circles to integrate vertical programs with horizontal service delivery systems.[10] However, the implementation of this attempted integration, like

9. William Easterly and Laura Freschi, "The World Bank's 'Horizontal' Approach to Health Falls Horizontal?" *Aid Watch* (blog, Development Research Institute, New York University), June 10, 2010, http://aidwatchers.com/2010/06/page/3/.

10. Gijs Elzinga, "Vertical-Horizontal Synergy of the Health Workforce," *Bulletin of the World Health Organization,* April 2005, 242, http://www.who.int/bulletin/volumes/83/4/editorial10405/en/index.html. See also June Weintraub, "Vector-Borne Disease

those of other similar recommendations, has been disappointing.[11] The major reason for the failure of this idea is the absence of critical factors such as a dependable horizontal infrastructure, an efficient system and adequate levels of funding from governmental health budgets, an adequate workforce, and strict monitoring and oversight. These conditions are not met in many developing countries, and certainly not in Pakistan, where most vertical programs have fared badly—the Lady Health Worker Program, the Malaria Control Program, the Tuberculosis and HIV/AIDS Program, and so on.

A Visit to the Chief

Today is our visit to the PWD's chief of foreign aid, who coordinates donor assistance for the Population Welfare Program activities. The trip starts off in stormy weather—literally. It is raining buckets; there is nowhere for the water to drain, so it just sloshes around and goes everywhere. The streets are like tiny, angry rivers ranting and raving to no effect. My companion, Lucymemsahib, continues to tut-tut about the state of the infrastructure in this chaotic city. And this is the main thoroughfare of the national capital! She cannot even imagine what the other cities must be like.

Lucymemsahib is growing into her role and is, by now, somewhat acclimatized to the culture. She is completely thrilled by the cuisine. The wonderful medley of deliciously spiced food, prepared with such skill and served with such care, and eaten at such leisure, has her in a "perpetual state of intoxication," as she puts it.

"I really do not know why this is an underdeveloped country," she says. "Any people that cook and eat this kind of food have to be high on the development ladder."

And she hasn't even tried *shabdeg* yet! That wonderful sweet and salty concoction of meat and turnips, slowly cooked to delicate perfection over a slow fire of smoldering coals, to be eaten with boiled basmati! Food for the gods. No wonder my grandmother had me convinced that the Kashmir Valley, where she and this dish came from, was heaven. As a child, I imag-

---

Management: Transcending Barriers to Sustain Global Health," October 7, 2009, http://knol.google.com/k/june-weintraub/vector-borne-disease-management/i2mzlbs52xfl/2.

11. Richard Skolnik, Paul Jensen, and Robert Johnson, *Aid without Impact: How the World Bank and Development Partners Are Failing to Improve Health through SWAps* (Washington, D.C.: Advocacy to Control TB Internationally, 2010), 25, http://c1280352.cdn.cloudfiles.rackspacecloud.com/results_swaps_report_0610_lowres.pdf.

ined God and His entourage of beautiful men and women sitting around in houseboats on the Dal Lake eating *shabdeg.* Or *saag ghosht!* Creamy spinach cooked with mutton. Or *paye* curry (goat's feet), eaten with piping hot *naan* straight from the tandoor. She would be converted for life! All these I have been eating at a cousin's house, to celebrate the end of winter. Lucymemsahib is blissfully content with the uniform fare at the hotel.

Later, after having encountered handmade silk rugs worked in exquisite detail, mirror-work embroidery, and hand-carved copper vases, her ideas about the development level of this country get more and more confused. "What in the world is going on here? Something is not right about this," is how she puts it.

For some strange reason, I am beginning to feel sorry for Lucymemsahib. What is this poor woman doing here? A country so outmoded and outdated, a bizarre patchwork of old and new, good and bad. Full of contradictions, with its people deprived of the basic necessities she takes for granted, living lives of unspeakable misery, yet so resilient and full of life, merrily cooking delicious food. This is a confused country, forever overtaken by events, natural and otherwise, teetering eternally on the edge of a precipice: Should it go this way or that? Because the country was created on ideological grounds, when allowed to vote, its people vote for secular political parties. Yet it has a solid fundamentalist religious streak that is manifesting itself, with devastating consequences.

As I grapple with these existential questions, Lucymemsahib is sensibly enough worried about the immediate: the torrential rain, and the city's obvious incapacity to cope with it. I tell her that her worries will find no end. They will sprout branches, dig in roots, and grow into huge trees that will block out the sky. The phrase *phalo phoolo,* meaning "bear fruit and flower," is normally directed at children, as a wish for their future happiness, but it could apply just as well here. Lucymemsahib's worries, if she lets them run, will bear poisoned fruit.

Is this rain a freak event or a regular occurrence? she wants to know.

Regular, I tell her, as regular as clockwork. This is the normal weather pattern for this region. In a way, it is manna from heaven: Without the rain, the rivers would not fill and the crops would not grow. Every year this happens, as it has continued to for the past so many years and will continue until kingdom come. Unfortunately, it will continue to wreak the same havoc every year, for the authorities are never prepared to manage and harness the monsoon rains. In spite of all the disaster management agencies and the agencies that monitor those agencies, when it rains. . . .

I tell her about the rain in Karachi last week. In that huge and roiling city at the mouth of the Indus River, several roofs collapsed, in Lalukhet, Landhi, and Orangi, killing a few hundred people in a span of ten minutes. (Of course, in the context of more recent events, the flooding and rains destroying wide swaths of the country, rendering millions upon millions homeless, it looks like nothing, but at that time these rains were considered quite catastrophic.) I could tell her how large portions of the city remained without electricity or water and telephone services, such as they were, for weeks. How the drainage system, such as it was, had already clogged up, and sewerage was floating in the street. People waded out their front doors through their own excrement and their neighbor's, just to get to work, to do the groceries, to continue their lives.

I could also tell her of the predicament of the housewives in the fancy Defence Housing Society, how they, in spite of living under roofs that did not collapse, had gone nuts because of the failure of electricity, and then of their private generators, which died because of working overtime, leaving the fancy freezers without the power to keep stuff cool. All the stored food, which was mostly meat—leg of mutton and rump of calf—going to rot. What a catastrophe! They were forced to cook all the choicest pieces and force-feed their families enormous quantity of tikka kebabs, giving them terrible stomachaches. Even the servants got to eat the fancy meat (the ungrateful creatures! still they give us a hard time). For this was soon after the Eid-ul-Azha, when Muslims sacrifice animals to commemorate the Prophet Abraham's sacrifice of his son Ismail to show his love for the Almighty.

I could also tell her how this cycle is repeated year after year, as it has been for all my life. It is in Sindh now, and later it will happen in Punjab, during that wonderful or wretched season—depending on your own orientation—the monsoon. This is the season that one of the greatest poets of the subcontinent, Mirza Ghalib, calls "the best of seasons and the worst of seasons"—best for those who can enjoy the weather while dry and secure under roofs that do not collapse, and worst for those millions who will lose their homes, their livelihoods, their children, and their cattle.

Take the case of Badin, one of the most underdeveloped districts in Sindh, which even today, in the twenty-first century, looks like it did when Mohammad bin Qasim landed on the subcontinent in the eighth century— the same skyline of trees and dusty fields and undernourished cattle and starving children and old-for-their-years women foraging for firewood or hauling drinking water from dirty little streams and desiccated men digging the land with bare hands or a rusty shovel. Then, when the floods hit Badin, people sat in the trees, for the waters were full of snakes. One heard stories of children, overcome by sleep, falling into the water, of mothers watching the bloated bodies of their daughters float by. And every year the chief ministers of all the provinces go around on inspection tours of the flooded areas, accompanied by television crews and reporters from all the leading publications—all transported in helicopters. The ministers sympathize with the people and, deeply affected by the sorry plight of their fellow human beings, magnanimously promise monetary help. They call for a high-level committee to "look into" the matter, thereby unleashing a scramble and an interminable, unabashed jostling for appointments to this committee, with every minister, even the president, muscling to get his own folks in—as is happening even today.[12]

But everyone knows that this help will never get to those who need it; even if the provincial government is able to find the money or obtain it from some donor agency, it will disappear in some pocket or other, either as administrative cost or overhead, or to pay for international study tours or something else, if it is not simply mismanaged. The people know all this, and so they wait for the skies to clear and the waters to recede and the snakes—and the officials—to go away, and then they pick up the washed-out pieces of their lives and begin again. This is what their forefathers did before them and what their children will do after them.

As we continue on our way, Lucymemsahib wants to know how ordinary people would get to work in conditions such as these. They do not, I tell her. "You mean on a day like this, people would just stay at home? But then how would any work ever get done?"

Oh, work, does it matter? Somewhere, sometime, somehow it gets done; we are a creative people. Remember our cuisine?

Take, for instance, the state of affairs in the district hospitals, which are severely overcrowded even under normal circumstances and are more so now, when patients refused to be sent home during the rains. They knew that they did not have homes to go back to, these having been washed away by the waters. Even the doctors and nurses would not be at work on days such as these. But that does not mean that the patients did not get "services."

In one hospital, the patients who were feeling slightly better looked after those who were feeling worse. It was said that the improvised staff members behaved extremely professionally. They donned the doctors' white coats, hung stethoscopes around their necks, and started writing prescrip-

---

12. Ansar Abbasi, "NDMA Moot Fails to Discuss Clean Commission," *The News,* August 29, 2010.

tions for the poor unsuspecting souls who wandered into the outpatient department. These improvised staff members were quite convincing, too, especially because they charged horrendously high consulting fees and wrote prescriptions in illegible scribbles. The more "experienced" staff members have been known not to be shy in attempting emergency surgery, such as a below-the-knee amputation, assisted by a few others. . . . And a patient's life had been saved, at least temporarily. Without this timely intervention, he would have surely died from the infection from a gangrenous foot. Setting broken bones is no problem. And the person doing the surgery was the local butcher, and an extremely skillful one, too.

I begin and then stop. It isn't going to make any sense to her. I have lived in this country most of my life, and it doesn't make any sense to me. At times I wonder. San Francisco sits next to the San Andreas Fault; a tremor is expected maybe every fifty years, yet the city's residents have made preparations for it. There are protocols to ensure the safety of people and property, and people continue to live and manage their lives. Why cannot the Government of Pakistan be prepared for the monsoons?

Lucymemsahib tells me she does not like these stories. Especially the one about the prophet Abraham—what kind of a father would sacrifice his son, and that too in such a barbaric fashion—using a butcher's knife? And she is not sure if they had knives in those times. Also, what if lacking a knife, Abraham (peace be upon him) had attempted to crush the boy's head with a stone? What then? Would Muslims all over the world be bashing in the heads of animals at Eid? And excuse her; she does not mean to be blasphemous, but what kind of God would ask this of His prophet? So we launch into the symbolism of it all, and the merits and demerits of a Christian God versus a Muslim one. And if God could be one or the other, and if it mattered.

As we drive bravely through waist-high water on Constitution Avenue, past the imposing dry and secure Presidency Building, serene atop its hill, Lucymemsahib gives me a detailed account of the different varieties of storm drains used by the government of Ottawa. Different drains are used in different cities, according to the terrain and other important geological considerations, such as the mineral content of the soil. She wants to know what kinds of storm drains are being used in Islamabad. They seem to be inappropriate, according to her diagnosis, or made of substandard material, or possibly both. She wonders about the suppliers of hardware and the kind of maintenance contract the city has with them. I cannot answer any of her questions and find them strange. I wanted to know how she knew so much about all this stuff. It turns out that her ex-husband was in the business of storm drains, and now her older son has joined his father's business, so she still gets to hear about this stuff all the time. Though she had managed to get rid of the man, she is not yet rid of the drains. She keeps her ears and eyes open, she tells me, for one never knows. . . .

As we turned into the parking lot of the PWD's office, our car runs into a pothole and we blow a tire.

"Oh bother," says Lucymemsahib, "I hope you have a spare and all your equipment with you. What a mess it'll be doing this change in the rain. Do you have an umbrella?"

She looks pityingly at me, also a little worried. And rightly so, because I know nothing about tires or changing them. If I need help, she can give me instructions through the car window, she says. She is quite knowledge-able about tires and stuff, because her current boyfriend has a used car business. What is the make of this car again? she asks. I want to choke her.

On learning that we will not have to do this ourselves, Lucymemsahib is quite surprised—yet another aspect of this underdeveloped country of which she was unaware. I half suspect that she does not believe me. But once we make it to his office and tell our host, Mr. V, of our problem, he sends three peons off to resolve it by merely nodding his head in the direction of the door. Without a word being spoken, these fellows understand exactly what is required of them. After this, Lucymemsahib forgets all about the drains and the lack of them, or the business of tires. We might not have storm drains or electricity or running water or schools or health care, but when it comes down to essentials, we know what matters.

Mr. V, the director of foreign aid for the PWD, is a large, loose, long, loopy man. There is an aura of entrenched sloppiness around him. His room is sloppy, his furniture is sloppy, and the curtains are sloppy, dangling half off the railing. The very air in his room is sloppy, the moisture hanging low and close. Mr. V is dressed in an off-color, grayish-greenish-bluish, crum-pled *shalwar-kameez* and is wearing open-toed rubber slippers one size too big—the better to slosh through the rain, I guess. One of his sleeve cuffs is unbuttoned, with the sleeve trailing six inches below his arm. His hair looks like it has been hastily hacked with a primitive garden appliance. In spite of his appearance, he is not at all apologetic or uncomfortable. He looks extremely cheerful and confident, with bright eyes and a ready smile. He moves his hands in wild gestures, including everyone—the peons, as-sistants, officers, and guests—in his conversation, as if all were one large happy family.

In a paradoxical twist toward fastidiousness, Mr. V holds a brand-new flyswatter at the ready, using it periodically to swat some thing or the other on his desk, the next chair, or even his own leg. Wary of his enthusiasm, I maintain a safe distance.

Mr. V knows why we are here, so he proceeds to tell us how the Foreign Assistance Section of the PWD works and about its impact on the program. The total foreign assistance provided to the Government of Pakistan amounts to 30 percent of the total budget of the PWD, the rest being the responsibility of the government. The United Nations Fund for Population Activities, Overseas Development Assistance, the Asian Development Bank, the World Bank, and the U.S. Agency for International Development were the major donors during the 1970s and 1980s. Because the U.S. government, under the Pressler Amendment, decided to stop its funding in the 1990s, the Social Action Program was expected to make a major contribution to the Population Welfare Program.

He goes on to tell us about the Population Welfare Program. The overall person in charge is the director-general, based in Islamabad, where most of the policy decisions are made. The policies are implemented in all the provinces through the provincial population welfare departments, where a provincial director of population welfare programs is in charge. The services are delivered through specialized outlets called family welfare centers. The program has its own specially trained peripheral health workers, called family welfare workers, who are trained at facilities specific to the Population Welfare Program, called regional training institutes, which are also located in the provinces.

The family welfare centers, as the most peripheral delivery units of the system, are crucial to the outcome of the program. It is here, though, that the confusion occurs—a confusion common to all the vertical programs— and one that adds to the inefficiencies and poor management. Though programmatically part of a vertical program, the family welfare centers and the family welfare workers fall under the administrative control of the provincial government and are supervised by the Health Department's medical officers. This dual management system creates unending problems, and service delivery is one of the first casualties.

"How does the foreign assistance affect service delivery?" asks Lucy-memsahib. "We are particularly interested in the funding for training and career development of the women workers."

"We had some little bit of problems in the past, but now with this recent Cabinet decision they have all been solved," Mr. V replies.

The Cabinet decision to which Mr. V refers was the high-level policy decision made by the government in 1991. This decision, as mentioned above, mandated the integration of the vertical and horizontal service delivery systems and the filtering of contraceptive services through all government health delivery outlets in the provinces, including all basic health units, rural health centers, and maternity and child health centers. Other federal agencies that maintain health services delivery outlets for their employees, such those administered by Pakistan Railways and the Water and Power Development Authority, would be also be required to follow this directive.

"And that should solve the problem," finishes Mr. V. He smiles a self-satisfied smile. We, I suppose, look obviously skeptical, for he continues in a reassuring tone. "Once a Cabinet—you realize, a Cabinet decision is taken, what was there to worry about?" he asks no one in particular, with a quick conspiratorial nod of his head.

If only this were not a rhetorical question, one could share with him the length and the breadth of one's worries!

"That is all very well," Lucymemsahib says. "But it takes us nowhere."

"Where would you like to go, madam?" Mr. V asks gently.

We would like to know how this foreign assistance works in the provinces. Is it all in the form of grant, or loans? Loans are serious; they have to be returned, no? Does the program provide for specific activities, or does the PWD have the flexibility to use the funds as needed? How does it help the program? And ultimately, how does the PWD intend to utilize the trained health workers? The training of female workers was a big part of the Social Action Program, as Mr. V well knows. Can the current assistance be used to redesign portions of the program, say to improve the utilization capacity of the service delivery outlets?

"You mean change the training programs?" Even he is clued into training programs!

"Those, too."

"Ah, yes, training," Mr. V begins, as if reciting a lesson. "Training is no problem for us. We can easily train people," he answers vaguely, looking over our heads. It seems he is trying to sort out, in his own mind, whether this is the right thing to say. "And another new thing we are doing, that you would like to know. . . ." He settles in to tell us, conversationally scratching his right calf with his fingernails, after hoisting his *shalwar* cuff a good six inches up his leg. I am reminded of the nuns in the Catholic school I attended as child, who went into a fit if you were seen in public scratching any part of your body, even if it was the tip of your nose. If it happened to be a part that was supposed to be covered—God forbid! Only tonga wallas and clerks did it. And here was the director of foreign aid for the PWD, calmly scratching away, exposing a large bit of hairy calf and patchy pink spots that looked suspiciously like chronic eczema.

"We have developed mobile service units, MSUs for short, which will provide services onsite."

"What services? And what do you mean by onsite?" asks my companion.

"Pregnancy and pregnancy-related services," replies Mr. V. "What else?"

I am thinking: Why is the director of foreign assistance involved with program development? He is supposed to administer the grants and loans provided to the program. The Population Welfare Program's elaborate structure for management as well as technical issues has designated directors and director-generals for each. There is a director-general for training, as well as principals for each of the regional training institutes. It is these people who are primarily concerned with training issues. And there are policy people who decide what needs to be done.

"How will these services be provided?" Lucymemsahib wants to know.

"The mobile service units that I just told you about, . . . they are the ones who will provide these services."

"But how? Who in the units will actually deliver the services?"

"The traditional birth attendants, who will be trained to deal with the immediate situation." He looks at us at last, pulling down the *shalwar* cuff and ending the scratching session, expecting to see all confusion cleared up. And he continues, obviously warming up to the subject: "All kinds of services can be provided through the mobile units. All complications of pregnancy can be handled onsite, . . . wherever the people need them, these units will be right there; . . . there is no problem. . . ."

"But I thought your agency was to deal mainly with contraceptive services?" Lucymemsahib is still trying to sort out who is to do what.

"Yes, we do that, too," Mr. V says, clearly in the swing of things. "But in a country like Pakistan, it is very important to deliver pregnancy-related services." He swats something on his leg. "That is why there is the Cabinet decision to deliver total services through health centers. Our mobile units will be based at the rural health centers, and any time a pregnant woman needs help, they will rush to her aid. For this purpose, we are training special field-workers chosen from that area only. Thousands of women will be trained under the Social Action Program to deliver these services."

"But you just said the traditional birth attendants will deliver these services. . . . I thought the family welfare workers. . . ." Lucymemsahib does not even finish.

"They will, they will. But what is the harm in more people doing a good thing, eh? All the village women can be trained to provide the services and deal with the complications related to pregnancy. That is no problem," Mr. V says.

I am now completely lost. Everything and everyone are all over the place. Everyone is trying to do everything—which means nothing will get done.

What are these complications that Mr. V is talking about? Those related to pregnancy, as he has said repeatedly, looking at us with infinite patience and the expression of an adult trying to explain a difficult concept to a child.

Pakistan's maternal mortality rate has not improved as significantly during the past few decades as one might have hoped; the adjusted maternal mortality ratio for 2005 was 320 per 100,000 live births.[13] The reasons for these high rates in Pakistan are the same as in other developing countries, including four major obstetrical problems: obstructed labor or difficulty in delivery of the baby; hemorrhage or excessive bleeding from the uterus before or after delivery; eclampsia, a condition peculiar to pregnancy; and infection.[14]

Any one of these conditions, superimposed on the generally poor physical condition of pregnant women due to anemia, malnutrition, and a lack of effective and timely health services, is a factor in 80 percent of maternal deaths in developing countries. These are the problems with which the mobile teams and the hastily trained health workers are expected to deal.

Imagine, if you will: An illiterate village woman is requested, coaxed, cajoled, or bribed to put down her plough, to leave her washing and her work and her children, and to come for days to listen to words and view pictures about the female genital tract. Then she is sent off, prepared to "treat all complications," such as those described above. This is what the director seems to think is needed to deal with the problems related to pregnancy and delivery.

Suppose such a health worker has to deal with a postpartum hemorrhage in a village that, like most of the rural areas of this country, lacks almost all

13. UNICEF, Pakistan statistics, http://www.unicef.org/infobycountry.pakistan_pakistan_statistics.html.

14. World Health Organization, "Maternal Mortality," http://www.who.int/making_pregnancy_safer/topics/maternal_mortality/en/index.html.

facilities—no sewage disposal, unreliable electricity, no running water, no supplies. How is she going to replace the lost blood? Does she even know that that is what is needed? And what equipment is she going to use? And all this is to be done under a tree, or by the light of a candle. She is to some-how do all this using the knowledge and skills given to her in four hours, or four days, or four weeks of "classes" based on a training course developed in Islamabad and Washington. Even if the course were appropriate, this methodology of learning is inappropriate for her. Most of these women are completely illiterate and have no experience with classroom learning. Four days of instruction are expected to prepare these poor souls to face and solve "all complications."

Simple problems and simple solutions! If only the well-meaning and misguided architects of the Alma-Ata Declaration could come and see "health for all" in action.

Actually, the situation of a well-trained obstetrician/gynecologist is no different from that of these peripheral health workers. Even if they had been trained in the most detailed and thorough fashion in the most sophisticated facility in the world, they would be unable to do anything in such a situation except want out—which is one of the many reasons that the medically trained physicians sent to government health centers in rural areas abandon their posts. Their medical and clinical training prepares them to work in a well-equipped hospital supported by a huge infrastructure of laboratories, blood banks, radiology departments, and other trained support personnel, which are the minimum resources needed to deal with obstetrical emergencies. Here, confronted with a twenty-year-old fifth-gravida, who lost the first four pregnancies and/or infants, presenting with a postpartum hemorrhage, superimposed upon severe anemia, even the best-trained doctors would be impotent. No wonder they give up and run back to the familiar milieu of the tertiary care hospital at the first available opportunity—advising the distraught family of the above-mentioned patient that that is where they should bring her, next time. And the poor devils actually do this, but the patient, if she isn't a corpse by then, will be one soon, having lost most of her blood volume or sick from a fulminating infection that has shut down her vital systems. The doctors curse these people, who should have had sense enough to seek medical help well in time, preferably during the first trimester of pregnancy. The woman should have been given follow-up assistance and evaluated regularly, she should have had nutrition support and rest, and all the standard recommendations.

There is no doctor available in my village, the confused husband tells the doctor. His wife has been seeing the traditional birth attendant, who was trained by the government's foreign experts.

The doctors continue to shake their learned heads. The relatives wring their callused hands and curse their fate. They are unhappy with the condescension they have encountered here in the city. It is exactly as they were told. The city doctors make them feel like ignorant fools. Village people die if you take them to the hospitals. They know that there are things that are out of one's hands. There is such a thing as Allah's will. And women have been known to die in childbirth. Almost all of them have lost mothers, sisters, and wives in this fashion. But still one must try, so the next wife or daughter or daughter-in-law is taken to the faith healer instead. At least he will not be condescending; he will not make you feel like a fool. And it will save on transportation expenses, and the time lost from work.

Man is a rational animal.

I come back to my companions involved in a discussion regarding the pros and cons of vasectomies, instead of more costly and time-consuming tubal ligations, as a method of contraception in developing countries. Lucymemsahib is holding forth on the financial advantages and technical simplicity of the vasectomy. Mr. V looks pityingly at her as she speaks, and shakes his head when she finishes.

"Not possible," he says, timing two whacks of the flyswatter with the shaking of his head.

"Not only are these people ignorant; they are chauvinistic, too," mutters Lucymemsahib. I see a dark cloud begin to settle on her fair brow. She is riled up. "Why must women suffer all the time, eh?"

"Ah, but Madam," says Mr. V, with the same infinite patience, as if explaining a critical point, "this is not suffering. It is good for them." He reaches across the table to swat a cluster of flies settling on the rim of a water glass; it clatters to the floor and breaks into pieces, which no one bothers to pick up all the time we are there.

"Good for them! Why, . . . what, . . ." sputters Lucymemsahib, visibly trembling in indignation. "And why is a vasectomy not good for a man?" She confronts him directly. "Sauce for the goose, sauce for the gander, and that sort of a thing. . . ."

Mr. V returns from another swatting expedition. "Oh, no, Madam," he explains, "you do not understand. There is no goose in Pakistan. We only have ducks and chickens. . . ."

Mr. V's little people have been walking in and out, all this while, bringing in this paper or that, mostly as a pretext to enjoy the spectacle, I am sure (at least one has entertainment value). Two earnest-looking females, and one of them a goree-memsahib, chatting with their boss. Some of them have managed to bring in some tea and spread it around casually, and Mr. V waves his flyswatter over the cups and plates to keep the flies away.

As I open my mouth to interject, he thrusts a plate of cookies in my face, and when I decline, he insists, picking one up with the same hand that had been scratching his leg. I must have one, he implores; these are chocolate chip, and his wife has baked them at home. She is taking baking lessons at the American Center.

Seven

Regional Training Institutes and Other Such Things

Regional training institutes (RTIs) are an integral part of the Population Welfare Program, a vertical program dedicated to training family welfare workers (FWWs), who provide services from rural outlets called family welfare centers. There are a total of eleven RTIs in the country, five in Punjab Province and two in each of the other provinces. Although located in the provinces, RTIs "belong" to the federal government as part of a federal program.

A typical FWW is a young woman in her twenties with a high school matriculation certificate, preferably with a science background—that is, she must have taken courses in physics, chemistry, and biology. It is also desirable that she be domiciled in an area with a service delivery outlet, so that once she graduates from the program, she can be sent back home and yet remain available to the system. This is important to help minimize attrition from the program, because most families are reluctant to have their women go away from home, especially for employment. The FWWs are trained at the RTIs for a period of eighteen months. The training is mostly didactic, using a curriculum developed by the staff of the RTIs with help from international technical experts. The curriculum must be approved by the Nursing Council, which is the examining and certifying body.

The staff of a typical RTI consists of eight to ten administrative and technical specialists. Each has a principal and an assistant principal; two senior instructors, who are physicians; two tutors; two assistant sister tutors (trained nurses who work as teaching assistants); and two FWWs. The physicians are assigned to this service as part of their work in the government's, that is, the Ministry of Health's, public health system, and they have the main teaching responsibilities. Most of the mid-level staff, the tutors, and the assistant tutors are women who are graduates of the program. Joining an RTI as a staff member is a desirable career choice for the graduates. Each enrolled student, during the period of training, is entitled to a stipend from the government, along with free board and lodging; the funding for this is mostly provided by donors. Once accepted into the program, students are rarely disqualified, even if they do not finish the program in time. The only reason for disqualification is, interestingly, pregnancy; a student is expected to leave the program as soon as she becomes pregnant. Like flight attendants in the old days, says Lucymemsahib, when she learns of this fact.

Our Visit to a Regional Training Institute

Today we go to see an RTI and meet its principal, Dr. R. The "main" RTI in Punjab is in Lahore, the colorful city that is Pakistan's cultural capital. This RTI has since moved to its own specially constructed building, but at the time of our visit it is still housed in a lovely old rambling building in Gulberg, which was then one of the city's fanciest residential areas. The building had obviously been a house, probably built around the middle of the century. It has a huge porch with ornate crumbling pillars, and cool verandas branching off on either side. The pillars are covered with magenta bougainvillea and trailing honeysuckle vines thick with age. The front garden, though dilapidated and unkempt, is bursting with flowers of all colors and kinds, which are growing everywhere, spilling over onto the cracked sidewalk and creeping joyfully up the middle of the cobbled drive. The honeybees are hard at work, and the air is full of their muted drone. It is definitely spring in Punjab, a short-lived but brilliant season, with a riot of colors, cascades of sweet scents, and mellow sunshine. Hardly a setting for serious work.

Lucymemsahib cannot believe her luck. It is 10 degrees below zero in Ottawa, and she is sorry that she could not convince her boyfriend to accompany her. He had been intimidated by reports of poor hygienic facilities and other primitive conditions. Boy! Is he going to be sorry when he hears about all this. She is glad she brought her bikini, in spite of being advised against it, this being an Islamic country and all. She wants to know which is the best place to sunbathe, the rooftop of the Holiday Inn where she is staying, or a public garden such as this.

We are shown into the office of the principal by one of those ubiquitous peons, a tall and well-built young man neatly dressed in a white cotton *shalwar-kameez*. His dark and immaculately groomed head is uncovered, and a trim moustache outlines his sensuous lips. When we arrived, he was deep in conversation with one of the ayahs in a shaded corner of the veranda, where the honeysuckle trails the most. Reluctantly, he interrupted himself to announce us, giving an apologetic look to his companion, a buxom young woman, who with flashing eyes jauntily tossed her long dark braid and gave him a brilliant—and promising—smile. It is, after all, spring.

The first impression one has of Dr. R's office is of entering another garden. The room is a riot of colors that seem to have leaped in from outside. Colorful curtains are fluttering at the half-open windows. Colorful flowers are all over the room, in all kinds of vases and containers placed in any available space every which way—on the desk, lying on the windowsill, atop the file cabinet, even on the floor. In the center of this sits Dr. R, the principal of the main RTI, who is no less colorful. She makes me think of a dowager queen of some princely state: She is easily over sixty years of age and looks majestic in her colorful and flowing *shalwar-kameez* and wide, sweeping, starched *dupatta,* which stands at attention on her shoulders. Her wrists are crowded with multicolored gold and glass bangles that tinkle merrily as she gestures with her hands. Her hair—an artificial raven black—is done up in an elaborate style calling for a lot of fresh flowers, including, believe it or not, a huge dahlia of the most brilliant blood red.

On the wall behind her hangs the standard framed photograph of Mohammed Ali Jinnah in his trademark attire of buttoned-up *sherwani* and Jinnah cap and enigmatic half-smile. On looking at this picture again, I think that the hollows in his cheeks seem to have disappeared, and there seems to be more color in his face. Modern photographic techniques—one more stroke and Jinnah would be rosy and chubby-cheeked, like the cherub on an old tin of English biscuits. We might be a nation of hungry and undernourished people, and he too may have been so in reality (at the time the photo was taken, Jinnah, dying of pulmonary tuberculosis, had a nearly cadaverous appearance), but we will not let the father of the nation appear starved and anemic. Certainly not in Dr. R's colorful office, not in spring.

Dr. R is very happy with the way things are going on in "her" RTI. This building is just a temporary facility. A modern building is being built in a new housing development; it will have much more space and greater training capacity. She hopes to move there in six months. The enrollment is going to increase from the current thirty to one hundred students in the entering class, a threefold increase, she tells us with great satisfaction.

Why would she want to increase her enrollment when even the existing number of trained graduates are not fully employed? Severely limited employment opportunities are the major bottleneck in most of the vertical programs.

That, Dr. R declares emphatically, is not her problem, or that of the federal Population Welfare Division. Her mandate is to produce "as many qualified girls as possible" in these eighteen months, which she is doing very well, thank you, and now it is up to the provincial Population Welfare Department or the provincial Health Department to employ all the graduates.

"But surely there is a rationale to the number of girls you would train?" Lucymemsahib begins yet again, the same question to another senior government official. There is a slight edge to her voice. "There are issues of need and absorption capacity of the system. The number also depends on the available posts. . . . There are questions of structured career paths. All these aspects of the program require continued resources from the government, the very issues that are creating the problems we see today."

"What do you mean?" says Dr. R, looking Lucymemsahib square in the eye. "Are you telling me that there is no need in this country for qualified women? In this country, where every man, woman, and child needs to be qualified?"

By the end of this sentence, the tone of her already high voice has risen an octave or two. Her words strike an internal chord with her somewhere, for she has worked herself into a queenly state, and before either one of us has a chance to say anything, she continues, as if at a political rally.

"My dears! Let me tell you, we did not separate from India to become a backward nation. The only way this country is going to progress is if it has qualified women." The flowers in her hair wobble precariously. She ignores them; they retrench as she continues. "The Quaid himself was a great proponent of educating women. . . . He has said so many times, if you care to read his speeches." She goes on to tell us in great detail about Jinnah's specific speeches, with the date and the location, that pertain to the subject of women working hand in hand with men. An impressive display of historical knowledge. She then moves on to the subject of her own mother, who as a young woman responded to the "Quaid's call" and dedicated time and energy to organizational work for the Muslim League in those difficult years leading up to the Partition of Pakistan from India. And she tells us how it is the result of such dedication and supreme sacrifice on the part of women—for it is a sacrifice to leave your families to work for the good of the nation

—that we have today a nation to call our own. And here we dare to stand before her and say that we do not need qualified women!

What could one say? And that too in front of various assistants, peons, and other office staff who look disapprovingly at us. For shame! Feeling quite humbled by this uncalled-for harangue, but not forgetting the realities of the situation, we ask her to tell us about the working of "her" RTI, the problems her graduates encounter as they seek to work in the system, and how the Social Action Program (SAP) may be able to improve their work environment.

This RTI is called the main RTI because, along with training family welfare workers, it provides training in contraceptive delivery to the technical staff of other programs, including the health system itself. It trains master trainers, the senior medical officers who work as supervisor in vertical programs like the Population Welfare Program or as faculty of the RTIs. Medical graduates in Pakistan have followed a strictly technical, "Western-style" curriculum based on hospital and curative care, and have very little training to deal with health and population problems in the community. The special training they receive in this institution means a working knowledge of gynecology and obstetrics (though they have learned this in medical school), and the skill needed to dispense contraceptives, especially intrauterine devices. Lady health workers also get specialized and advanced training from this RTI, after completing basic courses in their own institutions, the schools of public health.

"Is this a standard practice, for the RTIs to provide support to other training institutions, especially medical schools?" asks Lucymemsahib.

"It most certainly is not!" replies Dr. R, with a wobble of the red dahlia. Dr. R has been able to wangle this because of her "connections in the government." Only "her" RTI has this privilege, putting her squarely in the provincial limelight for providing this help to the government. There is no problem that she cannot overcome, she tells us, waving her arms and jingling her many multicolored glass bracelets, flashing rings, and painted fingernails. Anything that needs to be done by the government, she can get done with no problem.

While she is thus expounding, there is a phone call for her, as if on cue. Something to do with delayed supplies for the family welfare centers in Narowal; some intrauterine devices and midwifery kits, ordered a few weeks ago, have not been delivered. The FWWs are sitting idle while the women who have come from the surrounding villages to get contraceptive services have to go back unserved. Many potential clients will be permanently lost, because it is difficult for women to take so much time off from work. Dr. R calls some influential person at the head office in Islamabad. Someone (maybe the obliging Mr. V?) says that the supplies are on their way, and sorry for the delay. The way Dr. R is giving that person a piece of her flower-bedecked mind is nobody's business. And with a voice to match, too. Clearly she does not need the phone to talk to Islamabad.

The training curriculum for FWWs is something like a watered-down version of the standard medical school curriculum. The first one-third consists of gross anatomy, physiology, and some rudimentary therapeutics. The bulk of the training months are then spent on functional obstetrics and gynecology. There is enough gynecology to deal with the basic vaginal discharges and cuts and bruises of the genital tract. The obstetrical training is mostly in delivery practice. Surprisingly, there is very little information related to the range of contraceptive choices available. The portion of the curriculum dealing with contraceptive services is focused on the techniques for the insertion and removal of intrauterine devices.

After finishing their training, the students take the examination prepared and offered by the RTI. Those that pass are certified by and registered with the Pakistan Nursing Council. The graduates then start work as FWWs and are posted to a family welfare center near their homes. Although these facilities are also part of the Population Welfare Program, as are the workers, once the FWWs accept their posts, they are employees of the provincial governments, placed in grade 8 of government service at a starting salary of Rs 1,200 per month (at the 1990 exchange rate of Rs 21.41 to $1, this was about $56).

"Do enough of them graduate each year to fill all the posts in the province?" asks Lucymemsahib.

"Of course!" Dr. R responds brightly. "We actually graduate twice the number needed because some will choose not to work in the service outlets. Those interested in teaching join the RTIs as sister tutors, and most go to the Middle East." She says this without even stopping to think, as if going to the Middle East were a built-in option in the general career path and the graduates are only doing what they are supposed to. "The truth of the matter is," she continues with ill-concealed pride, "we make them little doctors, and most of them do function and practice as doctors."

I am thinking that this was not the original objective of the program, but before I can say anything, Lucymemsahib asks a critical question that highlights another major flaw in the service delivery system.

"If an adequate number of workers graduate and are available, why are there so many unfilled positions in the family welfare centers?" she asks.

Lucymemsahib and I had observed the rural facilities in operation in Punjab and the North-West Frontier Province. Each center is supposed to have a minimum of one FWW, along with a supervisor, who is usually a medical officer. This is in theory, however, and the reality is different. Most of the facilities we observed were closed—or to use the usual term, "vacant"—because of shortages of supplies or lack of staff. The usual reason given is that no qualified person, neither FWWs nor their supervisors, is available to work at the sanctioned posts.

Because the people in the area know these village centers will be closed most of the time or short of needed supplies, they circumvent the rural system and go straight to the city hospitals, usually much too late. This is one of the reasons that urban hospitals become severely overcrowded, and that minor health problems deteriorate into major complications. Most of the time, people just do without the services and let nature take its course.

"You tell me, what are these girls to do?" Dr. R almost wails in defense of her "girls." "They know so much. . . . Almost as much as any obstetrician in the city. They can conduct the most difficult deliveries, and yet they make very little money. They are only placed in grade 8 of the government pay scale, which is basically nothing. So they become frustrated and come out because of financial need."

"Come out" means that these women leave the Population Welfare Program and their government jobs, if they have them, or take long leaves of absence. Almost all set themselves up in private practices as obstetricians. They are known and addressed as "doctors" by members of their community. Almost 100 percent of their time is spent delivering babies, doing abortions, and treating minor gynecological problems—in short, doing things that are financially rewarding and personally prestigious. And—yes—useful, too.

"How can they do that? What do the regulations say?" asks Lucymemsahib. "That is not what they are qualified to do. Surely they need some accreditation, some license to set up a private practice." She turns to me. "Is there no regulatory or accreditation authority that monitors something like this?"

There is no such system. There are some vague rules and regulations, mostly on paper, that pertain to clinical practice, but because there is no way to enforce them, this kind of thing can easily be done. Lucymemsahib looks glum.

Dr. R brightens up. She has an idea.

"Because many posts continue to lie vacant because of a shortage of workers, that is why we are increasing the training capacity of our institution. This, you must admit, is a positive step." A general and sustained nodding of the oversize dahlia. "Because we lose so many of our graduates, we will just produce more. That way, at least some of those who cannot find jobs outside will stay in the country. And because donors want to do more training, this is good for all."

We have heard this justification repeatedly, but still something about the logic does not appeal to Lucymemsahib. She shakes her head. "But then these people who cannot find jobs outside may be of poorer quality than their peers who are hired internationally," she says.

"My dear Madam!" There is thunder in Dr. R's voice. "Let me tell you that no one from our institution is of poor quality! We produce first-rate material! Our girls can do the most difficult delivery better than any of your obstetricians." The dahlia nods along in emphasis as Dr. R tells us about one of the graduates, now practicing in Kamoke, who, in a remote village, without the help of any fancy instruments, using only the knowledge "we" taught her and the two hands God gave her, successfully delivered a baby with two heads.

Lucymemsahib is taken aback at this violent and emotional reaction to a very obvious aspect of migration. It is usually the smarter and brighter people who leave.

"Shouldn't this issue be raised with the policymakers in the government, now that we have the opportunity within the SAP?" I attempt to diffuse the situation. "Surely the objective of producing FWWs is not to have them work as obstetricians. Or to leave the country. They have, after all, been trained to provide a special service within the Population Welfare Program. Because they are attracted by financial rewards, would raising their entering grade, and thus their salary, help?"

Dr. R is not convinced that this strategy will work. "There is nothing the government can do in this regard," she says categorically, and goes on to explain why she thinks so. "If these girls are given a higher grade, the medical graduates who, after all, spend a total of seven years learning to be doctors, will not be happy. They will start agitating for a still-higher starting grade for themselves. And you know that no matter how much their grades are increased, there is no way the government can pay the kind of salaries these girls can get in the Middle East. This kind of a policy change will only create more headaches for the government." (Medical graduates start service at grade 14 of the government pay scale, which in 1990 meant Rs 4,800 per month. At the 1990 exchange rate, this was about $225.)

We try to analyze the problem from a different perspective.

"It seems that the curricular content is not consistent with the program objectives," says Lucymemsahib. "Maybe the curriculum should be changed so that these girls do not gain such easily marketable skills. Maybe then they will be forced, by their skill level, to work only in the family welfare centers."

"That cannot be done either. The curriculum cannot be changed," Dr. R replies with quick confidence.

"Why not?" Lucymemsahib is confused. "Because you design the curriculum—the content as well as the method of training—it should be easy. The certification is also provided by a government agency [the Pakistan Nursing Council], which I am sure will agree with you since it is the government's program."

"Then the girls will not be interested in joining the program." Dr. R knows well the mindset of her girls. "They are only interested in learning obstetrics so that they can deliver babies and make money, and enjoy the prestige of being doctors. That is why we have to hold that out as sugar to the horse, don't you see?" She looks at us as if we are indeed blind.

Of course we see, and have been seeing this all over the country in every program. After the training, the trainees pick up some curative skills and then practice these to their own financial advantage, preferably outside the country. The horse eats the sugar and still runs off the track. We see it only too clearly; we just wish that the policymakers and international experts would see it, too.

"Well, actually they do; it's just that they turn a blind eye to it," explains Dr. R.

"But why?" Lucymemsahib, who comes from a civilized country, is understandably confused. "I cannot understand this at all. Why does the government have to turn a blind eye?" She looks earnestly at us. "Most of the graduates, since they are on a government stipend and study without paying any tuition, should be bonded to the public sector for a certain number of years. This is standard practice all over the world wherever students study or train under these arrangements. This happens, even in the United States. Because it is the taxpayer's money that is being utilized, the government is in fact duty bound to hold them accountable. Surely it is easy to hold them responsible, at least for the years of their bond," Lucymemsahib explains, deliberately and patiently, to yet another senior government official. I have to admire her persistence.

"Oh, our girls have to sign a bond, too," Dr. R defends her government. She does not want to give the impression that the Government of Pakistan is ignorant of how these things work. "Each graduate has to sign a bond which is for three years of service."

"Ah! Then you have this continuous pool of workers for at least three years after they graduate." Lucymemsahib brightens, realizing that there is some means of control over the situation, something concrete to work with. Her hopes are quickly dashed.

"Just because they sign a bond does not mean that they have to fulfill it," Dr. R says candidly. And when we look incredulous, she adds, "Since there is no way for us to enforce it, why bother about a bond?" She smiles. "That will only create more headaches for us."·

The health delivery system and the officials of the Government of Pakistan appear to be very susceptible to headaches.

"But, . . . but, . . . someone, . . . some agency has to take the responsibility. . . ."

Responsibility. Accountability. Answerability. There is none of that here. No one is responsible or accountable. There is no process of accountability at any stage. Rules and regulations exist only on paper. Bonds are signed only to be ignored. No professional is held responsible for her or his actions. It seems even the government does not feel accountable to the taxpayers. Otherwise they would make an effort, wouldn't they? Lucymemsahib appeals to me. What can I say? She finds it strange and primitive because she comes from a country where even the prime minister can be held accountable, let alone a bunch of rural health care workers. Almost all the institutions of the health services delivery system in Pakistan are in similar situations—the same scenario is multiplied many times, as it will be again within the SAP.

Lucymemsahib has begun to look depressed. I am chronically so.

The Dilemma of Trained Workers

In addition to RTIs, there are other training institutions, such as the schools of public health, also under the jurisdiction of the provincial health departments, that do more or less the same things. Their graduates are recruited from the same pool, undergo the same kind of training, and are certified by the Pakistan Nursing Council. Then they graduate to grade 8 jobs, from which they too escape as soon as possible. The only differences are in their titles and the names of the outlets where they work. These women are called lady health visitors and work, or are expected to, in facilities called maternal and child health centers. Like their counterparts in other programs, these women also find other routes of work more attractive, and the maternal and child health centers thus lie "vacant" while these women are delivering babies (with mixed results) as private doctors, without any adherence to standards, supervision, or regulation.

Then there are the medical technicians, another set of health workers who were trained under a program funded by the U.S. Agency for International Development (USAID) in the mid-1980s. This program involved millions of dollars, with technical input from experts in Western Europe and the United States. Special medical technician training schools were built in all the provinces and produced a thousand or so men and women in six years, who, once they had their certificate of training, went exactly the same route. And these are not all. There are the control of diarrheal disease workers, the immunization workers, the malaria workers, the tuberculosis workers, and the AIDS workers. All are trained as peripheral health workers through vertical programs, financed by loans and grants from international agencies, and after some months of training they are left to strike out on their own with the tacit blessings of the government and their own parent departments. The cycle continues: In 2008, the Government of Pakistan proposed a Prime Minister's Hepatitis Control Program, announced by Prime Minister Yousuf Raza Gilani himself on a muggy July evening at the grand Marriott Wardman Park Hotel in Washington, to much thunderous applause by expatriate Pakistanis. Donor money will train hepatitis workers, who will then do exactly what their counterparts have done.

One fact stands out clearly in all this mess. No matter what the program, no matter what the training, no matter who the health workers, the end result is the same. The "graduates," having acquired marketable clinical skills, leave the country, go into unregulated private practice, or just fade away. They do anything except become available to work within the program for which they were trained. Who is responsible for this situation? How can it be rectified?

I suppose there are people who would argue that the issue of such programs running parallel and producing similar manpower is irrelevant as long as they all work, wherever, in or out of the system, and continue to provide services to the people. There is so much to be done and there are so few people to do it that even if they provide less than the best service, it is still worth it. The man or woman in the street, in the village, still gets the service that fulfills his or her needs.

But does he? Does she? That is what I am not so sure about. And if the service is one-to-one curative care, why not call it that and make sure that these providers are reasonably well trained in curative medicine and that they practice according to some regulation, with supervision and monitoring? There should be established guidelines with some kind of accountability. Financing options need to be considered at different levels of the delivery system. It is quite possible that the resources now used for inappropriate and half-baked training programs do nothing except fulfill some institutional agenda or mandate and thus could be better utilized.

And what of the doctors who are so jealously guarding their grade, their turf? Their professional trajectory, in fact, runs parallel to that of any other health care worker in the country. Although, on paper, there is a rule that requires all medical graduates to work for two years in the rural health system, very few of them actually do. Their first priority on graduating is to leave for the United States, Canada, Britain, or the Middle East, and many of them manage to do so—especially those from advantaged backgrounds or from elite medical colleges.[1] A case in point: The Aga Khan Medical College, which opened in 1983 with a commitment to produce physicians for Pakistan's health care system, and thus has obtained international assistance for its community health program, loses almost 70 to 80 percent of its graduating class to international markets. Similar figures are cited for other medical schools, like Baqai Medical College, which loses 50 percent of its graduates each year.[2]

Those who cannot leave the country, or are in the process of doing so, go into private practice or make arrangements to get themselves posted to large urban hospitals. The deployment of doctors in the government's system is regulated by the Pakistan Medical and Dental Council, a federal government institution that is fraught with perpetual internal squabbling and thus has little interest in or time for enforcing its own rules or reprimanding doc-

1. B. Senewiratne, "Emigration of Doctors: A Problem for Developed and Developing Countries," *British Medical Journal,* March 15, 1975, 618–20.

2. N. A. Syed et al., "Reasons for Migration among Medical Students from Karachi," *Medical Education* 42, no. 1 (2008): 10–11; S. Akbar Zaidi, "Undergraduate Medical Education in Underdeveloped Countries: The Case of Pakistan," *Social Science & Medicine* 25, no. 8 (1987): 911–19.

tors who do not comply with them. Doctors, like other health workers, would also seem to be tacitly encouraged to emigrate.

"I do not understand at all," says Lucymemsahib, shaking her head in wonder. "There are half a dozen institutions training women, doing the same things oblivious of all others, running into exactly similar problems, and yet everyone is talking continually about training more women. . . . Doesn't make sense." She is exasperated, tired of the common theme, the continuous merry-go-round. "Is there nothing that can be done to improve this situation? What can make these programs work? Given the environment and the constraints, surely there are some small problems that can be solved within the SAP?"

The question basically is this: What do they want, these women working in Pakistan's rural service delivery system?

The Ordeal of Mrs. B

In pondering this question, I am reminded of Mrs. B, a woman I met during a field visit to a school of public health some six months before, for a different project. Mrs. B was a loud, well-built Punjabi woman in her late thirties, who had graduated from a school of public health fifteen years earlier and had been working in the provincial health system as a lady health visitor. Her last posting was in a village named Rajaganj, some 150 miles from the city. She used to commute there Mondays, stay the week, and come back to her family on the weekend.

Mrs. B's family lived in Lahore, where her husband was an accountant, a midlevel worker at a local bank. She had three children, all in area schools. The family lived with her parents-in-law, because they could not afford to buy or rent independently. Her father-in-law retired as a teacher in a primary school. An unmarried and partially paralyzed (from childhood polio) sister-in-law also lived in the same house and was the responsibility of the family. Even if she wanted to, Ms. B could not have moved her family to Rajaganj, for the accommodation provided by the government, as stipulated in her contract, was a small cement and brick room attached to the maternal and child health center where she was posted. There was no electricity or running water, and toilet facilities were rudimentary. There was no school in Rajaganj for her children, if they were to relocate with their mother.

Mrs. B was able to survive because she was an incredibly determined and pragmatic woman who loved her work. As she said, "That's how our country is." She knew the separation from the family and the difficult work conditions were only temporary. Her posting was for two years, after which she was to be moved back to Lahore as faculty at the School of Public Health, a position for which she was qualified.

Mrs. B stayed the course. She did not leave the country or go into "private practice." She took courses at Jinnah Postgraduate Medical Center in Karachi, and though still in grade 12 due to bureaucratic snafus, she hoped to move into her earned grade of 14 very quickly and retroactively.

It so happened that a new medical officer was posted at the facility that supervised Mrs. B and her work. This medical officer, a young and vigorous man, in collaboration with the area's deputy commissioner, another vigorous man (though not so young), wanted to "have a good time" with Mrs. B and the other female staff at the maternal and child health center. She resisted their advances repeatedly, and eventually they decided to "fix" her. Using their influence, they had her transferred to a remote place 200 miles farther out, rather than back to the city and to her promotion.

"If you only knew what went on there, Dr. Sahiba," she said, touching her earlobes, first one then the other, and moving her head from side to side in the typical South Asian gesture used to ask forgiveness from God for having seen and heard things that pious people should not be seeing and hearing. "Two of the younger girls who worked with me simply stopped coming. One was unmarried, and she was afraid that if her family heard all this, no one would want to marry her, at the very least. Most likely her brothers would just kill her. . . ."

"Why didn't she bring charges against these men?" Lucymemsahib says indignantly when she hears all this. "This kind of thing perpetuates itself because women do not speak up."

"No, under no circumstances must anyone know the real reason for my transfer," Mrs. B had responded in genuine alarm when I, too, suggested this course to her.

"Why not?"

"I am only a poor defenseless woman, and they are powerful men. Who would believe me?" said Mrs. B candidly. Also, think of her husband—how would he feel? He has been so supportive of her working all along in spite of such difficulties and opposition from his family. His family would have preferred that she stay at home and take care of them. If it all came out in the open, her relationship with her husband might be in jeopardy. She, and he, would become the laughingstock of the whole community. She had a teenage daughter. What about her? Who would want to marry her? As it was, her community frowned upon her going off, leaving her husband to work and take care of the children. God knows where, doing who knows what. . . .

Lucymemsahib is truly incensed by this. (It was soon after the Anita Hill–Clarence Thomas sexual harassment case in the United States and the hearings related to it. And we all know the outcome of that.) We get more depressed. Lucymemsahib, who a little while ago was looking forward to lunch, has lost her appetite. She doesn't even want to sunbathe.

"Whatever the country, health conditions, and other systemic problems, men are the same all over," she says, to no one in particular.

But Mrs. B was an exception, for she hung in there for all these years, through marriage and children and other constraints that many women find difficult to overcome. Her hope was to have a career, and her ambition was to be a superintendent of the RTI in Lahore, the number three person after the principal and assistant principal, and the highest position to which a lady health visitor can aspire. (No lady health visitor can ever rise to be principal or assistant principal of a school of public health, posts that are always held by physicians.) Ms. B was one of a small percentage of women who actually stayed in the system, and she felt she should get her earned position. Was that too much to ask?

What would make more women stay with this service, I asked her. The reply came back quickly. They were, ironically, very minor things, some of which had already been agreed to on paper. First, there must be funds for transportation if a worker chooses to commute to work. (Mrs. B spent almost 50 percent of her salary on the weekly commute. The Health Department did not pay this, because it provided "accommodation" at the place of work.) Second, there must be protection of one's career and a well-delineated career path right to the top position, based on merit and not the whims of supervisors. And third, there must be physical security and a safe environment in which to work, with appropriate supervision and support. These are the basic things that all working people—men and women alike —expect, no matter where they work.

I noticed that she did not name child care, special leave, or other "women's things."

"We have to be realistic," she said, "as it is, it is difficult for women to show that they are serious workers. Let us start small."

That woman was brave and smart. I wondered if the system would finish her off or if she would manage to survive. I also wondered how many women like Mrs. B may have already fallen by the wayside. I found myself silently rooting for her. She wanted to know if I had an "in" with the provincial health director who would ultimately decide her case. She was contesting the issue of her right to be posted back to the city, to the School of Public Health. I wish I did, I told her. I was thinking of the Anita Hill hearings. All those serious and learned—and impartial (no doubt) men. This woman had the chance of a snowflake in hell.

Some years after that interview, as I write this, I learned that Ms. B was discharged from service. Eighteen years of hard work had gone down the drain. For along with her job, she lost her pension and all other accumulated benefits. She was charged with insubordination: She had refused to obey a direct order from her supervisor, a medical officer. No one could tell me the nature of the order. No one even seemed interested in that. Along with that charge, she had made her situation worse by failing to report in time at her new post, in spite of repeated reminders sent to her by registered letter from the office of the provincial director of health services of the Government of Punjab.

As it is, she could not have been promoted to the vacancy she had identified. That vacancy had been in the Population Welfare Program, in the Ministry of Population Welfare, and because she was a graduate of the School of Public Health program, she "belonged" to a different program in the Ministry of Health. A worker from one cadre cannot be posted in the empty slots of another, although both cadres come under the jurisdiction of the Provincial Health Services of the Government of Punjab. That post of superintendent of the RTI within the Population Welfare Program was still vacant three years later, because there was no qualified candidate.

"Rules are rules, Dr. Sahiba," said the little section officer in the Health Directors' Office who explained these intricacies to me, puffing out his chest like a rooster about to crow. "Nothing anyone can do about that."

Certainly not within the existing structure. But what about within the SAP?

"Whatever else the SAP does, the program should provide some way so that the women in the rural areas can communicate with the head office," Lucymemsahib proposes. "Maybe they should be given mobile phones that they can use if they need help." No one responds to this suggestion, this being a country where such appliances are a luxury. "I am certainly going to make it a recommendation, for one's physical safety is most important." (Now, of course, mobile phones are ubiquitous in even the smallest village —Lucymemsahib was just ahead of her time.)

Dr. R has, in the meantime, arranged for an elaborate lunch for us. This repast, complete with starched white tablecloth and matching hand-embroidered napkins, is to be served in an adjoining room. There are tandoori chicken and roghan josh and naan and raita, and chutney and achars, all mouth-watering and terribly distracting. So subtle and delicate that only a really sophisticated people could produce them. One wonders again why a country that has achieved such culinary sophistication is unable to do anything for its working women.

There are three people waiting on us. In my depressed state and with three pairs of silent eyes watching my every bite, I am thrown completely off. My companion is faring much better. She has perked up, realizing that so many people will pull out her chair for her, run to fetch her a glass of water, lift her napkin off the floor, and serve food right onto her plate. And many other such things. She needs to be made to feel good, she says.

Dr. R, the gracious host, tells us about her upcoming trip to the United States—to the School of Public Health at Johns Hopkins University, for a Curriculum Design Workshop organized by the Center for Development and Population Activities and funded by USAID. This is her third visit as a participant in this workshop, which is held every year.

What will she do there?

"Oh, nothing much," she replies airily, serving raita onto her plate. There is nothing those people can teach her, given her experience. And with a "My dears! Let me tell you," she launches into a long and glowing tale of the kind of experiences she has had in curriculum design for the past twenty years and then some.

"Then why are you going?" Lucymemsahib asks innocently. "Surely there are other staff members less experienced than you, who can benefit. . . ."

Yes, that is true. But this might be her last chance, she retires soon, and USAID is pulling out of the country. This stupid business of the bomb. She has a son in graduate school in Boston, and his graduation coincides with the dates of the workshop, . . . and "Why the hell not?" she says with a challenging shake of her head. She is, after all, the principal and has done so much for this RTI. We should have seen it before: . . . no supplies, no furniture, . . . nothing. . . . Girls attending classes in the yard, . . . and no one appreciates her efforts; . . . she deserves something. . . . And here the magnificent dahlia in her hair, which has survived heroically so far, finally gives up. It wobbles precariously for some seconds, falls, bumps off her shoulder, and lands on the floor.

Who are we to argue? I duck briefly under the table to retrieve the heroic dahlia.

As we leave, more confused if not more knowledgeable about issues concerning working women in the rural health service system in Pakistan, the little peon and his lovely companion are now seated on the grass under the shade of a mango tree in bloom. She is giggling at something he whispers in her ear, while they share a plate of samosas and the honeybees buzz around, heavy with nectar and the atmosphere.

An old Punjabi romantic film song escapes from the transistor radio of a passing cyclist, who accompanies it in a soulful voice, totally off pitch:

> Amb deyan booteyaan noo lagh geya boor nee
> Rut aayee milapaan waali
> Chan mera duur nee. . . .
>
> (The mango trees are laden with blossoms.
> It is the season for meetings . . . and [mating],
> My love is not far away. . . .)

Eight

A Day in the Life of a
Provincial Health Department

The Social Action Program (SAP), which is concerned with expanding services in the rural areas, is to be managed by the provincial health directorates, and so Lucymemsahib and I establish contact with the director of the Government of Punjab's directorate. However, I arrive at his office alone, for Lucymemsahib has abandoned me to go to the Anarkali Bazaar looking for lapis lazuli and garnets. These are the stones to buy in Pakistan, she had been told by knowledgeable people in Ottawa. Also, she is frustrated with the attitudes of the people we have met so far and the apparent futility of this whole thing and needs a break, for "cultural relief."

The Punjab government's Ministry of Health is, like that of the other provinces, responsible for health care services in the province. It does this through two distinct delivery systems. The first, the "urban system," is a one-to-one patient care system centered on the physician as the provider of curative services through clinics and tertiary care hospitals. This "Western model," which has hospitals, medical colleges, and the skilled staff to manage those facilities (doctors, nurses, and managers), caters to the needs of roughly 20 percent of the population and consumes 70 percent of the budget of the provincial Ministry of Health. The urban system is managed and administered by the Civil Secretariat of Health, under the provincial Health Ministry, and is led by the secretary of health, who is a nonphysician and a senior officer in the Civil Services of Pakistan.

The second delivery system is administered by the Provincial Directorate of Health Services under the provincial Health Ministry and is responsible for delivering health services to the province's rural areas. It is fashioned on the "primary care model," and thus provides community-based comprehensive care. It is meant to serve about 80 percent of the population and receives

99

18 percent of the budget of the provincial Ministry of Health.[1] Its outlets for preventive and curative services include rural health centers, basic health units, maternal and child health centers, and the district and tehsil hospitals. (A tehsil is the administrative unit below the district level and is the second-lowest tier of local government in the country. A tehsil is usually centered in a particular city or town and encompasses nearby villages and smaller towns.) These facilities are staffed by physicians, nurses, and peripheral health workers, such as the lady health visitors. The provincial directorate is run by a provincial director, who is a senior physician in the government service's Ministry of Health, although not an officer of the Civil Service.

Helping the Provincial Director Write His Speech

The Provincial Health Directorate of Punjab is on Cooper Road in Lahore, housed in a lovely old building that in the days of the Raj must have been the bungalow of the district magistrate or the deputy commissioner, the CEO of the district administration. Huge pillars support a deep, high-ceilinged veranda that encircles the main building, all surrounded by lawns that in another time would have been immaculate and lushly green. Even today, though dusty and rundown amid the clutter and confusion of the frenzied and unaesthetic concrete warrens that have been added to accommodate the expanding offices of the Health Department, it evokes memories of grandeur not long past. One can almost see the district commissioner sitting in an ornate chair, dispensing justice from the veranda to dhoti-clad villagers.

After I let the personal assistant to the provincial director (PD) know the purpose of my visit, he hands me on to another peon, probably lower than himself in this rigidly maintained hierarchy, who ushers me the three feet across the floor to the PD's office door. This he opens with a dramatic flourish, as if opening the door to Aladdin's cave, and wordlessly waves me in.

I enter a huge, cavernous, and cool room with wide windows and a high ceiling. At the far end of the room is a huge desk bearing nothing except for three telephones, and behind it sits a huge, imperious-looking man, his hands neatly folded on the surface. This is the director of the Provincial Health Di-

---

1. For a detailed account of the financing of the health system, see M. Akram and F. J. Khan, *Health Care Services and Government Spending in Pakistan,* PIDE Working Paper (Islamabad: Pakistan Institute of Development Economics, 2007), 32.

rectorate of the Government of Punjab. He is an extremely influential and critical person, though at this moment he reminds me of Orson Welles. I half expect him to say "We shall serve no wine before its time," from the TV commercial Welles did in the early 1970s. The PD is wearing an expertly tailored plaid suit, in an absolutely sparkling color combination—army green, mustard yellow, and red. A blood-red silk handkerchief, with a tie to match, peeps jauntily from his breast pocket. As I draw near, and even before I have had a chance to speak, he waves me to the chairs set up against the wall around the whole semicircle of the room, dance hall style. I am for some reason startled to see enormous rings adorning his pudgy fingers.

After I explain the purpose of my visit, he looks more imperious, and a bit bored. But because he is obviously a gentleman raised in the old tradition, he gives me whatever attention he can. What is it, again, that I'd like to know? Ah! Yes, the issues involved in the training and employment of female rural health workers. And the issues in recruitment of appropriate personnel. Certainly. He stifles a yawn and says, "Yes, of course, we are working on the various issues, . . . and the recruitment of female workers is very important. . . ."

It never fails to impress me, this instinctive ability of bureaucrats to say things that sound so right yet mean nothing. Hopefully, we shall get to the concrete points of the discussion, for as an experienced officer of the Ministry of Health, and the director of public health services, he must know them. It is only many days later that I learn that the PD is as clueless as his federal colleagues. What I had interpreted as boredom and condescension was plain ignorance. I do not mean this in a derogatory sense; the process of maintaining and designing a large, complex public health system is simply not his area of expertise.

The PD is by training an orthopedic surgeon, and he has worked as a clinician for the past thirty years. He has been, and still is, a professor in and chairman of the Department of Orthopedic Surgery at one of the large urban hospitals. He is also the same hospital's deputy medical superintendent—an extremely demanding administrative post, in which the day-to-day running of the hospital as well as its long-term policies and plans are his responsibility. On top of all this, he has a busy private practice—he operates through various private clinics throughout the city. He has been in this job for a brief period on the basis of "seniority." This period of four weeks is all the time to which his seniority entitles him, before another physician will achieve the needed seniority to occupy this post.

"And under the new SAP initiative, we are going to recruit thirty thousand female health workers. . . ." The PD continues with our original conversation. "As you are well aware, this is a very important project, very important for females. Females, as you know, are the critical workers in the health system and the backbone of our society."

"How does the Health Department plan to utilize all these trained people?" I ask. "Thirty thousand workers is a lot of people to be accommodated. Have their salaries been included in the annual provincial budget?"

This is the major stumbling block in most of the donor-funded projects. Jobs for trained workers and placements in the system, as well as staff salaries, are the responsibility of the provincial governments. No donor agency gives aid or grants for this purpose, and so the government fails to utilize the trained workers. This is also one of the reasons why, after all the capital outlays, all the training, and all the good intentions, almost all health projects run aground. In spite of this recurrent problem, the government has never really developed an adequate infrastructure to address this issue, or even plans for one. Our assumption is that the SAP's objectives, if operationalized correctly, would do this: develop the utilization capacity for the trained workers.

The PD looks at me for the first time since I asked this question.

"Naturally, these people will be volunteers," he says, "and they will work in their own villages. We will give them the basic training for which the donor agencies are providing funds. After they are trained, these people will happily do the work. There is, as you can see, no need to worry about salaries." He delivers this information with a charming naïveté, seeming surprised that I didn't know and had to have it explained.

"Why would they work without being paid?" I am really curious. Maybe there is a dimension to the human psyche of which I know nothing.

"They'll get moral satisfaction," says the PD, taking my remark seriously. "A good feeling for helping their fellow men in pain, and some degree of importance. That should be enough for them. . . ." His manner and tone imply that this should be enough discussion for me, too.

Does moral satisfaction put food on the table and clothes on your child's back? A little voice inside goads me on. "If moral satisfaction is such a good thing, why don't you and I work for moral satisfaction and good fellow feeling?" I begin, tongue slightly in cheek. He looks blankly at me for some 30 seconds, and even before I'm finished talking, picks up the in-house phone to order tea and refreshments.

I have many more questions that the PD has no time to answer, for he is busy, as he tells me in great detail over a cup of tea, writing a speech to be delivered at the opening ceremony of a new urban health center in Rang Mahal, an area inside the old walled city. In fact, all his staff members are working on this—the deadline is tonight. And this is no ordinary health center, I am told. This center happens to be in the constituency of the local member of the National Assembly, who happens to be the younger brother of the country's prime minister. This same member will be the chief guest, and the PD will be the host. What an opportunity to rub shoulders with the high and mighty! No wonder even busy clinicians want to be in such a post, for however brief a time. After this explanation, the PD feels magnanimous, and he shares the first draft of the speech he hopes to deliver. He is a bit anxious, and for some strange reason invites my comments to "make it better," because "you people from America know a lot about speeches and stuff. . . ."

I tell him I know little about speeches, having made none and tuned out most that are given by officials, but would be happy to help, and with much trepidation I make some suggestions. It is my lucky day, for the PD likes these comments, and his demeanor changes. To solve my problem (and his too!), he invites me to attend a major strategy meeting with his senior staff the next day. This meeting is being held to finalize the details of another five-year project being undertaken by the Government of Punjab. This effort, called the Family Health Project [FHP] II, which is to be implemented in Punjab and Balochistan, is the second phase of the FHP I, which is already being implemented in the North-West Frontier Province and Sindh.

The FHP is designed to complement the Health Manpower Development Project. Both these projects, which are funded by the Asian Development Bank, hope to improve the quantity of manpower available to provide health services. They are focused on recruiting and training female staff to provide specific maternal and child health services. To me, it seems like a duplication—or multiplication. It seems that all anyone—the donor agencies, government officials, and their advisers—can think of is to train female workers, whether it makes sense or not. All programs are beginning to look like similar messes.

"Oh no, this is different," says the PD. How? "It has a different source of funding." He looks beseechingly at me. "You will get a chance to see this when you come back tomorrow to participate in the meetings. Also, you will meet with the core staff of the directorate. They are very experienced people and will answer all your questions readily." So I leave, planning to turn up the next day.

Meeting the Staff—and the Curtain Rises on "The Making of a Project"

I turn up the next day at the appointed time and am ushered in the same grand manner, again alone, for Lucymemsahib has gone off in pursuit of rugs and carpets. She found someone during her wanderings through the Anarkali Bazaar who has promised to take her to a wholesale dealer of handmade rugs, provided she makes it there before noon. "This is my only chance," she says. After today, who knows what will happen? "It is, after all, an unstable country. . . ."—and with this cryptic comment and a wave of the hand, she steps out of the taxi at the junction of Cooper and McLeod roads. Also, given the time constraints of the consultancy, we have decided to split the work and "do" different provinces. Lucymemsahib is to take Balochistan, and Punjab is mine to sort out.

This time, the PD greets me expansively, as if he is actually glad to see me. I suppose having his "core staff" around him gives him a certain amount of confidence. Or maybe it is the afterglow of last evening's meeting with the prime minister's brother, which by all accounts was a great success.

Dramatis Personae

The PD's core staff consists of several interesting people. The second in command of the office is Mr. A, the deputy director of Provincial Health Directorate and chief of the Asian Development Bank's FHP II. Mr. A has a bachelor's degree in statistics from the local university and a degree in health education from Leeds. Programmatically, he reports to the Bank's director of the FHP, who sits in the Bank's Resident Mission in Islamabad, about 200 miles away. Administratively, being an employee of the Provincial Health Department, he reports to the PD here. Mr. A, like almost everyone who works in the public health sector, has two bosses. This does not seem to perturb him at all.

Next is Mr. S, the program planning and development officer of the Provincial Directorate of Health Services, whose job, as his title indicates, is to help develop and plan all the programs of the Health Department. Mr. S looks smart and is dressed smartly too, in a three-piece suit and jolly tie.

He speaks very good English, and tells me, when I comment on this, that he was hired for this job mainly because of his ability to speak English "like a native." He has a master's degree in English from Government College Lahore—one of the most prestigious institutions in the country in the 1960s and 1970s. Whatever he has learned about program planning and development, he tells me, has been "very much on the job." Both these gentlemen are in their early forties.

Then there is the bearded and turbaned Mr. C, whose tag indicates that he is the operations officer for the World Health Organization (WHO). He used to work in the transportation wing of the Provincial Health Department until two years ago, when he applied to work in a WHO-funded vertical program, the Traditional Birth Attendant (TBA) Training Program. He has been "seconded" (temporarily transferred) to help the Department of Health as WHO's representative. (WHO has been providing grants for TBA training programs in Pakistan for more than three decades, and the countrywide TBA training program was the backbone of the international commitment to help reduce maternal mortality rates in Pakistan. Some years later, this program morphed into the Safe Motherhood Initiative, and the same women who had been trained as TBAs started getting the same training with new funding under a different name—midwives. More recently, these same women—those still alive, or their counterparts—have been given more training under the midwives' programs funded by the U.S. Agency for International Development and the U.K. Department for International Development.)

Mr. C deals with the logistics and transportation issues within the TBA Training Program. In his own words, he is to make sure that "all vehicles pick up whoever they are supposed to pick up and take them wherever they are supposed to go." Mr. C is a soft-spoken, cultured, heavily bearded man who looks much younger than his age, fifty-five. He has two grown-up daughters, he tells me—proudly, I think, until he adds with a little sigh, "of marriageable age." His basic degree is in religious studies from a prestigious religious institution of undivided India. He graduated in the 1950s and had hoped to teach religious studies at that institution, like his father before him, but after the 1965 war, he finally migrated to Pakistan and had to make his way as best he could. He is very happy working for WHO and hopes to someday work abroad for the organization, perhaps even in the head office in Geneva.

Last, there is Dr. N, a graduate of King Edward Medical College, one of the country's oldest medical schools. Dr. N joined the Provincial Health Department seven years ago as a rural medical officer, the starting position for graduating doctors, and has now worked his way up to be an evaluation officer. He has a postgraduate degree in public health from a school in London, and is a tall, well-built, rather handsome man in his late thirties, with big, almost lashless eyes in a broad face. This characteristic, combined with an intense expression, gives him a mildly demented look. He has a vague resemblance to a character in a Russian novel.

The assorted characters of this core group have gathered together around the ornate office table, as if on stage—under the chairmanship of the PD. There is a general shuffling of papers, pulling of chairs, and clearing of throats, and the curtain rises on "The Making of a Project."

Scene I: Health Workers

"Do you think, Mr. C," says the PD, looking at him, "that your TBAs can be involved in the FHP as female community health workers? For female community health workers are the core of the program. Nothing will get done if we do not have enough community health workers, and you know we need a lot."

I worry about the gentle Mr. C feeling this is an unfair question. How can he, sitting in an office in Lahore and assigning vehicles on unseen routes, know the technical intricacies of TBAs functioning as family health workers out in the rural areas? But the good Mr. C knows the system, and the system's expectations of him, much better than I do. So he, too, plays his part.

"Yes, of course, Sir," he replies deferentially, "without any problem. They are already doing things for the family as well as for the community, so why can they not be called community health workers?" Why not indeed! Because it seems to be only a question of semantics. A rose by any other name, and so on.

"That is good, very good," says the boss. "This will solve a major potential problem for the Health Department. Because the TBAs already work as volunteers, it is better to go with them rather than any other government people."

"Why, what's the problem working with government people?" I ask.

"The main problem is the government people do not work." This from the horse's mouth, so to speak. "Since they are assured of a regular salary, they have no need to work." The people in the group nod their heads as one.

The PD seems oblivious to the fact that all the people in the room except me, and certainly including him, are government employees, with his being the longest period of service.

"What we, the Health Department, should do is open one or two training schools in each district, train these women as recommended by the Bank. But there is no guarantee of jobs," he continues. "If we concentrate on illiterate village women or these *dai*-type people, they won't bother us about jobs. It is usually the young people who create problems for us." (*Dai,* in many of the local languages, including Urdu and Punjabi, means "midwife.")

"But surely these people will also have expectations of being employed somewhere once they have acquired certain skills—indeed, as they should. At least within the maternal health program—otherwise why waste money on training them?" I ask, for no one else seems to think the PD's pronouncements sound unrealistic. In reality, one of the biggest motivations for men or women to join training programs—in addition to the stipend for the training period—is the expectation of employment in the government's health care delivery system.

"You plan to train the first batch of six thousand women in three months; where will they all go?"

"Maybe they will go to the Middle East," the PD says, with complete seriousness, "just like a lot of our nurses and health technicians have done. And that way there is no problem for the government, and these people can earn good money, too. You know," he faces me, warming to the subject, "just in the past year, four of my operation theater nurses have gone to work in Saudi Arabia, and within six months their families here were able to build houses with modern toilets."

What this says about the state of affairs in the operating rooms of the hospital is another question altogether—but I cannot resist asking. The answer is predictable.

"Oh, I can easily operate without theater nurses," says the ever-resourceful PD, puffing out his chest. His staff look at him with awe. His credibility has obviously increased in their estimation. Not only does he operate every morning before coming here, but he does so without help from a theater nurse. He has certainly scored some brownie points.

"But surely that defeats the purpose entirely," I start to say, for the whole rationale of the FHP, and certainly of the SAP, is human resource development for Pakistan, not for the Middle East, but I am preempted by Mr. A, the director of the FHP.

"With all due respect, Sir, if we do not sanction jobs, the Bank people are not going to be happy; you know they always talk about this business of jobs. . . ."

"Let them be what they like to be; they are economists, and so they have to talk of jobs," booms the PD with a wave of his mighty hand, rings flashing and sending a kaleidoscope of color dancing across the room, disposing of the Asian Development Bank and the World Bank and their people in one sweep. "The infrastructure is ours; they can't do a thing without our cooperation," he says confidently.

"In my humble opinion, if I may be permitted, Sir," says the polite Mr. C, "the best way to handle this problem is to find older couples who are already working, and so won't harass us for jobs. Also, because these people have families and obligations, they won't be tempted to run away to the Middle East either. This way we can kill two birds with one stone."

He looks around, almost surprised by the brilliance of his own suggestion, for the others at the meeting are nodding their heads in what can only be interpreted as enthusiastic agreement. Mr. S, the English whiz, is writing away frantically in the most exquisite longhand I have ever seen. Somehow, such beautiful handwriting—such jaunty Ts, such voluptuous curves to the Gs—seems wasted on such a bizarre scheme.

"But older people in rural areas are mostly illiterate and very difficult to train," I blurt out in a panicked state, for it seems that events are moving very fast.

The PD turns to me indignantly and, puffing out his chest, says, "Madam, you do not know. Everyone in our villages is educated—no one is illiterate anymore."

Then what is contributing to the poor showing of our literacy rates?

"Also, I think it is very bad on your part to run your own people down and say they cannot learn." He wags a bejeweled finger at me, almost playfully. "What will the international agencies think of us if we talk like that, huh? And about our own people. . . ."

All look at me with mild disapproval and shake their heads. I can almost hear them tutting.

I want to tell him that it is not a question of running anyone down. The evaluations of the TBA programs all over the world agree that one reason for the programs' lack of success is the age and background of the health workers. TBAs are old and set in their ways, besides having had no previous experience of didactic teaching, and it is impossible for them to learn by this method. And because nothing else in the system changes, even after getting trained, the TBAs' practices do not change much. Not to mention the fact that most of the people who, according to our Mr. C, "already have jobs," usually work twelve to sixteen hours a day, mostly in agriculture, and have very little time for any other "work," especially if it is unpaid. Or maybe that is the whole point of this suggestion.

Scene II: Routine Business

While this discussion has been going on, the PD has only had half an ear toward us, for his staff have been walking in and out with the routine business of the day, which has to be disposed of, and which the PD certainly disposes of without losing a beat anywhere. Like an expert juggler tossing three, now four, now five balls at the same time, he signs papers, responds to phone calls, and gives his assent or denial to things whispered in his ear.

At one point, the little peon ushers in a loud and huge man in a loose, shimmering *shalwar-kameez,* his entrance preceded by a wobbly abdomen. He has a bulbous nose and a face pockmarked with scars from childhood smallpox, and he is extremely agitated. This gentleman brings the application of his nephew, a grade 5 employee of the tehsil hospital in Sargodha. He asks the PD to write promotion orders for his nephew, to be promoted to grade 7 as a supervisor of the district's Control of Diarrheal Disease Program.

Cannot these issues, of the posting of a grade 7 worker, be handled by the district health officer, without this man traveling a hundred miles? Absolutely not. All postings and promotions and transfers come directly from the office of the PD.

"He'll have to await an opening," announces the PD's assistant, a withered old man who has accompanied this newcomer, without consulting any documents or verifying anything when the PD looks inquiringly at him.

"I am here with a letter of recommendation written personally by Mr. Khagga, the MPA [member of the Provincial Assembly] for Sargodha, who assured me that this will be done. There was no talk of any opening. . . ." Our shimmering man has done his homework. Assuming that his luck has turned with this announcement, he adds, "And Basheer Mohammad, the current supervisor, needs to be reprimanded at once, for he is using the official motorcycle for taking his son to school, a purpose for which it is not intended." A swipe at the absent Basheer Mohammad. Might as well get the most out of this trip.

There is cutthroat competition for the supervisor's positions in most of the vertical programs, for the sole purpose of having access to an "official motorcycle" or some other small vehicle bought with donor funds. Access to an official vehicle, however, places the supervisors totally at the mercy of the district health officer, who has the authority to sanction POL—petrol (gasoline), oil, and lubricants. That is, the daily running and maintenance of these official vehicles remain the responsibility of the provincial government, and this power can be misused. It is not uncommon to see these motorcycles, along with the supervisors, sit idle for months on end because they fell afoul of the district health officer, who in turn may or may not have fallen afoul of someone else, and thus failed to sanction the quota of designated POL. Or, as happens equally frequently, the supplies are just not available, or the paperwork for its procurement was not completed in time. Or the oil tanker that was to bring these supplies from wherever is still sitting offshore awaiting a berth, or there is some other hitch in the long and convoluted process for procuring supplies. Or maybe some document got washed away by the rains.

The PD seems to take this man a bit seriously after the announcement regarding the letter from the member of the Provincial Assembly and sends him off with a nod and pat, along with one of his many peons "to do the needful." In this system of patronage, the actors follow the script.

Scene III: Doctor's Dilemma

Soon there is a phone call for the mighty man. It is from the district health officer of Kamoke, a small town 50 miles outside the city, who is desperately searching for a new medical officer assigned to one of his rural health centers—a Dr. Rasheed, who was supposed to show up for duty a week ago and has not. The next day, this district health officer is having a visit from "a big World Bank–Overseas Development Assistance delegation," whose members want to see a rural health center in operation. The lady health visitor, the female rural health worker assigned to the center, is on extended leave because she lives in Lahore and finds it difficult to commute to Kamoke. The center is "officially" functioning, and on at least one morning it has to be seen doing so. The district health officer has made arrangements with another lady health visitor who has a "private practice" in Kamoke to make an appearance that particular morning, but he cannot, as he puts it, "get his hands on a medical officer." This absconding Dr. Rasheed was transferred from the Services Hospital in the city.

"Where is Dr. Rasheed?" the PD asks of his staff, while still on the phone.

"He is lost, Sir," is the reply, and it is not facetious. "Lost," in the context of Pakistani health workers, is a definite category, along with "employed" or "unemployed."

"Well, find him," says the PD, and reassures the district health officer that this little doctor will be found and sent to him as soon as possible. And if not, "send him someone else for a day, just so the World Bank people are not unduly alarmed."

Two of the PD's peons scuttle out in hot pursuit of this lost doctor, or another warm body as a temporary replacement, and I have visions of them looking high and low, behind each tree and every bush, at last pouncing on an unsuspecting medical officer who will be "it" for the day in this complicated game of tag.

Actually, everyone, including the PD, knows that this is standard practice. The government has made it mandatory for all doctors, after graduating, to serve for two years in the government health system. This means working as a medical officer in one of the rural service delivery outlets. These posts—inadequately equipped, lacking supplies and infrastructural support, with almost nonexistent living arrangements—are, however, designed to fail. In the rural health system, salaries also decrease (despite the fact that these are difficult positions, akin to hardship posts), because the cost of living is lower in rural areas. Nor does the work experience count toward postgraduate qualifications offered by the College of Physicians & Surgeons Pakistan, which accepts only candidates who have worked under expert supervision in busy tertiary care hospitals. A tertiary care setting is the only one in which these medical graduates are equipped to function, and they are unable to work on these kinds of problems in an unsupported environment. Doctors are therefore understandably reluctant to take up the rural posts.

The standard practice, then, is to get "lost" for a few weeks, during which uncles, fathers, and other influential relatives pull strings to rescind the orders, usually with success, following which the lost professionals are transferred back to the urban health delivery system and the large teaching hospitals. Alternatively, they use this time to make arrangements to leave the country, to go to the Middle East, Western Europe, or the United States—a practice to which the government turns an encouraging blind eye. Or two years are spent in the effort to do all this and the mandatory period is exhausted anyway. Those who cannot escape or have no influential uncle just remain lost and set up their little shops wherever they can, mostly in the large cities, where the economic returns are higher and living standards are relatively better.

An Aside on the History of the Medical Profession in Pakistan

The medical profession and medical education in Pakistan, like the country, have an interesting history. They are part of the overall health care system, which was designed and set up by the British in the second half of the nineteenth century to cater to the medical and health care needs of the colonial rulers—first, the officials of the East India Company, then, when India came directly under the Crown in the late nineteenth century, the British colonial residents. At that time, the state was responsible for providing all the services to its own people. It did this through the system of hospitals and dispensaries, which employed doctors and nurses who came from Britain. Initially, this manpower was imported to India, but as the need increased, training institutions and medical and nursing colleges were set up locally, also designed following the British model of medical and nursing education—that is, a disease-based, one-to-one, curative system supported by laboratories and other allied services.

The standards of education and regulation for these facilities and the certification of personnel and other quality assurance responsibilities were also fulfilled by the state, with much-coveted final and higher certification awarded by the London-based royal college of the particular specialty. This system worked well during the colonial period because it was set up to provide services to a select group—the military, the people associated with the colonial administration, and their families.

After India gained independence and Pakistan emerged as a separate state, the national government inherited this system and continued to expand it over the years. The College of Physicians & Surgeons Pakistan, modeled after the Royal College of Physicians and the Royal College of Surgeons in London, is the nation's highest postgraduate degree-granting institution and the seal of credibility for physicians. This seal is no mere stamp: With it come increased salaries, promotions, better practice opportunities, and overseas assignments.

Unfortunately for the people of Pakistan, policymakers and the medical professionals themselves fail to see that this model for organizing health services and producing personnel is no longer appropriate. The government has also proved inadequate to sustain it, yet continues to do so for two main reasons. First, the model is financially rewarding for the people involved. The skills acquired (at the taxpayers' expense, as in all government-administered medical colleges) can be leveraged very easily in lucrative markets such as the Middle East and the United States, generating personal rewards.

Second, and equally important, this model produces valuable foreign exchange for the government. When the Pakistan People's Party came to power for the first time in the early 1970s, with Zulfikar Ali Bhutto (Benazir Bhutto's father) as the prime minister, it adopted a policy of "exporting" qualified medical manpower to generate foreign exchange. Five new medical colleges in the public sector were started within two years. This effort was not entirely out of context with the reality of that time in Pakistan: The foreign exchange remittances generated by overseas workers during the years following the implementation of this policy were more than those generated by the combined earnings of the country's traditional exports.[2]

The first priority of most Pakistani medical graduates is to go to the United States or Britain. This is especially true at elite schools: 95 percent of graduates from Aga Khan University and 65 percent from Baqai University "intend to proceed abroad."[3] This migration happens in spite of the recent difficulties caused by the complicated, time-consuming qualifying examinations and visa restrictions for countries such as the United States and the United Kingdom. Any professional who stays back in Pakistan is considered a failure. It is assumed that this was not a choice.

Scene IV: Drug Procurement Professionals

Yet another harassed person now comes in, wailing and flailing. "Sir, the medicines at the Rural Health Center, Noorshahbad, have not arrived. . . . And there is a major malaria epidemic in the villages. People are dying like flies."

(Recently, while working for the U.S. Agency for International Devel-

2. This situation is not uncommon in developing countries even today; e.g., see Roger Ballard, "Remittances and Economic Development in India and Pakistan," chap. 4 in *Remittances: Development Impact and Future Prospects,* edited by Samuel Munzele Maimbo and Dilip Ratha (Washington, D.C.: World Bank, 2005), 110.

3. N. A. Syed et al., "Reasons for Migration among Medical Students from Karachi," *Medical Education* 42, no. 1 (2008): 61.

opment, USAID, I heard exactly the same lament on a monitoring visit to the same area. People were dying like flies, and the malaria worker lamented the fact that "people had not been provided the mosquito nets they were promised by the Health Department." And no, it's not a matter of simple delay; the staff members of the nongovernmental organization—the local partner of an international nongovernmental organization—were instead selling them in the market. Noorshahbad is a lovely old rustic village on the left bank of the River Chenab, 14 miles from Sahiwal, which is the setting for the romantic and tragic legend of the ardent lovers Sohni and Mahiwal. Associating such a setting with a mismanaged malaria epidemic seems to me somewhat sacrilegious, but now the two are, in my mind, forever linked.)

The PD does not even bother to answer him. Instead, he tells his peon to take him to some relevant person or other to "do the needful." The poor fellow looks bewildered. He hasn't even finished talking. I can still hear him raving about the malaria epidemic—of flies, mosquitoes—as he departs the stage.

The drugs utilized at all the rural health centers are usually supplied by the Provincial Health Department according to a centralized procurement system, which works—at times. Over the years, donor agencies have invested substantial funds to help the government improve the drug procurement system. Most recently, USAID and the U.K. Department for International Development jointly funded a $7 million Health System Improvement Program to help streamline the financial and administrative processes and bring efficiency to provincial procurement systems, including those for medicines. All indications that this program would not meet its objectives were clear even at its start. USAID, after determining that the program was not likely to meet its expected targets, did not extend it, but it had already incurred both direct costs and many opportunity costs. The program's managers determined that its poor design had led to mismanagement and corruption.

"Who was that person?" I want to know. He is a malaria control worker, a person trained for the Malaria Control Program. His job description? I ask my knowledgeable neighbor. It is to "help control malaria in the villages." With a job description such as this, what can one do, except what he is doing. Most of the time, one sees these malaria control workers, like those of other vertical programs, floating around aimlessly, giving some tablets or injections, even if they do not know if the syringe is sterile. For no one else knows that either.

This person seems to be committed and serious about his work, I think. Committed nothing, says one of the gentlemen around me. He has a roaring medical practice just outside Kamoke and sells off all the government medicines to his private patients for personal profit.

"Why isn't anything done about it?" I am compelled to ask, though I know the answer.

A sigh. What can you do? How can you control these things? There is no system for doing so. There are some lukewarm regulations on paper, but there is no way to enforce them. The monitors themselves will write any report for Rs 10. Besides, the people have confidence in him—he is there when they need him. He gives them medicines, they get better, and they come back. He seems to be doing some good.

As it is, there is not a single doctor in Noorshahbad.

Intermission

Before the PD can turn his attention to anything else, we learn that someone needs to see him urgently. There are sounds of a major commotion outside. Apparently, this someone is trying to bring a buffalo into the room. The owner is adamant that he will bring the animal into the room with him, for there is danger of its being stolen. We learn that this visitor comes from the PD's ancestral village and has traveled all night to see him. The PD makes an exasperated gesture and assigns someone to stand guard outside over the buffalo and bring the man in.

In comes a tall, gaunt villager in a mud-spattered dhoti and *pagri,* typical of Punjab. He has been traveling by bullock cart for the past sixteen hours. His face is lined and browned and caked with the dust and grime of unpaved roads and a difficult life. He looks around frantically, with the gentlest eyes I have ever seen, for a familiar face. He is obviously tired and worried. His young son, seventeen years old, has a problem with his right leg that has not been resolved in spite of many treatments by the doctors at the local rural health center. He even took the sick young man on a pilgrimage to the shrine of the famous *pir,* or local saint, and to any number of *hakims* (physicians), as advised by the village elders, but nothing seems to have helped. Now the PD, as the son of the village, is his last hope. The man has tears in his eyes. This is his only surviving son, the other two having died in childhood. If anything should happen to him, who will take care of him and his wife in old age? He will not be able to bear the loss of this boy. His voice drowns in his throat.

In one hand, he holds a poorly made X-ray film in a tattered, mud-spattered covering, and in the other a shiny copper tin of homemade *ghee* (clarified butter), which is considered a special delicacy in South Asia. This is a gift for the doctor, sent by the boy's mother, who churned it herself from the milk of the very buffalo now tied to the pillar outside.

The PD has the frail, pale boy, who limped in on improvised crutches, lie on the velvet-lined couch by the wall, and then in no time he is kneeling on the floor beside him, oblivious to his fancy trousers and silk tie. He examines the boy sympathetically and expertly with gentle hands and small reassuring sounds. He touches the boy's feverish brow and wipes off the beads of sweat clinging to his matted hair with a silk handkerchief. He counts the boy's pulse using the gold Rolex strapped to his wrist. He holds the poorly developed and faded X-ray film to the light. His diagnosis is immediate: osteomyelitis, secondary to a compound fracture. It's a miracle that the boy has not died of tetanus, for this injury was sustained in the field.

The boy needs to be admitted to the hospital to have the pus drained, and he needs an intravenous infusion of antibiotics continuously for at least two weeks, the PD explains to the boy's father, who is apprehensive. He does not trust these large city hospitals. He has heard that people die in hospitals, and to die away from one's home and hearth is the worst fate that could befall anyone; one's soul is lonely in the afterlife and wanders forever looking for its own people. Cannot the doctor give him some "strong" medicine and let them go home? It does not matter how expensive it is; he is ready to sacrifice anything for his son. He has brought the family's sole asset, the buffalo, a healthy female, much more expensive than a male, in case he needs to raise money for medicines. She is an extremely healthy animal, and yields almost two buckets of milk two times a day, . . . and again his voice dies, as he looks at the floor to hide the tears that spring to his eyes. He has already lost two boys to "childhood diseases."

The PD puts his hand on the man's shoulder and reassures him in a soft and gentle voice. He will make special arrangements for admission; the chances of recovery are almost 100 percent if treated now; there is no residual damage, either; there is no need for any financial sacrifice; this is a government hospital, and the treatment will be free of cost—the PD will see to it personally. The father should keep his buffalo to continue to provide milk for his son. His son will not die. Soon he will be big and strong, and asking his parents to find him a bride before they even have time to breathe. Soon he, the father, will be a grandfather.

The father begins to calm down. He wipes his eyes with a trembling hand, blows his nose loudly into the dangling end of his *pagri,* and a shy smile begins to play around his parched lips as he looks lovingly at his son, and to their future. . . .

The Final Scene: Time for Tea

While the PD is thus occupied, the well-trained staff takes the opportunity to distract us with refreshments. As if on cue, three peons walk in, one after the other, carrying trays full of clanking china, clattering silverware, an ornate tea service, and steaming samosas. The tea is laid out on the PD's desk after the three telephones are removed and placed in a heap on the floor. We start eating and drinking with great gusto, with much passing back and forth of the sugar and milk pots. My companions ladle in generous amounts of each, stirring energetically and smacking noisily. Mr. C looks mildly offended when I refuse both.

The PD comes back after dispatching the father and son safely to the Services Hospital, escorted by his most trusted peon. He has given instructions to the junior doctor to see to the treatment of this patient immediately.

The FHP II is reaching its final stages "between the taking of a toast and tea."

Having resolved the "larger issues," as Mr. S puts it, "it is just some minor details that are left," which are actually "no problem." There is "little need for any more discussion on that, for we have already done this countless number of times, even with our eyes closed." To overcome the problems of infection during delivery, "let's just give new razor blades to these women to cut the cord," is Mr. C's suggestion. Are new razor blades sterile? The vast amount of literature documenting the pilferage of new blades by the family members of health workers in developing countries is of no concern to us either. No one pays attention to me. We really do develop these projects with our eyes closed—and apparently our ears, too.

"There can be one supervisory team for three mobile teams, and we can provide vehicles for the supervisory teams (four-wheelers) as well as the mobile teams (small vans)"—the same old gas all over again.

Mr. A sips his tea noisily while passing a plate of goodies to the PD, who waves it away and says, "Vehicles, make sure you put in vehicles. Four-wheel-drives, vans, jeeps, pickups, even motorcycles and scooters. You never know what the project might need."

His eyes shine as he looks toward the horizon, seeing spanking new vehicles rolling off the line toward him. Vehicles are a great favorite with all program managers and policymakers, for aside from imparting prestige and status, they are obvious, tangible evidence of the "something" that "has been done."

"We should make sure that these women get a hands-down experience, and have the know-how to clump the cord," Mr. C continues his train of thought, while I try to figure out what "hands-down" means. He seems to be quite taken up with the cord and its "clumping," and understandably so, for this has been the mantra of the TBA training programs all over the world.

Dr. N, who has not uttered a word all morning, continues to stare at one or the other person, looking more and more demented as the morning wears on. He is not even drinking tea.

"So is everything ready?" asks the PD, smiling encouragingly at all of us after putting the phone down; he has been making sure that his latest patient has been admitted as per his instructions.

"Oh yes, Sir, the project is complete," responds Mr. A, the chief of FHP II. "XXX thousand women will be trained for our province. We need XX hundred four-wheelers and XX vans and XXX jeeps. These will be used for transporting the participants who come for training as well as by the 'officials.' After all, people cannot come from the remote rural areas on foot. In terms of budget, make sure we set aside X million of the XX million for consultants who will come from outside as curriculum developers and trainers." Yes, yes, all agree, there has to be a set-aside for technical assistance, for consultants, for without this the project will not go forward.

Mr. A has all the breakdowns and figures ready. He knows the game well, having played it so many times in the past. He can, as he had said earlier, "make a project document with his eyes closed, and in less than a day." He also knows all the ways to get a project accepted.

"Just remember to budget in a large sum for outside consultants," he reminds us. "Quite a few of the consultants are already involved and are hoping for continuous involvement."

"The number of vehicles seems a little short to me," says the PD. "Can you not justify some more?"

"We can, Sir. That is no problem," explains Mr. A, patiently, "but if we do that, Sir, it might cause some other problems. The POL will become a big headache for us." The POL, like the staff salaries, remains the responsibility of the provincial government. No funding agency gives money for maintenance or the day-to-day running of these vehicles. And no jeep or SUV, no matter how fancy, can run without gas. We are all aware of, if we haven't actually seen, the shiny ambulances, bought with donor money and handed over to provincial government departments with much fanfare and speeches and photos, that soon sit idle in some official's backyard housing chickens and goats, or end up vandalized in the lot of a government department.

"Not to worry." Mr. C comes to the rescue again, as the group members look a little pensive. "WHO, in its TBA Training Program, has one-time funds for POL that are more than what the program needs. And as a special one-time offer, Sir, you are welcome to use these."

"But the funds of one program cannot be used for another. . . ." Usually, there is very strict compartmentalization of each vertical program. Transferring funds from one program to another is not permitted.

"Usually not, but we need to show and set a good example of collaboration for international agencies, no? This will also take care of the issue of coordination of program activities that the donors are always talking about, no?" Mr. C smiles a benign smile. Having been in the program for so many years, he knows some special tricks, and goes on to explain to the PD's satisfaction how this can be done. "This shows cooperation between WHO and the Asian Development Bank—something that everyone wants to see, no?"

Yes! Yes and yes! And so we have our many vehicles.

"Good work, good work." The PD beams all around, rubbing his hands. He looks triumphant as he is handed the red velvet folder containing the FHP II document rather ceremoniously by Mr. A, who, it is obvious, had come to this "planning meeting" with the document already prepared. The PD will take it to Islamabad the next day for the final meeting with the federal government and the donors.

Chairs are pushed back, pens capped, arms stretched. The peons come in to remove the remains of the tea service.

End scene. Exeunt.

Meeting Postmortem

I am a bit bewildered as I sit in Dr. N's office afterward. He looks like he is sulking. I ask him why he didn't participate; after all, he was expected to contribute. No use, he tells me. No one would have listened to him. And the proposal was already prepared. What he had to say would have raised many difficult issues, which would have needed to be resolved before any money could start coming in.

"And that would not be in the interest of either party—the donors or the recipients. The government is interested in getting the money—the first phase of the project is already under way in two provinces. And the donor agency, the Asian Development Bank, wants to get it onto its "done" list. These people want their vehicles and other little perks. So it works for everyone. Who is interested in what I have to say?"

"But the PD seems to be such a nice man. So concerned and so competent. I was impressed by the way he had handled that young man with osteomyelitis. Such a superb clinician."

"That's just it," says the doctor, still sulky. "He is a clinician, has been for the past thirty years, and he has no notion of the larger health problems or design issues in large-scale programs. What do you expect him to know about public health issues? Like most policymakers, and given his short half-life here, he too thinks it is just a matter of training and vehicles and all the problems in rural areas will be solved."

"Why is he here, then?" I ask.

"According to the government's governance and personnel rules, the post of PD goes to the most senior physician in the Health Department, and at the moment he is it."

"But surely he can decline, saying that this is not his area of expertise; it is obvious that he does not need this job—financially or otherwise. . . ."

I am being a bit naive, I realize, and Dr. N looks strangely at me.

The position of PD is one of the most powerful and influential in the province. Aside from giving him direct control of all Health Department personnel, to say nothing of the budget, it gives him immense political clout. Not one of those seven thousand vehicles would be able to roll an inch without a direct OK from him. People can be hired, fired, transferred, lost, found, and all else in between, at his command and pleasure.

"What I cannot understand is how perfectly sensible professionals start acting like 'quacks'—pretending to be experts in a discipline in which they are not. And this phenomenon is most common in clinicians. Just because they can diagnose and treat osteomyelitis or hepatic failure or cardiomyopathy, they think they can use the same knowledge and skills in diagnosing and 'treating' public health problems. And who can tell them otherwise?"

Who indeed!

The PD, we learn, will be the personal guest of the prime minister's brother during his upcoming visit to Islamabad to hand over the finished FHP II. Would he even be able to meet the prime minister's brother if he were only an orthopedic surgeon, like two hundred others in the province?

Maybe, if the brother's son had broken his leg and had not been able to find a doctor for days. Otherwise, not very likely.

But what interest can the prime minister's brother have in the PD? A lot, it turns out. The PD can, by executive order, and overnight, open ten service delivery outlets in the brother's constituency, thereby increasing the latter's goodwill.

And so the wheel turns.

Dr. N hopes that once it gets to Islamabad the project document will be rejected by the Ministry of Planning and Development, and recommendations made for improvements. "For anyone can tell, it is just a rehash of old stuff, and stuff that never worked to start with," he says morosely.

Having already met the heroes who usually review and improve these proposals, I know what is going to happen, but I do not have the heart to tell Dr. N, who looks even more morose as he tells me he has decided to migrate to Australia. While his application is being processed, he is seeking the help of his uncle, who is a close friend of a local member of the Provincial Assembly, to secure a position in the Pediatrics Department of Mayo Hospital. It's just no use; he shakes his head, his lashless eyes burning intensely in his handsome face.

Hanging on the wall above his head is a framed Urdu verse by our much-revered national poet, Allama Iqbal. The verse refers to the famous legend of the star-crossed lovers Shirin and Farhad. Farhad seeks Shirin's hand in marriage, and the only way he can prove his love for Shirin is to cut a river of milk through the stone mountains. Farhad dies in the process, and Shirin is given in marriage to another. The verse reads:

> Zindagaani kee haqeeqat kohkan kay dil say pooch
> Juu-e-sheer-o-tesha-o-sang-e-giran hai zindagi
>
> (Ask the mountain cutter the meaning of life,
> It is the stream of milk, the stone-cutting tool, and the heavy boulder.)[1]

Some tasks are impossible and futile. And yet there are some, passionate lovers, who continue to try.

---

1. This translation is adapted from that found in *Allama Iqbal: Selected Poetry,"* by K. C. Kanda. (Elgin, IL: New Dawn Press Group, 2006.), p. 202.

Nine

The UNICEF and UNDP Workshop
and the Sindh SAP Proposal

If you do not know where you are going, any way will get you there.

—Lewis Carroll, *Alice in Wonderland*

The Sindh Provincial Social Action Program (SAP) Committee, based in the province's Department of Planning and Development, had the Sindh SAP Proposal draft prepared with technical assistance from the UNICEF offices in Karachi, and then invited the relevant government departments— such as Health, Education, and Population Welfare—to review and refine the proposal before it was sent to Islamabad. This review was done jointly with officials of the line departments and the SAP's consultants in a three-day workshop held in Karachi.

How Do You Refine a Rehash?

The workshop is being held smack in the center of the seaside Clifton district of Karachi, at the Metropole Hotel. The Metropole, which saw better times in the early years of the country, is now boarded up, awaiting the resolution of a property dispute between the city and the hotel's legal and many illegal owners. In 1991, at the time of this workshop, it is barely serviceable, though not as a hotel. In keeping with the atmosphere of the city, it is dusty, dry, and cluttered, yet full of sunshine and good cheer and lots of noise—from the neighboring school, the screeching and screaming of children, the wailing of street vendors, and the steady unrelenting drone of traffic—along with choice four-letter words from irate motorists. Decrepit and derelict portions of it have been rented out to hole-in-the-wall travel agencies and barbershops, giving it a greasy and vaguely shady appearance.

The ground floor is still imposing, in a sad sort of way. Until well into the 1970s, the Auditorium, the venue of the workshop, was the Ballroom, where elegantly dressed women in off-the-shoulder gowns or brilliantly colored saris danced with men dressed in tails. With their hair perfectly coiffed and pomaded, they paraded around to live music played by Goan or foreign bands. The room has a high, ornate ceiling and lovely French windows, which open onto what was once a courtyard garden but because of the perpetual water problem is now just a dusty, scrappy yard. The French windows are covered with red velvet drapes that are stiff with dirt and mildew, but still valiantly swish back and forth with a theatrical flourish, evoking memories of those grand and decadent times. The same moth-eaten red velvet also covers the numerous ornate chairs scattered around the room.

Because UNICEF is providing the technical assistance for this workshop, its presence is very visible—its personnel and equipment are all over the place. One corner has been designated the "Computer Room," where half a dozen desktops and attached printers are in constant noisy motion. (At the time of this workshop, computers, desktops only, were still a technological novelty in Pakistan. They were mostly used by international agencies and corporations and had not yet made their way into government offices.) These large, clunky things, used for word processing—that is all most people had as yet been able to master—create an aura of unquestionable credibility and authenticity.

UNICEF's "technical help" consists of loaning its staff and computers to help with writing the technical aspects of the Sindh SAP Proposal. The United Nations Development Program (UNDP) is paying for the participants in the workshop, including their travel and living expenses, as well as those of the three outside consultants, one each in education, human resource development, and health/population. I am the consultant for health/population issues. We are to give our input on the programmatic details of the proposal, to make sure that it is "technically sound" and consistent with the SAP's overall objectives.

The participants in the workshop are the district-level staffs of the line departments, which include the managers of the Health, Education, Population Welfare, and Sanitation departments—all those directly responsible for service delivery. These are the people who face the day-to-day problems of operations and management. For example, the medical officers who work in the rural health centers or the tehsil and district hospitals are responsible for providing supervision and technical support to the rural health workers—those who will be trained under the SAP. Similarly, there are population welfare officers who are the supervisors of family welfare workers. All in all, this seems like a good group to be part of the proposal preparation process.

The chief of the provincial Ministry of Planning and Development of the Government of Sindh is the chief of the Provincial SAP Committee and is in overall charge of this workshop.

UNICEF Karachi's project officer for monitoring and evaluation in the Health, Population, and Nutrition Department, Mr. J, is the technical expert representing UNICEF in this workshop. And that worries me. I knew Mr. J well while working for UNICEF in Karachi as the project officer of the Traditional Birth Attendant Training Program from 1986 to 1988. Mr. J's background is interesting. He has a master's degree in history from a university in undivided India and was a midlevel bureaucrat in the Sindh Education Department before joining UNICEF. Though he is extremely knowledgeable about how the offices of the provincial government function, and also about international organizations, he knows very little about the problems of female health workers in the field.

I have seen Mr. J in action many times, and his strength, as he himself says with great pride, is to "smell out in one second what the boss wants" and then do it. No doubt this is a wonderful ability, but not one that is particularly useful for designing health and population services for rural areas. I once requested Mr. J's assistance in developing the monitoring tools for the Traditional Birth Attendant Training Program. He had advised me to pick up eight or ten program documents from previous projects—any projects—choose the things that seemed reasonable to me, and splice them together. Simple. And he went on to tell me, again not without a hint of pride, that he could now come up with a project proposal in an hour. Mr. J is the main architect of the draft proposal prepared for the Sindh SAP.

The draft proposal presented to the consultants on the first day of the workshop is an impressive document: bright logo, good format, very few spelling errors, perfect binding. I open my copy and read it—and read it again. Then I shift a few pages and read again. I get a cup of water and read again. It flows well, an easy read. But it makes absolutely no sense. It is a bunch of words, and then a bunch of sentences, strung together in neat and perfect paragraphs that make, again, no sense.

And then it hits me. Of course! This document has been spliced together.

It consists of old proposals from the Traditional Birth Attendant Training Program, from immunization workers' training programs, from the training programs for community health workers, the village health workers program, and the Family Welfare Workers Training Program. Some bits from the now-defunct Medical Technicians Training Program have also been thrown in; for instance:

- "Mobile teams of eight to ten female health workers will be deployed in each village. . . ."
- "Each team will be accompanied by a supervisor and a health educator and. . . ."
- "Health workers will be trained in obstetric methods and contraceptive methods. . . ."
- "Workers will be belonging to the same village so they can be available on the spot. . . ."
- "The workers will provide the preventive and curative health services as needed. . . ."

All these are high-sounding ideas and well-meaning words and phrases. Who can argue with them? Who in their right mind is liable to say no to any of this? And so the proposal goes on and on about the support for the training program for the workers—the capital outlays, the vehicles, training curricula, curriculum development experts, stipends for training, and other budgeted items crucial for any large-scale training program. And so the SAP for the health and population sectors is all ready. The same kinds of things are given for the education, water, and sanitation sectors. As I said, it is an impressive document. Everyone is sufficiently impressed.

But I am perturbed.

I am perturbed because this draft proposal is a repeat of the past four decades. This is exactly what happened with the government's Accelerated Health Program, with the Medical Technicians Training Program, with the Traditional Birth Attendant Training Program, and with a host of others. After the workshops and the curricula development process have been completed, after the experts have gone, after the vehicles have been ordered and the stipends have been consumed and the reports have been written, one sees the curricula sitting on shelves gathering dust. Frustrated and misused health workers, those who are unable to find jobs outside the country, roam the streets, or put to work whatever crucial skills they may have learned, unsupervised, without any standards, without accountability. They give injections of this and that for five bucks a pop for everything under the sun, and dispense pills—antibiotics, hormones, steroids—to people who for lack of any other provider come to these "doctors." The fancy vehicles are driven by the family members of the project personnel, and the four-wheelers are used to cart farm animals or their feed from the market to the farm, or for other such errands, if they don't simply sit idle and rot for lack of gasoline, oil, and lubricants.

"What are we to do, Dr. Sahiba?" a senior officer in the Department of Planning and Development responds, when I raise the issue with him of the SAP draft proposal being a rehash. "We are on a tight schedule, and also, if things are already available, why not use them?"

"The SAP is basically speaking of establishing a health delivery system for a disadvantaged population. This is a complicated program. There are sustainability issues that are likely to have an impact on the budget of the provincial government. At the very least, there are issues of regulation, financing, and monitoring of services," I say, thinking that I have a sympathetic ear. "Do we not need to sort out these issues first before we get into simply training more women to do more of the same? It seems we are setting ourselves up for failure if we do not do so."

"Who is talking of failure? God is with us. He watches out for His own. We shall have all the success, Inshaallah!" the senior officer replies, with hair-raising faith.

"But. . . ."

"It is all very well for you to say these things," he interrupts, looking accusingly at me, "but we have to meet a very short deadline. The Consortium meets on the loan process in two months, and we must have the financial outlays completely outlined."

"But how can you only have the financial outlays without. . . ." Before I can finish, he interrupts me again.

"Yes, yes. . . ." He holds up a hand while his attention is already beginning to wander to someone more important, "there will be time enough for all that later on. . . . We need to get this out first."

I refuse to be blown off. Seeing my expression, I suppose, he goes on to explain his views of the situation in an even voice, looking me straight in the eye. "We are talking about millions of dollars, Dr. Sahiba, millions! We have very strict instructions from high up, so all systems must be 'go' in that direction; there is no time to think!"

I am reminded of a brief encounter I had with another senior officer in the federal Ministry of Planning and Development in Islamabad at the beginning of this assignment. He was too busy to meet with us, but paused long enough in the colorless corridor of the P Building to say, when I raised the same issues with him, in exactly the same even voice, "This, Dr. Sahiba, is a done thing. This money is coming in as long as we are able to come to the table with a document. . . ."

"If you have a shoddy document, the money will be completely wasted," I had retorted to his rapidly retreating back. That had made the senior federal officer stop in his tracks, turn around, and look me in the eye.

"This money is not going to be wasted at all," he said in that level voice. "It will be put to extremely good use."

"Which is?" I asked. I was in an argumentative mood.

He relaxed, smiled indulgently, and said with a naughty twinkle, "Maybe it will help build the bomb. . . ."

I had thought the senior federal officer was joking, but now I am beginning to think that maybe his remark was not facetious. So I detain the SAP Committee member. "Surely you, as well as the lending agencies, want a realistic document," I persist, "one that achieves some objectives of much-needed development, or at least starts to move the service delivery system in the right direction. . . ."

"Who says this is not the right direction?" he says, with much authority.

Realizing that this is the only opportunity—and a fleeting one, no doubt —that I shall ever get to put my perspective across, I look him straight in the eye, take a deep breath, and say, "I do," with equal authority.

"That is not your problem." He brushes off my response quite calmly. "You have to stay within your defined parameters and help develop the program."

"This is within my parameters," I say evenly, being on sure ground. I attempt a clinical analogy to drive the point. "Suppose you brought me someone with a stomachache and asked me to remove the appendix, because it is common knowledge that a bad appendix causes a stomachache. And I, as the expert, tell you that though this person has a stomachache, it is not because of a bad appendix. It is something else."

My companion looks perplexed; he frowns and opens his mouth to say something.

"I would tell you in this case that your diagnosis is incorrect, as is your recommended solution," I rush on, "and I, as the expert, have made a different diagnosis, and the prescription may be different as well."

"Who is talking of prescriptions and stomachaches?" the SAP Committee member interrupts impatiently, looking as if he has a headache. "We are talking of the social sectors, which have nothing to do with this. . . ."

I can tell that the analogy has passed him by.

"And don't worry too much," he says as he moves away. "This money will come in. For after all," he adds, a bit pompously, "the [World] Bank is also under pressure to loan. . . ."

Under pressure to give, under pressure to receive. It seems that a cement mixer has been turned on and a building will soon rise—even without a foundation.

Soldiering On

So I, too, join the surrealistic exercise of putting together the program design for the SAP. It is being done in a participatory fashion, with everyone contributing. One of my fellow consultants looks at the whole thing and walks out, saying that it is an insult to his intelligence. He will have no part of this exercise. He will not rubber-stamp a Mickey Mouse document to which he cannot make a meaningful contribution.

"Then contribute," I say to him. "This is our chance to maybe try and change something. We are, after all, the technical experts. Surely we have a say."

"This is the first time you are doing this, isn't it?" He looks pityingly at me. "You'll find out how impotent you are in spite of your technical expertise. I've done this too many times to be sucked into it again. It is no use. I'll see you when this is all over." With that, he leaves the workshop—on the first morning.

And find out I do. Each day for the next three days, twenty-five people— the social-sector department managers of the government of Pakistan and us, the technical experts brought in by international agencies—divide into groups of five to discuss and reach a consensus on the programmatic details of the SAP. The group consists of one member from each department— Health and Population, Education, and Water and Sanitation—along with one or two technical experts and a representative of some national or international nongovernmental organization (NGO). The parameters have been rigidly defined by the draft proposal, and we know that our discussion is supposed to stay within them.

For example, a section on population welfare states: "To increase the contraceptive prevalence rate in rural areas, village women will be trained to dispense contraceptives." Then this general statement is worked out: XX number of workers per XX number of women in the village will be trained for XYZ number of days using a specially designed curriculum. The curriculum will be prepared by international curriculum development experts. The training will be done in such and such a place—usually a five-star hotel in the city—by a team of trainers, young women from population welfare departments or the lady health visitors, supervised by maybe a medical officer or a representative of a prominent NGO. These trainers will undergo a master-trainers' training before conducting the training of village women, and so on and so on.

A heated discussion ensues about this activity within the program. Someone says that a group of XX is too large; it should be no more than X. Well, it's a trade-off, says another; there is such a thing as economies of scale. The logistical problems of transportation and other operational issues make it worthwhile to have a large number of participants in each training session. Then the duration of five days of training is debated. One expert feels that a week of training at one go is too long. These women cannot take off that much time from their homes and families and other work. Another is worried that it is too short, for there is a lot to learn and these are illiterate village women. They have never even gone to school, never learned in a didactic fashion, and have no idea of how to use textbooks or lessons.

Then there is a long discussion on refresher courses. Should there be refresher courses? If yes, how often? Would this have budgetary implications? But this is critical, no? Everyone needs to have their knowledge updated. These women should be called back every three months for refresher courses. Ah, good! Good! Refresher courses are good, they really need them. And one very knowledgeable medical officer launches into a story of how one traditional birth attendant in his jurisdiction came back seven times for the same course. Even then, she did not learn the basics. That is why refreshers are so important. It is almost impossible for these people to pick up the skills the first time around.

"They are actually not serious about learning anything," says the medical officer who has been involved with the UNICEF-supported Traditional Birth Attendant Training Program for the past three years. "They just join the training program for other reasons. Some do it to oblige the officials; most do it for the stipend and to get away from the drudgery of their homes. As you know, their lives are not a bed of roses, . . . just cooking and cleaning and tending to animals and children and then being beaten by their frustrated husbands for some trivial mistake or other," he explains.

"That may very well be true, but this training program is not supposed to be a paid holiday," someone mutters. People shake their heads. These people are so ignorant, so difficult to train. Tut-tut-tut.

A Health Department lady who has been quiet all along, her head covered by a *dupatta,* her eyes lowered, becomes emotional. "Why should they not get a break?" she says, her eyes flashing, challenging us. "Even the chiefs and the rest of us go off on all kinds of training programs and workshops, don't we? Aren't those paid holidays? And in London or Washington, too." She looks deliberately at each of us, and we lower our eyes. "Why should these women be doomed to days of endless drudgery? If God has willed some relief for them, why should they be denied that? And this money has to be spent. . . ."

All look sad and solemn for a while, a bit sheepish. The Health Department lady, embarrassed after her outburst, lowers her eyes and adjusts her *dupatta,* which had fallen off her hair. Ah! What can we do? The situation is terrible, we all know. It is terrible all over the country, and much worse in rural areas. But these are cultural problems, no? What do these have to do with health programs? A straightening of the chairs, a shuffling of the papers, and back to work. Come on, people, we have a lot of work to do. So is seven days of initial training agreed upon? With maybe at least one refresher course after three months? Yes, let's compromise. The group agrees, nods, yes, . . . yes, . . . all right.

Then the discussion moves on to the curriculum. Should a new one be designed, or should we use the old ones?

"I say we should use the ones we have. Why waste money?" says Dr. K, the assistant director of the provincial Population Welfare Division. "There are millions of curricula lying around the country. Even UNICEF has one, which, though not used, is very good."

"Because the curriculum under discussion has never been used, how do you know it is good?" I ask.

"Well, my dear, it comes from the head office," she replies, unfazed. "From New York! Prepared by Johns Hopkins University!"

There is a visible intake of breath. New York! Who dares question this seal of authenticity. They look at me: Satisfied?

Not quite. "Why was this curriculum not used? The Population Welfare Department paid for it with a loan or grant money, no?"

"There was no need to!" Dr. K replies, with a decidedly triumphant note in her voice, ignoring the last part of my question, and explains: "Before it could be delivered, we had developed our own, each agency according to its needs. That worked quite well. It is not difficult to design the basic curriculum, for we know our population and we know our problems."

Then why incur the enormous cost of paying international consultants? Because curriculum development is part of the overall program, and has already been budgeted in, no? Dr. K nods, while the others look out the window.

On to the question of the trainers. The experience of using lady health visitors has been very good in the past, except for one thing. Because they are younger than the women they are expected to train, their youth can at times cause problems. In this culture, younger people do not tell older people how to do things. It is usually the other way around. For a minor issue, some managers had been able to resolve this problem quickly. It depends on the manager and how he or she handles his or her staff. Also, these lady health visitors are Health Department employees, so they will do what the department tells them to do. Some of the NGOs are willing to help, and they provide their own experienced trainers. The Family Planning Association, one of the oldest NGOs in Pakistan, had been very active in this regard, with funding from the London-based International Federation for Family Planning.

And so we go down the list, discussing each activity methodically, discussing each component of the activity, and reaching a decision by consensus. In this way curriculum content, teaching methodology, number of trainees, stipends for trainees—oh yes, stipends are the most critical; otherwise, why would they come?—are considered and incorporated into "the project."

Then on to the other infrastructure needs of the training program as part of the general "financial outlay." Vehicles, a specific number, are clearly stipulated, because they still are the most crucial (and expensive) item. It is impossible to work in rural areas without adequate transportation, the group agrees. The project is going to need four-wheelers, minivans, and jeeps, and in the hundreds. The proposal looks more and more operational. What about maintenance costs? And petrol (gasoline), oil, and lubricant (POL)? This, like all other maintenance costs—such as staff salaries—remains the responsibility of the provincial government, and is never part of the assistance. This poses some problems, for we all know that the provincial government is chronically short of funds. All are silent—and thoughtful for a while. So many vehicles will need a lot of POL.

As we are struggling with this problem, the officer of the Department of Planning and Development (P&D)—the same gentleman who told me ear-

lier to concentrate on the program and forget the larger issues—passes by.
We flag him down and pose this problem to him. No problem. He gives his
OK—the department will make sure there is enough POL. But this group is
not one to be appeased so easily. The government departments, including
P&D, are terribly strapped for funds, and the program mangers have heard
this refrain before. The Health Department's purse, the field staff are told
again and again, is quite depleted. We remind the officer of the innumerable
vehicles for the immunization program sitting stranded because of a lack of
POL, and of the unsatisfactory results of that program. We do not want the
new SAP's activities to meet the same fate a few months into the project.
Without batting an eye, the official puffs out his chest: "For the SAP, we
shall make the money," he says with a theatrical ring to his voice.

He might as well have said that we should "eat grass" while they're doing so—so eerie is the echo Prime Minister Zulfikar Ali Bhutto's declaration after the Indian nuclear tests in 1974 that Pakistanis would do whatever
it took and suffer whatever deprivation in order to develop a nuclear bomb.
I was a final-year medical student in 1974, and at the time Bhutto's grand,
outlandish statement stirred me to the depths of my soul. Time has tempered
things, however, and the statement has taken on new meanings. Just as the
people of Pakistan have been forced to—metaphorically and literally—eat
grass over the past four decades, and as they will keep on eating it, the government of Pakistan will, as its responsible officer says, "be constantly making money. We refuse to learn from our mistakes, and thus will continue to
repeat them."

By the end of the afternoon session, as it is getting close to the break for
tea—with chicken patties and other yummies, arranged courtesy of UNICEF,
and paid for from proposal preparation funds—a major section of the Sindh
SAP Proposal supporting the Population Welfare Program has been put together. It discusses the program at the district level along with all the details, such as the services to be provided by trained rural health workers,
with an approximate amount of money given for each item. This program
is to be implemented with the collaboration of three crucial—and rival—
departments, Health, Education, and Population, with the P&D Department
being the coordinator and adviser. UNICEF and UNDP will arrange for or
provide technical assistance as needed over the future life of the project. International consultants will be called in to monitor and review, as part of the
technical assistance. Of course, of course, all concur. Everyone knows that
no assistance program would be accepted without this provision. Let's just

hope it is a reasonable amount, is the dominant thought, for there have been projects in which a substantial portion of the assistance has gone back to the parent country in consulting costs.

During the tea break, the "experts" from UNICEF continue to thunder away at their desktops, with Mr. J flitting about energetically, now looking over the shoulder of one, now giving gentle instructions to another. "Let me show you how to do the spell-check here," he says to one, who looks on in awe at this wonder of word processing. Soon the printout of "our" project draft is placed before us. All look at it with a certain amount of satisfaction and sense of accomplishment. It looks good, doesn't it?

The senior program officer of UNDP saunters over to me. She is an extremely attractive woman in her mid-forties, her hair perfectly done in a hip bob, wearing a perfectly tailored, trendy *shalwar-kameez.* A beige pashmina, with its intricately embroidered end trailing gracefully behind, is thrown over her left shoulder. She has spent some years working for the UN system based in New York, so she is well known on the international and national development circuits.

"So what do you think?" she asks me, delicately sipping tea and fluttering eyelashes heavy with mascara. But before I can reply, she tells me that she is "cheesed off" with the other consultants for not taking their responsibilities seriously enough. If she and other senior officers from international agencies could find the time to participate in this effort, why couldn't they? I can only concur. She and the SAP Committee are looking to me, she says, for some "solid recommendations" for the health and population sectors. "For these are very serious issues with the government," she says.

You could have fooled me. In any case, her attention is soon claimed by the chief of P&D, who has a crucial point to discuss with her. I am strangely relieved to see her go, for her way of fluttering her eyelashes, which apparently does things for the senior officers of the Sindh government, does nothing for me. In truth, I find it quite distracting.

And so, over a period of three days, all the other sections of the proposal are "done" in a similar fashion. Activity by activity—in health, population welfare, education, and water and sanitation—each task is discussed and debated, and then a consensus is reached. For you see, the participants are experienced in this kind of exercise and know what is expected of them. Who can find fault with this process? It is as democratic and participatory a process as you could ever hope to see. Thus, four provincial proposals were prepared and presented to the Federal SAP Committee. There was some snipping and cutting, some changes were made here and there, a consensus was reached, and a final proposal was presented to the International Aid Consortium–World Bank team. The SAP was on!

No Impact: Faulty Programs, Then and Now

I found fault with the SAP proposal in 1991, however, and I have found the same fault with those designed since then, including those prepared after 2003, while I worked for the U.S. Agency for International Development in Pakistan. If you look at the history of development programs in the health and population sectors in Pakistan, you will see that this same program has been prepared in exactly the same way during the past four decades, and the results have been, are, and will be the same. Almost all the health and population delivery programs have been designed the same way, with capital outlays for vehicles and for training workers; with plans and budgets based, always, on supply, without an adequate analysis of the nature of the demand or the utilization of the finished project; and without any thought given to sustainability.

Almost all these programs have failed; even a cursory review of the social-sector indicators will corroborate this point. The most recent data from the 2006 Pakistan Demographic and Health Survey confirm that the social-sector indicators have not improved much during the past fifteen years, in spite of continued donor assistance to health, education, and women's development.[1] The SAP alone cost $8 billion over ten years, with nothing to show for the money or the time. The programs being implemented now will also fail to achieve any sustainable improvements in service delivery. At best, these improvements—mostly in the form of trained manpower, which demonstrates "capacity building"—will last only as long as the life (i.e., the funding) of the project. We are repeating the mistakes of the past, and seem likely to keep doing so into the future.

There are project completion reports that speak of so many thousand health workers trained, so many thousand village health workers available in the villages, so many thousand skilled birth attendants available to pro-

---

1. National Institute of Population Studies and Macro International Inc., *Pakistan Demographic and Health Survey 2006–07* (Islamabad: National Institute of Population Studies and Macro International Inc., 2008).

vide obstetrical services, so many thousand trained to do something else, and so many millions of condoms distributed to family welfare centers or intrauterine contraceptive devices inserted. The reports also give details of hundreds of new service delivery outlets opened in rural areas funded by one donor agency or the other. Yet there is no impact. What is the problem?

"You know, the problem with our country," a field officer of the Population Welfare Division, from Tando Allahyar, says in reply to my question, "is people lacking in education. Especially women who are completely illiterate."

Like most development experts, I couldn't agree more, and tell him so.

"Our women, . . . they, poor things, must have children. . . . Otherwise, what they will do? Their husbands will divorce them," says another, and I agree with him, too.

"And most of the time their children die in infancy, so they must try again and again for a pregnancy even at the cost of their own health," someone else volunteers.

Social scientists agree that in a society like Pakistan's, where a woman's social standing and identity are tied to the number of her surviving—male—children, where there is no other means of security for old age, and where the infant mortality and childhood mortality rates are high, people are forced to choose large families over smaller ones. For disadvantaged people, children are an economic asset, and in Pakistan, for most people a larger family is still the more logical decision.[2] Another factor behind large family size is the importance of sons; numerous studies have shown that contraceptive use and family planning only become serious options once a couple has had one or more sons that have a reasonable likelihood of survival.[3] This state of affairs has existed on the subcontinent for many years,[4] and even as of 2007, it had not changed as dramatically as those involved with development programs might have hoped.[5]

2. Zeba A. Sathar, "The Much-Awaited Fertility Decline in Pakistan: Wishful Thinking or Reality?" *International Family Planning Review* 19, no. 4 (1993): 142–46; the citation here is on 144.

3. Tasnim Khan and Rana Ejaz Ali Khan, "Fertility Behavior of Women and Their Household Characteristics: A Case Study of Punjab, Pakistan," *Journal of Human Ecology* 30, no. 1 (2010): 11–17; the citation here is on 14.

4. E.g., see David A. May and David M. Heer, "Son Survival and Family Size in India: A Computer Simulation," *Population Studies* 22, no. 2 (1968): 199–210.

5. National Institute of Population Studies and Macro International Inc., *Pakistan Demographic and Health Survey 2006–07*.

The people in the group nod their heads in understanding. They see—and live—this reality every day. So, I ask these officers of the provincial government, if the problem is one of illiteracy, infant mortality, and women's status, why are we blindly dispensing contraceptives and doing training?

"Ah! Don't you see this will eventually alleviate all these problems?"

But that is exactly what we had expected would happen with programs A, and B, and C, four, five, or ten years ago. That is why all the health workers were trained at huge costs, and yet we can see that the problems have not been alleviated. Isn't it time to find out why? Shouldn't we analyze and maybe pose the question a different way? Maybe the problem is different from what we think it is. Maybe the solution is not another training program. Maybe the problem needs a different solution.

The answer they give me: Ah! But that training program, you know, the one that did not produce the desired results, was developed under a different minister or prime minister or project director. *We* are now doing it for the first time.

"You are so fluent at this," I say to Dr. K, the assistant director of the Population Welfare Department. She is rattling off the details of the Population Welfare Program's training project, taking the lead in all discussions.

"I should be, my dear," she says, not without some pride, while chomping on her *sipari* and jauntily tossing her sari *palloo*. "I have done this five hundred times. I bet you I can even come up with a training project in my sleep."

"What do you mean?"

"Well, I've been working for the Population Welfare Department for over fifteen years and we must have developed this or a similar program at least that many times," she replies. "We've done the same thing for CIDA [Canadian International Development Agency], for UNICEF, WHO [World Health Organization], and another Swiss NGO. Not to mention our local NGOs and our own department." She counts the funding agencies on her fingers. "In fact, even for this workshop, UNICEF asked us for our older proposals. I can see a lot of the same materials being used. The same training strategy. . . . I know this stuff by heart." She gives a girlish giggle, as if ready to recite again all that she knows by heart.

"This means that this is a good program and works in the field, which is why you use the same material repeatedly?" I ask, trying to convince myself that there must be some sense in this.

"Actually, in the field, it is another story," Dr. K says with deliberation, bobbling her head from side to side from the base of the neck, a gesture that means neither yes nor no but points to something serious that should be of concern to all those listening. And then she explains.

"You know, there are many problems in the field. The major problem is dealing with job expectations. Most of the women, especially the traditional birth attendants and other community health workers, join the training programs in the hope of eventually getting a job—preferably within the Health Department or the Department of Population Welfare. They do not think that they need any training or that their skills are deficient at all, for they have been delivering babies for years—some of whom survive and some of whom die. It is 'Allah's will' or 'Bhagvan's *kerpa.*' How can you neutralize this divine power, they tell us, with the skills of mere mortals? Many participants, when they finish the training and are expected to go home and fend for themselves, feel they have been misled and misused.

"The other big problem is one of support from the system. The parent departments, Health or Population Welfare, do not have the personnel or the infrastructure to provide the rural health workers with backup support. At least our girls [she means the family welfare workers] have us looking out for them a little bit. But the rest of the girls, from other departments, are on their own. And you know how difficult it is for them to be out in the field. They are not even guaranteed physical safety. You can train these people till kingdom come, but this does not increase their income, and so they get frustrated. Many of the participants leave the system and establish themselves in private practice or go to the Middle East."

Dr. K goes on, citing the same problems identified by the other evaluations.

"Then why do you not say so?" I ask. "Why are you endorsing the same program under the SAP?" And I realize, much to my chagrin, that I too am doing exactly that.

Dr. K looks startled. She sits up and looks around, as if awoken from a dream, and looks as if she may have said too much.

"This . . . this program," and she looks at the SAP draft proposal in her hand, so neat and so impressive in its velo (strip) binding with the green logo of the Government of Pakistan at the top and the baby-blue logo of UNICEF at the bottom of the title page. "It has already been developed, no?" She looks from one to the other in the group for confirmation, for some help. They avoid eye contact. She continues valiantly, "And . . . and . . . we have to have a training program. How else you can meet the objectives? We must have trained people to provide the needed services in underserved areas. . . ."

"You have firsthand experience that, time and again, a program like this has not been able to achieve improved services—so in a sense the overall program objectives are not achieved," I continue mercilessly, putting her on the spot. "The people you train at such cost are just not there, or are unable to provide the service that the program expects them to."

"Yes, but they still do something, and that is better than nothing," Dr. K says doggedly.

"Is it really?" I ask.

She does not pay attention to me, and continues defending her position or that of her office. "And anyway, it is a federal government program," she finishes lamely. "We in the provincial setup have nothing to do with the policy. We just implement the policies they make."

"Then why are we here?" I ask her. In a sense, I am asking myself, and the rest of the people around the table, the same question.

"But the P&D Department has developed this with international assistance." A fellow worker comes to our rescue.

"Yes! And UNICEF has provided the technical assistance," says another, as if that should be enough. "And our mandate is to stay within the parameters. The discussion therefore has to be within the plan that is laid out here. It has been done by experts in UNICEF; they are very experienced."

"Who in UNICEF?" I ask. There is no answer.

The next time the UNICEF expert, Mr. J, comes around to ask if we have anything new that needs to go in the word processor, we raise our concerns with him. We want to find out if we can question the basic parameters of the program as it is laid out in the document under discussion. We tell him that in light of the hundred years' combined experience of the people around the table in managing and implementing social-sector delivery programs, this program is not likely to meet the objectives of the SAP.

"You have to ask the P&D Department," Mr. J replies evenly. "This is their proposal. UNICEF has only provided the assistance they requested." He saunters off to the next table.

So we do ask P&D—being as determined or foolish as we are. We raise the same concerns with none other than the chief of the P&D Department. He, much to his credit, listens patiently and graciously, and he looks seriously and laboriously at some of the program details under discussion. We request that he focus on those calling for training female health workers to provide health and contraceptive services, with expensive plans for training.

"Well, I am not a technical person, as I will be the first one to admit," he begins, with elaborate self-deprecation. "This program was developed by the technical staff in the UNICEF office. You know that they have many years of experience in this area. They have been developing training programs for years, maybe longer than the number of years you have been born." He directs this, with an indulgent smile, at all of us. "And you know they have been working day and night on this for the past two months. They have not charged the government a single rupee; they have even used their own technical people and their own computers," he says, emphasizing "coompooturs" with a near-reverential tone.

"Which technical people?" I ask him.

"All of them. . . ." He waves a hand, indicating the whole room, and stopping for a second at the computer corner, where everyone and everything is humming away with a credible aura thick as the foggy program in front of us. The technical people to whom he points consist of three stenographers who are experts in the use of the word processor, two office assistants, two drivers, and Mr. J.

"I am a technical person, and I disagree with the overall program. This will not help to achieve the objectives of the SAP," I reply. I have taken a kamikaze dive and made a categorical statement, knowing that I am risking my neck, and at best sounding horribly arrogant. But bureaucrats are such wonderful creatures.

"So change whatever you feel needs to be changed," the chief says, with a magnanimous sweep of the arm. "That is why we have asked for your expertise. That is why we have only provided the parameters. . . ."

"But it is the parameters that I do not agree with. Those are exactly the items that need to be changed," I say.

"How can you say that?" he says with a plaintive gulp, sounding genuinely hurt, as if this were a personal attack.

"Because, as you have pointed out, I am an expert in this field and I should know."

He still looks unconvinced, and he eyes me a trifle suspiciously. "But this has to go to Islamabad by the end of the week, and . . . and everyone is here. . . ." He ends on an appealing note. Come on now, why spoil the party?

"Suppose I was a surgeon." I again go into a clinical mode. Maybe it will work with him; he is, after all, the chief.

"Suppose you bring a child to me with pain in the abdomen," I begin patiently. "And you ask me to remove the child's appendix in the next two days. I, as an expert, say it is not a problem with the appendix and make a diagnosis different from yours. Suppose I say that the child has roundworms." He nods his head, having followed the argument so far. Encouraged, I come to the punch line: "Would you then accept my diagnosis and the recommendations that would logically follow from there?"

At once, his brow clouds with a familiar darkness. It looks as if he is getting a headache. But before he can respond, the great man's attention is claimed by the deputy chief, who wants the boss's opinion on a very crucial matter—one of life and death, judging from the way the deputy is wringing his hands. The provincial minister for P&D is expected to preside over the successful completion of the hard work of this past week; it is the issue of seating at the dais that needs to be decided. The chief must attend to this immediately.

But the chief is courteous enough to still half turn in my direction, and to say with genuine concern, "I am sorry to hear your child has roundworms. . . . I am afraid I cannot recommend a surgeon, for none of my children, God forbid, ever had roundworms." He sounds apologetic. "But my wife's younger brother works in the Civil Hospital, and I can have him make inquires for a good surgeon for you. . . ." And with a sympathetic smile and a gentle wave of the hand, he is gone.

Similar exercises have been conducted at all other tables, and so by the end of the afternoon, a series of program plans for the development of the health, population, education, and water and sanitation sectors have been designed and "costed" within the overall framework of the SAP.

The afternoon is rapidly drawing to a close. The sun is slanting in the dusty yard, and there is a feverish rush inside to finish everything. The tables at one end have already been moved to make space for the dais. Colorful buntings have been strung around the dais and tied to bamboo poles erected for only this purpose. Huge ornate chairs, each with its own, equally ornate footstool, have been placed in the center of the dais. The stage is set, complete with sound effects. Behind a curtained space, there is the familiar tinkle of china and silverware.

Some of the minister's security staff members, rotund mustachioed men with hairy ears, wearing crumpled *shalwar-kameezes,* shiny ammunition belts slung ostentatiously across their chests, are poking in and around corners and the heavy and dusty velvet curtains, grinding cigarette butts under their heels, sniffing loudly, and spitting expertly in the flowerpots from the corners of their mouths.

The function in the evening was a great success. There were many flowery speeches by all the chiefs of the Sindh Provincial Government's departments—of Health, of Population Welfare, of Water and Sanitation, of Education—and then more speeches from the chiefs of the provincial offices of the UN agencies—UNICEF and UNDP. The speeches were followed with a delicious tea, with chicken patties and scrumptious chocolate cakes brought specially from the now-no-more Bombay Bakery in Hyderabad, a poor, sad city torn by senseless ethnic violence, where there is no potable water, or sanitation facilities, or proper roads, or hospitals, or schools. These cakes, with real chocolate, and that too in a country that does not produce any cocoa, are transported to Karachi, another sad city torn by the same ethnic violence, Karachi, too, which has no drinking water, broken roads, failing schools, miserable hospitals. . . .

While we are busy enjoying the cakes—shades of Marie Antoinette—and tea, the UNICEF experts and their machines are still whirring away. Before the last cup of tea has been drunk and the final piece of cake has been consumed to much tongue-smacking delight, the final version of the Sindh SAP Proposal, warm from the printer, complete with its velo binding, is placed before the minister for P&D, personally, by the chief of UNICEF.

The minister puts down his cup. There is a palpable hush as he pulls a gold Parker pen from his inner breast pocket and, with a dramatic flourish, signs the document. A little assistant moves in quietly from the shadows to affix to it the gold seal of the Ministry of Planning and Development of the Government of Sindh.

Ten

The Punjab Proposal and the Firing of the Learned Dr. Sahiba: . . . And That's the Way It Is . . .

A process similar to that undertaken in Sindh was to be used for the preparation of the Punjab Social Action Program (SAP) Proposal. As usual, the members of the Punjab SAP Committee, within the Department of Planning and Development (P&D), had the overall responsibility to prepare the Punjab SAP Proposal. UNICEF was to provide them with technical help. As it happened, I was the technical help that UNICEF sent to the Punjab SAP Committee. On the appointed day, I showed up with a copy of my contract at the Office of P&D of the Government of Punjab.

The building that houses the Punjab P&D Department is off the lower end of the famous Mall Road in Lahore, the romantic and tree-lined Thandi Sarak of another time and another place. Back then, it was associated with fashionably dressed ladies and gentlemen, strolling leisurely, stopping at Shezan in the horseshoe-shaped Ganga Ram Building for a hot cup of tea on a winter afternoon.

Or perhaps the ladies and gentlemen were on their way to shop for hand-crafted shoes at Hopson's—the Chinese shoemaker who spoke fluent Punjabi and was the nastiest shopkeeper south of the Himalayas. For many years, I thought all Chinese were genetically a bad-tempered people. Or perhaps they were going for a trim at Hanif's—the hairdresser of Lahore where my mother, in defiance of all the prim old matrons in the family, got the "Jackie Kennedy cut," which had become all the rage as soon as Jackie stepped into the White House. Then on to the famous Anarkali Bazaar with its treasures of glass bangles and assorted sandals, along with many other things known and unknown.

For a long time, that end of the Mall marked the beginning of Lahore for me. Crossing the Ravi River, turning south away from Jehangir's Tomb—Jehangir, the romantic Mughal prince who fell in love with a courtesan, giving her the now-famous name Anarkali, and, vowing to marry her, invoked the wrath of his father, Emperor Akbar, who had the poor girl entombed alive for this transgression—past the spectacular yet serene dome of the Badshahi Mosque, with the walls of the Lahore Fort in the background, competing for visual space with those of Ranjit Singh's Gurdawara, the living evidence of communal harmony. Avoiding the tongas and the bullock carts, and the kamikaze bicyclists, skirting the outer wall of the famous Government College, its gardens full of flowers and handsome young men, you came upon Zamzama, the ancient cannon made famous by Rudyard Kipling in his novel *Kim*. Here was the Mall and thus Lahore.

It was here that I would sit up to see the enchanted city unroll itself before my childish eyes during those innumerable trips in the little Hindustan-10 when the country was new and hopeful and good things were on the horizon. With their children packed in the back seat, my parents came up to the city from Sialkot, a sleepy little hick town some 80 miles away, for shopping or doctor's visits or just to be in the city. It was at Kim's gun that Lahore, the magical city of my childhood, spread its arms to gather me in its warm embrace. It is still the magnificent city of the Mughals, of gardens and mosques and minarets; the vibrant city of colleges and learning; the colorful city of courtesans and music and poetry and art and wonderful food. A city that, though plundered and looted, bears proudly the myriad scars of its tormented history and has now spread itself in all directions, with haphazard, unregulated development and shady housing schemes, and shadier schemers of these schemes, with garbage strewn all over, and no social services to speak of, shiny and loud and beckoning, like an aging whore done up for one last fling.

A Short Meeting with the Chief of Punjab P&D

The office of the Punjab P&D Department is off the Mall in a rundown, "modern" six-story building, its walls still stained by the last monsoons. It is dusty, dingy, dirty, and strangely depressing. The chief of Punjab P&D, Dr. S is a woman with a PhD in economics. She is also the chief economist and chairman of the Punjab SAP Committee. Unlike the building, she is well groomed and smart, wearing a salmon-pink sari, matching pumps, and delicate gold jewelry.

"Please have a seat, Dr. Sahiba, Madam will be with you," says the peon who had shown me into her office. He points me to a sofa in one corner of the room, diagonally across from Madam, who gives a luminous aura to her corner—or maybe that is just the effect of the mellow sunshine streaming in through the window. Madam is busy with some paperwork as lots of little fellows flit around her, like moths around a candle, to use a favorite phrase of South Asian poets.

It is quite a pleasant room, with two large windows and clean furniture. One window opens south onto the courtyard, where people are huddled together in the sunshine, smoking and chatting. It is January, and Punjab is cold enough for the sunshine to be enjoyable. After a wait of a good forty minutes, Madam is done with whatever it is she was doing and turns her attention to me. From across the room, she would like to know what she can do for me. I tell her that it is I who have been sent here to do things for her—specifically to help in the preparation of the health and population sections of the Punjab SAP Proposal.

Madam looks at me calmly for a full minute before saying, "Who says so?"

I must admit I am taken aback at this response. Surely she knows what is going on. Of course government officers are overworked and can be distracted—but this?

"It is my understanding that your office had requested technical assistance from UNICEF, and I, ahem, I am that assistance." I finish, a bit self-consciously.

"We had requested no assistance," replies Madam, calm and serene. "They, it seems, insist on giving it to us." With a roll of her eyes and a shake of her head, she goes back to some more work that has appeared on her desk.

I take out the copy of my contract and point out the signature of the federal SAP adviser, feeling rather stupid. Madam ignores all this and continues to work. Not knowing what else to do, I begin to make preparations to leave.

"You can write up the project as you see fit and send it to our office." These words are directed to my back, from the general direction of her desk.

Still confused and not knowing what to make of her previous remarks, I think it best under the circumstances to ignore whatever has happened and get on with the work. Maybe it is just the way she works, or maybe this is just a bad day.

"I'd appreciate if we could set up a time to meet with you and with some of your staff to get a sense. . . ."

Before I get any further, I am interrupted by a thunderous sound. Madam has banged her pen down on the table.

"Dr. Sahiba!" she minces out the words before I can go on, "let me make this perfectly clear. Neither I, nor my office staff, nor anyone else here is at your disposal. We are very busy and have our own work to do. And I would suggest you do the same." And if I catch you not doing it, it's off with your head! she might as well have added.

What am I doing here? I ask myself. Clearly, there is some confusion somewhere, and I have no intention of wasting my time. So I leave. Madam does not look up as I go. This whole exchange has taken place within earshot of Madam's assistants and peons and such, who have been walking in and out. I run into one or two of them in the corridor, and they look sheepish, averting their glances.

If at First You Don't Fail . . .

The next day, at the briefing meeting at the UNICEF office, I relate the events of my meeting the day before.

"Oh-ho-ho," says Mr. T, UNICEF's resident program officer in Lahore, smiling indulgently. "Do not take that so seriously. Everyone knows that Dr. S is rather a difficult person to work with. She is just all bark and no bite. And she is under a lot of pressure; . . . all senior P&D staff are in a time crunch. Also, she is not the person who has hired you; it is the chief of the Federal SAP Committee. So you should just go ahead and do the required work. You have your terms of reference, and we shall sign off on the completion of your work."

This does not seem like a good arrangement to me, given my experience of the past days.

"But it is her department I am supposed to work for, and she clearly does not feel the need. She has told me in no uncertain terms. . . ."

"Oh come now, you are just being emotional," the resident program officer insists. "UNICEF has made this commitment to the Ministry of P&D in Islamabad that we shall provide the technical assistance for the preparation of the Punjab proposal. And we intend to go through with it."

"Maybe it is better if you hire some other consultant, for it might be that for some strange reason, Dr. S does not want to work with me." Although this is the first time in my life I have ever met Dr. S, there might be something about me that has turned her off. My grandmother, may her soul rest in peace, used to say that my nose was too big for my own good.

"We have hired an education consultant, who will be coming from Islamabad in two days. He is responsible for developing the education portion of the SAP. But as far as health and population are concerned, you should handle it. Also, there is no time to look for alternates; we are all working under tight deadlines," Mr. T says, soothingly.

I should not have been, but I was reassured.

The next day, I call Dr. S's office. Her administrative assistant answers. I introduce myself and tell him that, for the purpose of doing the work assigned to me, I need the basic health and health services system data—especially the data related to personnel and rural health facilities.

"What kind, please, madam?" he asks deferentially.

I tell him.

"Please hold." Off he goes. After about five minutes, he comes back. "Please, Madam, I think you can get all this from the project offices themselves. . . ."

The information I am looking for most likely is indeed available at those offices, but that would require going to every facility and every outlet for each program office scattered throughout the city. Given the way things work in Pakistan, it would take me weeks of footwork and shifting through dusty ledgers if I tried to get it piecemeal. It is certainly compiled and easily available at the P&D office.

"Look," I say to the man on the phone, "I shall not expect you to find it or compile it for me. Why don't I come into your office, and I am sure I can find all this in a day and be out of there."

"Oh no, no, Madam, please," his panic-stricken voice pleads, "you must not come here. We cannot give you any information."

"Why not?" I ask.

"Please, Madam, try to understand, I am doing a job," he says softly. "I am a poor man, and have a family. I do not want to get into trouble. . . ."

What can one say to that?

There is nothing to do but bite the bullet. I spend the next two weeks going from office to office to office, each one more disorganized than the last. I go from the Health Secretariat on the Lower Mall to the office of the Provincial Directorate on Cooper Road, at opposite ends of this crowded, cacophonous city, fighting traffic, wasting time, and cursing myself, and then on to the offices of the Population Welfare Division, to the office of the director of the Expanded Program of Immunization, to the offices of the Control of Diarrheal Disease Program, and so on and so on.

Everywhere, perplexed people tell me that the P&D Department has the whole thing, for all the past decades, why don't I just get it from them? I say yes, but because I am here, can I get it together now? Of course, they say, and they offer whatever can be found, which is not always much. Some files have been partly eaten by rodents or washed away by floods. Some have been misplaced—the person who knows where it is has just been transferred or left for the Middle East—his No Objection Certificate was approved unexpectedly, so he had no time to tell those left behind where things were. Or I am told that the information is in huge ledgers stuffed on crumbling shelves or locked in cupboards, the keys to which have gone off with some person or the other—either to say the Zohar prayers or to the village to bury an uncle who died suddenly. Documents that are available are outdated and incomplete. Still, at the end of the period, I have gathered the basic information about the health services delivery system in Punjab, and about the number of health facilities and the placement of female health workers in the system.

It is, as expected, bizarre, and consistent with what is happening in the rest of the country. During the past decade, with donor assistance and in response to some program or the other, there have been massive, haphazard investments in building rural health facilities, whether feasible or not. True to form, buildings are sitting empty—"vacant." Equipment lies unused and vandalized, while people from those areas spend money and effort getting to the cities for health and contraceptive services. Medical officers are running errands for the deputy commissioners in exchange for promised transfers to the large urban centers. And our lady health visitors trained in the last batch have set up neat little shops and are doing deliveries and abortions and everything else that they can, whether part of their training or not.

A Kafka Story, Featuring Mr. G

I have prepared a draft outline of the Punjab SAP Proposal related to service delivery for the health and population sectors, and I take it to Dr. S's office on Monday morning. I had called earlier to get an appointment with her, and, much to my surprise, it was granted. She would be happy to see me whenever it is convenient for me, I am told. That honeyed welcome should have been my first clue that something was not quite right.

Dr. S, dressed in a lime-green sari—with shoes to match—meets me cordially and even sends for a cup of tea and some greasy samosas. I feel as if I have stepped through the Looking Glass, and the Queen, instead of ordering her minions to chop off my head, is offering me samosas. Or I am like the poor sucker invited to a fancy dinner by the Mafia boss, and after being wined and dined, I will be driven out to a lonely sugar field to meet with an unfortunate accident.

And sure enough, after a few minutes' chitchat about the weather and the traffic jams on the Mall Road—so different from what it used to be, sighs Dr. S—as I begin to relax, she announces, with an impressive calmness, that because I have not been able to meet the deadline to produce the first draft, she had no choice but to hire another consultant at the last minute, . . . has no choice but to have me beheaded, I hear from far away.

"For this work is top priority, very critical for the government," she says, and "time is of the essence," and some other words in a similar vein. Then, pointing to a rather dark corner of the room, she is pleased to introduce the new consultant.

I now realize that someone has been sitting in the shadows on the other side of the room all through the tea and samosas. This is a gray-looking gentleman in his mid-sixties in a steel-gray *shalwar-kameez* and a round-collared jacket—the outfit that was de rigueur in government circles during the era of the third of Pakistan's four military dictators, General Muhammad Zia-ul-Haq, who in his zeal to institute the Islamic mode had changed the dress code of government officers to "Islamic dress"—and this was it. Mr. G fits the picture of a government functionary of that time, sporting a luxuriant, too-evenly black "Muslim beard" (the beard neat and evenly trimmed, the upper lip clean-shaven), and reading the national Urdu paper, *The Daily Jang.* This is Dr. S's new consultant. He folds up the paper and crosses his arms on his chest, looking blankly at me over thick-rimmed glasses. I feel as if I have stepped into a short story by Kafka.

Dr. S is most disappointed in the quality and commitment of consultants being hired these days—all the good ones seem to have left the country; not that she blames them. It seems that my colleague who was responsible for the section on the education sector has not delivered, either. And so Mr. G has been asked to take care of that work as well. He is to bring this whole thing together in time for the five-day workshop to finalize the Punjab SAP Proposal, scheduled to be held three days from now with the participation of all the staff members of the line departments. This is a huge commitment on the part of the Punjab administration, to let its managers off for five days —and she, the chief of P&D, is not going to let this opportunity be wasted, for the opportunity cost—maybe I, being a noneconomist, do not understand? I do; good—is too high. The chief minister of Punjab has kindly consented to be the chief guest, and her department was committed to present a finished document.

"And it is tremendous good fortune," expands Dr. S, "that Mr. G here has accepted and was available." Otherwise, she has no idea what she could have done. Never in her career had she encountered a situation like this. But what can you expect from these so-called consultants, eh?

I learned later that my absent colleague, the consultant for the education sector, had received similar treatment from her and had left for his home in Islamabad the very day they met.

Mr. G, I now learn from Dr. S, had retired from the P&D Department the year before. His last posting was in the position now occupied by Dr. S. She was his subordinate for ten years. Since his retirement, Mr. G has volunteered his time as an imam at the mosque in Multan, where he owns land and where his older son, by the grace of Allah Almighty, is a subdivisional magistrate—a very influential and powerful officer in the district's judicial system. Mr. G, as is obvious, has no need for work, but he came at a moment's notice to help his country and a colleague who was really in a bind.

While Madam explains all this to me, Mr. G sits perfectly still, with his arms crossed over his chest, calm and quiet as a sphinx, running his fingers alternately over a set of green prayer beads, which he has produced from his shirt pocket, and on his luxuriant beard—and shimmying his knees discreetly from under the overhang of his long gray shirt. At one level, this is an incredibly impressive theater piece. I am also quite awestruck by the marvelous maneuvering of Dr. S.

Mr. G will now put together the whole final proposal because the subject specialists, including me, have not delivered on anything. OK, he can look at what I have done—for I have begun waving my draft in the air—but he really has to do all the rest of the stuff all on his own. In a way it is good, I think to myself, that this person will have the ultimate responsibility. Being an ex–member of the department, he will know how to get through the bottlenecks of the system and get the job done, and because he is Madam's consultant, she will be supportive of the overall effort.

Feeling somewhat relieved, and grateful that my head is still on my shoulders, I turn to Mr. G and say that it would be helpful if we could meet one to one and reach some common ground. Because I have already done the work according to the terms of reference, he might want to take a look at it to see if it fits in with his vision of the SAP proposal. I tell him I'd be happy to make any changes he would recommend.

"That is entirely up to you," he says in a measured voice. "You can give me whatever you like."

"Surely it is not a question of what I like, but what is required." I have started to feel disoriented, but I shake it off and continue. "You must have an idea of what you want the end product to be. . . ."

"Oh yes, of course I do," he interrupts, his knees speeding up and his hands running faster over his prayer beads, "but that has nothing to do with you." And now, for the first time, he smiles in what is meant to be a benign manner, showing a wide expanse of white underlined in thick brilliant black.

I think that maybe this is the way the Punjab P&D conducts its business—a bit off-center. Or maybe there is a language handicap, for Mr. G, in spite of his impressive credentials, does not seem to be very comfortable in English. I pose the same question in Punjabi. This time, Mr. G does not even bother to answer. With an explosive Allah-ho-Akbar (God is great), he lifts himself from the depths of the sofa and, taking out a gold watch attached to his coat button, mumbling something about being late, he makes for the door.

Down the Rabbit Hole?

I'm late, I'm late—for a very important date.

Alice in Wonderland

"Wait for me! Wait! Mr. Rabbit," I want to say, for like Alice, I am intrigued by where Mr. Rabbit—er, Mr. G—is going. He is going to his office. Office? Here? Where is his office? I ask. It is few rooms down the hall from Madam's. As he walks out, I follow him, although clearly I am not meant to feel very welcome. This office thing, I've got to see.

Mr. G's office is another pleasant little room with a large window facing south. Because it is still winter, an electric heater glows cheerily in one corner, though the room is bathed in the afternoon sun. Through the window, I can see the group in the courtyard smoking and chatting away. That scene has become strangely reassuring.

Mr. G's office contains all the trappings appropriate to a senior government official: a polished desk with a telephone sitting in the middle, an upholstered desk chair with curved legs, a bookshelf, and an in-tray and out-tray; a couple of chairs for visitors; a framed picture of the Ka'aba, the Muslim place of pilgrimage, on one wall, and the one of Mohammed Ali Jinnah in his *sherwani* and Jinnah cap and paternal half-smile on the other. An undernourished assistant hovers nearby, stacking papers on the desk, aligning "chits," those little scraps of paper that lend such authenticity to government offices, and opening and closing files. A consultant hired for a task cannot even dream of an office like this.

There are telephone messages for Mr. G, who sets them aside impatiently and then sends the fellow off to fetch a prayer mat, *jaldi,* for it is close to the time for Zohar, the noon prayers.

I cannot contain my surprise and have to ask, "How have you managed to get an office?" I don't know how my other colleagues have fared, but I couldn't have gotten a scrap of paper from here even if my life had depended on it. Let alone the heater and the assistant and the big desk with a telephone and chairs and the chits, a whole stack of them pierced neatly by that special chit-piercing pole.

"This office has been assigned to me by the P&D Department," Mr. G explains patiently, as if I am mentally retarded. "As a consultant on the project, I need to work closely with the office and the chief of P&D. I need to meet with the other officers in the department and peruse the files of the immense data set kept in this office. If I am expected to do all this for the department, where else should I have an office, if not close by?"

Where else indeed!

I have no answer to any of this, but am quite agitated.

"But Dr. S told me her staff was too busy to provide any assistance to the consultants," I manage to sputter hysterically, while Mr. G looks pityingly at me.

"That is between you and her," he says absentmindedly, and one has to admit rightly, beginning to roll up his sleeves and his *shalwar* cuffs after another "Allah-ho-Akbar." Taking off his shoes and socks in preparation for making *wudoo,* the ritual ablutions required before offering prayers, he meticulously cleans out the interdigital spaces between the splayed toes of both hairy feet. Having finished with that, he ambles off to the adjoining toilet.

A toilet! And adjoining, too! I would have had a heart attack right now, if the horrible thought of my children left motherless to fend for themselves had not been uppermost in my mind.

The little assistant returns with a fiery red velvet prayer mat, which he places pointing west before propping the door half-closed. He moves the heater close to the mat, and with a respectful angle to his neck, leaves the room. I sit stunned in a chair, holding the copy of the draft report, listening to the ablutions of Mr. G, who in the adjoining toilet is snorting and gargling ferociously, clearing his throat, coughing loudly to bring up stuff from great depths and then spitting it out with religious determination. All the while, he is reciting appropriate Quranic verses in the most melodious and pitch-perfect voice I have ever heard.

Postscript

Exactly a week after this, I receive a registered letter in the mail. It is a copy of a letter from Dr. S, the chief of the Punjab P&D Department and chief of the Punjab SAP Committee, to the chief of the Federal SAP Committee. This letter says, most regretfully, that the consultants for health and education—and it names the consultants, just in case—have submitted to her office work that is substandard, incomplete, "time bard (sic)," and therefore, as such, unacceptable.

As a result of this irresponsible behavior, she, Dr. S, and her office had been placed in the embarrassing position of having to scramble around at the last minute to prepare the SAP proposal for the Federal SAP Committee as required. And, thank the Almighty, Mr. G was available and kind enough to drop the critical work he was doing and come to the rescue of the department. Otherwise, Allah alone knows what might have happened. And it was only because of Mr. G's in-depth knowledge and twenty years' experience of working with the government that he was able to put together an outstanding proposal within twenty-four hours, thus saving the nation from a terrible loss.

If she had relied on the proposal prepared by the "learned"—and this word was in quotes—Dr. Sahiba, we, the Government of Pakistan, would have been in a most embarrassing position at the upcoming meeting with members of the International Aid Consortium. But, by the grace of Allah Almighty, who watches over true believers, the government has been spared this potential loss of billions of dollars to our poor nation, which is in such dire need of this kind of help.

At the end of the letter, Dr. S recommends that the learned Dr. Sahiba, because she seems to be incapable of handling a task of this magnitude and seriousness, be relieved of any further duties related to the SAP. These specifically include those duties having to do with the upcoming five-day workshop in the ballroom of the Pearl Continental Hotel to finalize the Punjab SAP Proposal. Dr. S, as the Punjab SAP chairman and the chief economist of the P&D Department, as of the date of this letter, unfortunately has no choice but to "de-recognize" Dr. Sahiba "as such."

She ends by requesting the permission of the chief of the Federal SAP Committee to wish him all the best, as she prayed to the Almighty to watch over him and his dear ones. Amen.

This letter is also copied to Mr. T, the resident program officer from UNICEF, who tells me again not to take it seriously (!), and that the UNICEF staff members have reviewed my report and are satisfied that it has met all the requirements of the terms of reference. The office of the federal SAP chairman does not respond to my phone calls. A letter of protest to his office also remains unanswered.

A dear and wonderful friend, who has many years' experience working with the P&D Department at both the federal and provincial levels, laughed when he heard my account of this bewildering business, thumped me on the back, and said, "So you got a taste of the Punjab bureaucracy and got to see it in action. Don't take it so personally; that's just the way it is. . . ."

Eleven

The Immunization Program in the North-West Frontier Province

The mood is upbeat as we travel northwest on the famous Grand Trunk Road from Islamabad to historic and turbulent Peshawar, the capital of the province that now has a new and controversial name (Khyber-Pakhtunkhwa) but was known as the North-West Frontier Province (NWFP) from the days of the earliest British forays into the region. One of the oldest cities on the Indian subcontinent, Peshawar lies at the foot of the historic Khyber Pass, a centuries-old passage for invaders and traders, once upon a time considered the gateway to the subcontinent. Many a conqueror entered India through here to set up empires that had a long-lasting impact on the subcontinent and its people. Persians and Greeks thundered down this road, watched by the wary eyes of the Pathans, the region's dominant ethnic group. Then came Mahmud of Ghazni, and the Mughals led by Zaheeruddin Babar, who marched to Delhi to set up an empire that would last for three hundred years. With the invaders came writers, artists, scholars, musicians, and philosophers, who brought with them the culture and knowledge of their regions and helped enrich the life of the subcontinent.

Peshawar is also home to the famous Qissa Khwani Bazaar, or Storyteller's Market, where the mountain-dwelling people come in winter to liven up the city, to rest and eat, to buy and sell, to hear and tell stories:

> When spring-time flushes the desert grass,
> Our Kafilas [caravans] wind through the Khyber Pass.
> Lean are the camels but fat the frails,
> Light are the purses but heavy the bales,
> As the snowbound trade of the north comes down
> To the market-square of Peshawar town.
>
> —Rudyard Kipling, "The Ballad of the King's Jest"

154

In many ways, the city's role has not changed very dramatically. Peshawar is now, many say, the center of the war on terror, and life in and around the city has taken on a new dynamic. In the spring of 1991, on the other hand, the city and the region were recovering from the recent ouster of the Soviet Union from neighboring Afghanistan, and there was an aura of the conqueror about things.

Lucymemsahib is traveling with us—my two boys, their nanny, and me. We have taken my car to cut back on travel expenses, and also because Lucymemsahib is "still nervous about this thing, whatever it is." She would like me to brief her on "this whole business," as well as on Pakistan—on the status of women in an Islamic society, the problems of working women in Pakistan, and the historical development of the health sector as well as its specific functioning within the development programs. Talk about a tall order.

Lucymemsahib, aside from being lost, is genuinely worried. She has heard and read of the trigger-happy nature of the Pathans. "I understand that everyone in Peshawar carries a Kalashnikov," she says, peering out of the window at the bullock carts and brightly painted trucks on the road. "Even ten-year-old children and they are not afraid to use one. In fact, that is the reason the Pathans have been able to defeat the Russians." She looks suspiciously at my older boy, four, who gives her a cherubic smile.

She has gathered all this from the Western popular press, which covered this region extensively after the 1979 Russian invasion of Afghanistan; their coverage generated exposure for the Pathans in general, and Muslim fundamentalists in particular, as a militant culture. However, to their credit or discredit, the Pathans, who live in the areas between Pakistan and Afghanistan, have been carrying some kind of arms for centuries, long before their current notoriety.

I tell Lucymemsahib not to worry. In my experience, if it counts for anything, Pathan men are some of the gentlest creatures in God's world, in spite of appearances. While working as a clinician, I saw ferocious-looking, guntoting Pathan men, with a row of bullets strapped to their chest and a dagger to their waist, and not loath to use either, collapse like soap bubbles at the mere sight of a syringe and a needle. Lucymemsahib thinks I am joking.

Arriving in Peshawar

We are booked to stay at the Pearl Continental, the city's recently built five-star hotel. I would rather stay at Dean's, one of the chain of hotels built by the Raj around the turn of the century and known by the names of their proprietors:[1] Flashman's in Rawalpindi, Faletti's in Lahore, Cecil's in Murree, and here, in Peshawar, Dean's. (Laurie's in Agra and Maiden's in Delhi were also originally part of the chain.) For me, these hotels are inextricably linked with memories of childhood. When I was young and our family went to Murree to escape the Punjab heat in summer, or to see the snow in winter, we would go from Faletti's to Flashman's, where we would stop for tea before heading on to our destination, Cecil's. Faletti's, though, is unfortunately right across the road from the Punjab Assembly building, and rumor has it that it is soon to be pulled down to make way for a new hostel for the members of the Provincial Assembly. This is a pity, I think, for though it is no longer the "hip" place of the 1960s, it still exudes an old-world charm that should be preserved, to say nothing of its Ava Gardner suite, where the actress stayed when in Lahore filming *Bhowani Junction.*

I take Lucymemsahib to Dean's, but she scrunches up her nose as we walk through. The rooms are small and almost windowless, and the bathrooms are huge and drafty. There is actually a door to the bathroom from an alley in the back! Lucymemsahib shudders at the implications, though this was simply so that soft-footed servants could enter discreetly to clean the toilets and leave water for the sahibs and memsahibs. The furniture is outmoded, the rug is grimy and bald, and there is no central air-conditioning. She walks gingerly, holding a handkerchief to her nose. The air smells of something nasty, she says, and she does not want to catch it. It does not look good, she says.

But look at the walls, I tell her. Each one is as thick as an arm's length, blocking out all sound of the outside world, enveloping you in a protective cocoon. And the little window opens onto a lawn full of spring wildflowers, with a climbing rosebush that creeps surreptitiously into your room. And there's your personal trellis-enclosed veranda, where you can sip your afternoon tea (I drink coffee, she says darkly), lounging in the old-fashioned wrought-iron chairs. . . . And you don't even need to get into an elevator, just out of your car and into your room!

"Nah," she says, with the handkerchief still to her nose, "this is too . . . too inconvenient." And so she goes off to the Pearl Continental, to her room on the sixth floor with its new furniture and clean rug, its central air-

---

1. For an excellent description of these buildings and others, see Jan Morris and Simon Winchester, *Stones of Empire: The Buildings of the Raj* (Oxford: Oxford University Press, 1983/2005).

conditioning and tiny bathroom. One woman's sense of adventure is another's inconvenience!

So I am left to enjoy alone the decrepit charms of Dean's. I stay in this quaint old rambling, crumbling place, reeking of the Raj, of sahibs and memsahibs lounging in silk dressing gowns and smoking on the veranda as they call for barefoot bearers to bring in the morning tea. I wonder if I will have time to visit the legendary Qissa Khwani Baazar, where fierce Pathan men in billowing *shalwars* and voluminous *pagris* still gather on the stoops of their shops as their ancestors did through the centuries. Sitting on their haunches or reclining against bolsters, smoking the communal hookah, they spit *niswar*-laden gobs that barely miss your feet, and drink endless cups of the local green tea. They narrate stories from far and wide, stories from Kafiristan and from the caves of the Hindu Kush, of brave men and beautiful women, of courage and endurance—and now, probably, of al-Qaeda and the "*farangi* soldiers" in their midst and of the "stuff' brought in and taken out of the area; and they look at you with eyes blue as the sky and as remote as the mountains from where they come.

> We cleaned our beards of the mutton grease,
> We lay on the mats and were filled with peace.
> And the talk slid north, and the talk slid south
> With the sliding puffs from the hookah mouth.
>
> —Rudyard Kipling, "The Ballad of the King's Jest"

Learning from the Director of Provincial Health Services

The next day we meet the director of provincial health services (DHS). The offices of the Provincial Directorate of Health Services of the NWFP are in a colorless and characterless new cement building. Its walls are moist from recent rains, and the corridors are dark, dank, and smelly. The DHS is a regal-looking man with clear skin, an aquiline nose, and the most innocent-looking green eyes I've ever seen in a man his age and with that many years in government service. He is dressed in a *shalwar-kameez* of rough cotton (*khadar*), buttoned right up to his chin, making him seem childlike.

He is cordial, courteous, and attentive, and also extremely knowledgeable about the health services delivery system in the province, knowledge that he generously shares with us. At present, he says, almost 40 percent of posts in the rural health sector are lying vacant. These posts are specifically meant for female health personnel, lady health visitors, and maternal and child health workers. At the same time, qualified women are roaming around unemployed, scavenging for jobs in the urban health system, where one job has twenty qualified applicants.

The reasons for this paradox are exactly the same as in the other provinces. Women are reluctant to take up their posts in rural areas because of security concerns and a lack of infrastructure support. The provincial government, which is ultimately responsible for the rural health workers, cannot provide the kind of support—basically, secure housing and transportation—that is needed. The DHS also tells us, very candidly, that the three main issues related to the health sector that are part of the Social Action Program (SAP)—the recruitment policies of the government, a career structure, and incentives for work—will remain difficult to resolve unless there is a fundamental change in the way the federal and provincial governments function.

The issues in the SAP, he says, cross over between more than one government department; the Department of Planning and Development, the Health Department, and the Department of Finance are all involved, with the last usually having the final say and veto power. Because the budget for salaries and other financial incentives comes from the federal government, the provincial government is bound by the resources they have been given. With limited resources, there is never any money to sustain a project that starts with an external grant or loan. The SAP, in any case, is not likely to bring about any fundamental change in the health care system or in the way that the Health Department's budget is submitted and approved, and until this changes, nothing else in the delivery system can improve. This effort, like similar ones before it, will be wasted.

He says all this kindly and gently, conveying respect for both us, the consultants, and for the donors. The upshot is very clear, though—that he seems to say, is basically that.

"But you have to begin somewhere," says Lucymemsahib, very serious and professional.

(She tells me later that she is a little surprised by the somewhat "casual" way people treat her here in Peshawar. No one seems to give her any particular attention. This is quite different from her treatment in Punjab, where even senior government officers scampered around and made her feel very special. "Maybe it is because these people have colored eyes," I tell her, somewhat but not entirely facetiously. She seems partially convinced.)

"Yes, you have to start somewhere," the DHS says in response to

Lucymemsahib's remark, "but you must start from a solid base if you want a structure of some permanence. We should start at our own pace, strengthening the crucial infrastructure. We should do one thing at a time, without this pressure of doing this, that, or the other in two months, or four, which unfortunately has been the situation for the past so many years and continues to be, in spite of evidence to the contrary." He sighs a tired sigh. "All this does is leave us a mess, which we have to clean up after the consultants and grants have run out."

"Those are larger political issues," says Lucymemsahib with an imperious wave of the hand, "important no doubt but out of our jurisdiction. Surely there are microlevel problems in the field, which once solved can have an impact on the work of peripheral health workers."

"But Madam, that is just the point," the DHS says again, patiently. "It is exactly those microlevel problems that cannot be solved by these ad hoc means."

Lucymemsahib looks unconvinced. "In an area where there are numerous problems, surely some can be fixed," she persists. "We should identify these special problems faced by field-workers. These can certainly be addressed within the SAP."

The DHS nods wearily, and says he will help us as much as he can in completing our assignment.

An Evaluation Team led by an expatriate epidemiologist is here for the year-end review of the provincial Expanded Program on Immunization (EPI), and the DHS's office has been busy with them lately. The team is going to do field visits and meet with rural health workers, in this case the vaccinators. The DHS advises us to join the team if we are interested in learning firsthand about the problems vertical programs encounter in the field.

The EPI, being one of the priority programs within the SAP's objectives, at this time is one of the better-organized and better-conducted vertical programs in the country. Most provinces cite coverage rates close to 70 percent in the urban areas, usually for the first round of vaccinations, with those for subsequent rounds being much lower. Whether the children are, ultimately, protected or not is another matter, and dependent on many other factors, not least the nutritional status of the child and the viability of vaccine. These variables are not part of the EPI evaluations, which concentrate on the shots dispensed to determine coverage rates.

"But is that not the objective of the program?" asks Lucymemsahib. "If in the long run the children are not protected, and all one is able to show are coverage rates for the first round of shots. . . ." She looks at me. "Why is there such a drop in coverage rates between the first and the second rounds?"

Before I can reply, the DHS responds: "Madam, I am afraid there are many things you do not understand. Our people are superstitious and illiterate. . . . It is the immediate experience that determines their actions."

It is the observation of program personnel all over Pakistan that mothers are reluctant to bring in children for the second round of shots because of their "negative" experience with the first one. A healthy child is given something that makes them "sick." Children develop fevers, stop eating, and become cranky; babies refuse the breast.

"But this is clearly a question of education!" I say, having encountered this issue in both developing and developed countries, like the United States.

"That is true. No parent wants her child to die or be disabled with disease. It's a question of educating them about the necessity of prevention from these," adds Lucymemsahib.

"You are very right, Madam; it is a question of education," replies the DHS, "the education of women. Otherwise, no health program, no matter how well conceived and how brilliantly executed, will succeed. . . ."

That the literacy and education of women make a critical contribution to the successful implementation and the ultimate impact of health programs is a well-documented fact. I have seen it firsthand—the same program, but different success rates. I worked, for example, on the same maternal health program, developed and run by the same agency, in two Indian states, Bihar and West Bengal. The program produced very different results in these two states. In the early 1990s, the female literacy rate for West Bengal was over 40 percent; for Bihar, barely over 20.[2] Along with other members of the Evaluation Team, I agreed that the higher literacy rates for women in Bengal contributed to the program's relative success there, as opposed to its performance in Bihar.[3]

"Then I think SAP should concentrate only on trying to improve the education levels in women, rather than get into this elaborate service delivery program that it looks like is not going anywhere," says Lucymemsahib rather grumpily, for she is tired, as she says, of going around in circles. "Can we make this a recommendation?" she asks me.

---

2. Victoria A. Velkoff, "Women of the World: Women's Education in India," U.S. Department of Commerce, Economics and Statistics Administration, Bureau of the Census, October 1998, p. 2.

3. Samia Waheed Altaf, "A Critical Review of the Traditional Birth Attendant's Program in Southeast Asia," Report SEA/MCH/202, Regional Office for Southeastern Asia, World Health Organization, New Delhi, October 1992.

I suppose we could, in a way, and we really should. Unfortunately, we are bound by the terms of reference that speak clearly of issues related to the workers in the rural health system—specifically the recruitment policies, career paths, and incentives for working women.

"Then the terms of reference need to be rewritten," says our Lucymemsahib, not one to give up. Amen, I say.

The members of the EPI Evaluation Team, who have been listening to this exchange, look helplessly at each other. "Oh no, that should not be recommended," says one, with some concern. "We do not want to be left out of our share of the SAP grant."

What can one say? We are all human, and bread-and-butter issues take precedence for the individual.

We learn that a team of female vaccinators is going to set up a mobile camp in Mardan, a small city about 50 miles outside Peshawar, so we decide to visit the camp. The provincial director of the EPI generously offers to escort us.

Visiting a Vaccination Camp in Mardan

The next morning at six o'clock, the EPI director is at the hotel in a fancy four-wheel-drive jeep provided to the EPI by a UNICEF grant—it has UNICEF's blue logo on one side. The director, an internist by training and now a senior officer in the Health Department, has been seconded to the EPI from Lady Reading Hospital in Peshawar, where he was the medical superintendent. He has many years of administrative experience in the health system, and he is professionally very well respected and personally well known and well connected—a definite asset to the EPI.

The director is somewhere around fifty years old and of medium build, and has a rather dark complexion for a Pathan. His face is pockmarked, again from childhood smallpox, and it gives him a rather somber look that belies his pleasant and jovial nature. He jokes good-naturedly with Lucymemsahib about the simple mindset of the Pathans, poking fun at himself and dispelling her notions of the ferocious nature of the Pathans. It turns out that he is not a "true" Pathan, which explains his darker complexion. But his family has lived in this area for four generations, and so by default they have become Pathans.

So the director was not attracted by the salary and the perks of this job, which are the main attractions for most people? Lucymemsahib asks. He laughs good-naturedly at our ignorance of his situation. The remuneration for this position is a pittance. Given his lifestyle, the salary is just enough to cover the cost and upkeep of his drivers, he tells us. He has brought his personal driver for us today, because the project's driver had to take the Evaluation Team into the field. Not many people could provide this kind of assistance to the project.

We set out for Mardan, picking up Major (retired) Shershah, the EPI field supervisor, from the EPI zonal office. Major Shershah is also a Pathan, but "kosher," judging from his light-colored hair and moustache, to say nothing of his bright green eyes. He is tall and lanky and the softest-spoken person I've met in a long time; it seems as if he could not say boo to a cat, in spite of his abundant mustache and his wonderfully evocative name (Shershah means the king of lions, and Shershah Suri, an Afghan, was one of the bravest of rulers on the subcontinent in the sixteenth century). When he learns that I used to be a surgeon before getting into this business, he scuttles away to the far side of the seat and continues to marvel at my ability to cut open human beings. The fact that I have given it up is not of much consolation. It is as if I have blood forever on my hands.

Major Shershah, as his title suggests, retired early from the army to take this position. This move was orchestrated by his younger brother, who is one of the leading cardiologists in the city and very well known—and useful to all the top government officials; as middle-aged and old men, they need to be on the right side of a good cardiologist. The major is extremely proud of his brother and generously offers to introduce me to him, a useful conduit to the powers that be in the provincial government.

To get to Mardan, we drive to the northeast on a newly paved portion of the Grand Trunk Road. On this stretch, originally built in the sixteenth century by Shershah Suri, the road almost lives up to its name. It is truly grand, or at least evocative of past grandeur. We weave in and out of the assorted vehicles, towering trucks painted and tassled in the most vivid colors, spunky little Suzuki vans, bullock carts, and pedestrians, all traveling at their own peculiar speeds. We zoom past the formidable Bala Hisar Fort and the army barracks, where scrawny recruits with identical buzz cuts, clad in identical khaki pants and white vests, are diligently digging holes in the ground in the early morning sun—holes that another set of similar recruits will fill up at sundown. It is said that this exercise builds the habit of unquestioning obedience in soldiers.

The EPI, funded by donor agencies, has trained close to five hundred female vaccinators in the past two years, and although the turnover has been high, because there are not many job vacancies the program is able to put together, at any time, four teams of two vaccinators each per district. This is not a small feat, for the NWFP also suffers from the same resource constraints as the rest of the country. The recruitment pool is extremely small and poor, the admission standards are unrealistically high, and the training is erratic and donor dependent. The career structure and the work conditions of the NWFP vaccinators are also no better than those in the rest of the country.

The team we meet today consists of six young women in their late teens or early twenties, fair skinned with light-colored hair and eyes. Bowing to the cultural traditions, their heads and the lower halves of their faces are covered in voluminous chadors, with only their eyes showing—eyes that are outlined in bold strokes of black *kajal* and flash with youth and vigor. They are busy setting up "camp" in the courtyard of one of the village notables, who has been gracious enough to provide the space. Major Shershah supervises the whole operation in a most un-major-like manner. Coaxing one, politely requesting another, he is quickly elbowed and jostled to the margin. He supervises a pair of assistants setting up the freezer that contains the vaccine to be used today. The freezer, along with the generator that will help power it, has been brought to the campsite by donkey cart. The freezer, generator, and donkey cart are just as integral to the project as the vaccines and syringes. These need to be carried everywhere so that the cold chain can be maintained. Half the freezer is stocked with cold drinks— Coca-Cola, Pepsi, other drinks of assorted colors—for the team.

The vaccinators divide into two groups. One set forms a mobile team that will walk from house to house, escorted by Major Shershah, for young women cannot be walking around the streets alone, even in their own village. This team will encourage families to bring their children to the vaccination camp, or it will give the shots to the children of families that cannot come. For this purpose, the team members carry little icepacks with packets of syringes and vaccines. Given the conditions in the field, this is a very-well-organized operation. I mention this to the director. It is, he admits with some pride. He was the architect of this strategy, and thus he can very modestly take credit for the relative success of the program.

Meanwhile, the director sits in a red, velvet-cushioned chair looking over all this with a benevolent, paternal eye—chatting now with one, now another, holding a minicourt, for when people learn of his presence in the area, they come to pay their respects. He receives them with a natural comfort and indulgence, which shows his status in this society and that he is used to all this. In between, he finds time to chat with the girls, encouraging and teasing them in a paternal way, which thrills them no end.

"Oho!" he jokes, commenting on the dark eyeliner that the girls have applied so generously, "it seems the bazaars of Mardan will soon run out of *kajal*. It is being consumed in such enormous quantities. It seems I shall have to order some from outside, probably from Geneva, and have it brought up along with the next supply of vials of vaccines. It will have to be smuggled up here in the major's freezer and then I shall sell it on the black market and get enormously rich. . . ."

The girls titter and blush and duck and hide their faces behind each other's shoulders, flashing their brilliant eyes, stuffing wads of chador in their mouths to silence their laughter.

One Girl's Story

"And how is your father?" the director asks one girl.

She smiles shyly, with lowered eyes, and securing her chador on her head, says he is well. He is almost recovered from the fever that had nearly killed him, a result of pulmonary tuberculosis. The hospital staff was very good to her father, thanks to the personal reference of the director. Once her father learns that the director is here (and learn he will, for the whole city learns of it in no time), he will come to pay his respects.

This tall, slim, intense-looking girl, with delicate hands and luminous skin, tells me her father is a fruit vendor. She is the first person in her family to get an education. She has two younger brothers, who are enrolled in the local school. Another one, who would be older than both other boys, died in childhood from a "fever," probably the same one that her father has now. Her father, though uneducated, was determined that his children, even the girl, would get an education. She is a good student, she says with a collective pride in her brave father, in her brothers, and in herself. She won a provincial scholarship for the High School Matriculation Examination and was able to join the girl's college, where she opted to study premedical subjects. She did well enough on that exam, too, and was accepted by the medical school in Peshawar with a government scholarship for five years.

Why, then, does she not go to medical school, I ask, knowing that she must be exceptionally bright, and hardworking, and lucky, to have made it so far.

She does not, she says without bitterness or anger, because her future in-laws objected. They did not like the idea of their future daughter-in-law studying medicine, let alone in a coeducational institution.

Why didn't she go to Fatima Jinnah? I ask again. My alma mater, Fatima Jinnah Medical College in Lahore, is an all-female medical college set up precisely to overcome such hurdles. It has an all-female student body as well as a largely female faculty. It is a federal institution, and has quotas for admission from each province, especially from disadvantaged areas. Because she has done so well and is from a "backward" district of the province, she would certainly find a place.

Well, . . . she says, with a break in her voice, her eyes lowered. She did, but her in-laws did not think that was such a good idea either, for a young unmarried girl to go so far away to a large city, to live by herself in a hostel. . . . Also it is not good for a wife to be more educated than her husband. Her fiancé will finish high school this year, and then they will get married.

What about her parents?

"What could they say," she answers, looking me in the eyes for the first time. Her father is not in good health. He would like to see his children settle down as quickly as possible, especially his grown daughter. Her fiancé is a "good boy," from a good family. His father has his own business, which the "boy" will inherit. Their business, though modest, has enabled them to buy a house—their own house, with four rooms and a "modern" toilet. Her parents realize that it would not be wise to lose such a good match. She will have to resign from this job soon, for she is to be married in three months, she tells me, brightening up and inviting us to her wedding.

I am too sad to respond. This was such a waste, and in so many ways. Would she want to continue with this work? I ask. She does not think her in-laws would permit her to continue. Even for these two years, to get the vaccinator's training and work as a vaccinator in her own town, close to home, her father had to beg and fight her in-laws tooth and nail. Once she is married, . . . her voice trails off into the folds of her chador.

I do not ask what is on the tip of my tongue: What about her? What does she want? For I know, without asking, that she has no choice. She has no control over her life.

"This is barbaric," Lucymemsahib says when I translate all this for her. "Why can't the government do something about this? This is precisely the kind of candidate you want to keep. Boy! If I had a chance of going to medical school—and that too on a state scholarship! Wow! I wouldn't care a hoot about any boy! Good or bad or any other category!"

"Our women, as you can see, are like cattle," says the director, who has been quietly listening to this exchange. "Their primary purpose is to marry and produce children. They, poor things, know of no other options. . . . Women in America and Canada can make their own decisions, do things differently, but not our women."

"But this is exactly what your country needs!" says Lucymemsahib, with obvious exasperation. "You need trained and technically qualified women. . . . How will things get better if women, and especially the ones as smart as this one. . . ."

"Madam, you do not understand," the director interrupts. "There are many issues here that are more immediate and personally critical than what the country needs." And he explains: "It is true that this girl cannot be more educated than her husband. It will create tremendous problems. For her."

"Surely she can find another husband, who hopefully will be more educated than her, or more understanding," Lucymemsahib argues.

"That is not the point," says the director.

"And this, what about this?" asks Lucymemsahib, pointing to the paraphernalia of the EPI spread out around us. "Why must she give all this up, especially since there has already been an investment in her training, and it is right here in her hometown? This is certainly a viable option."

"Is it?" asks the director with a smile. "Compare the situation and the status of a girl happily married living in her husband's house, the mother of his children, with that of an unmarried one. One is secure, with a position and a status. But the other is roaming the streets, working to earn money, open to all kinds of suggestions. Very soon, she will become an outcast, and no one will want to marry her. Her own family would refuse to have anything to do with her, having been humiliated and belittled by her behavior."

"Well then, let them marry and live with their husbands and have their children and then work." Lucymemsahib, much to her credit, will explore all possible options. "What is the harm in that?"

The director shakes his head. "Madam, you do not understand," he says again. "A married woman leaving her children behind, neglecting her husband and her home to roam around for work!" He looks at us in mock horror. "It will reflect badly on her husband, suggesting that he is not able to feed his family and has to send his wife out to earn money. He, the poor man, will not be able to show his face anywhere; he'll be the laughingstock of the whole town." He shakes his head again. "Not possible. This is a conservative society. Besides, she will not have the time," he says matter-of-factly. "She will be too busy having and raising children."

If she survives the delivery, I say to myself, for the maternal mortality rates in Pakistan have been and are among the worst in the developing world. And they have not changed, in spite of innumerable donor-funded, government-implemented programs.

"Surely there are women who have families and yet find time to work, and their husbands do not become laughingstocks?" Lucymemsahib looks pointedly at me.

"Yes there are, but most of them have not one but many servants to look after their children," the director explains, smiling indulgently at me. "These women," he says, pointing generally in the direction of the vaccinators, "cannot afford that kind of luxury."

What a strange paradox! But how true. Lucymemsahib is bewildered. "Then why is the government investing millions of dollars in trying to train women to work in the health sector when you know that they will leave at the first opportunity?"

The director sighs. He seems tired, as if he's run out of gas, and distracted. Two withered old men in grimy *pagris* claim his hands and his attention—the former to shake, and the latter to put in a request for a job for some nephew or son. The director mumbles absentmindedly while attending to them. "Because the World Bank advises so, and . . . and the country needs them," he says on autopilot.

Another Girl's Story

A slim, doe-eyed young woman, who is addressed as Baji by the other girls, has also been listening to this exchange. She is married and has a year-old son. How is she able to work? She has no choice: Her husband, who worked in the emerald mines in Swat, was injured six months ago and has lost his job as a result. Their family has no means of support. She decided to take this course, which offers a stipend even during training, and she now earns close to Rs 1,000 a month (a bit less than $50, according to the exchange rate in 1990)—almost twice as much as her husband earns doing odd jobs, which are all he can do in his condition.

"He must be relieved that you have been able to help," I say.

The young woman bursts into tears. Her husband is extremely unhappy.

He feels like the laughingstock of the whole community because he is sitting at home taking care of the child (a woman's job!) while his wife earns money for the household (a man's job). He is sullen and depressed most of the time and is not nice to her anymore. Her in-laws also disapprove, and her mother-in-law refuses to take care of her child while she, the daughter-in-law, "goes gallivanting" all over the place.

"But how would the family survive otherwise?" Lucymemsahib asks with concern.

That is why she does this, Baji says. First they pawned off the jewelry from her dowry. Even the sewing machine, and the radio. Then they borrowed money from family members for a couple of months—but you know how expensive things are; just the milk for the baby, one tin of Similac, costs Rs 80. The baby could easily drink two of those in a day, although she adds extra water to make it last, but. . . . And then the doctor's fees and the medicines for her husband! She is really at her wit's end. She had great trouble convincing her husband to let her do this. She has promised to do it only until his condition improves.

"Would you like to continue regardless, for every little bit of money helps, and you have learned a very valuable skill," Lucymemsahib asks gently.

She shakes her head, smiling wanly. "That is not possible. . . .

How did she learn of the position, Lucymemsahib wants to know.

Her friend, the fruit vendor's daughter, told her about it, and the vendor himself helped convince her unhappy husband to let his wife participate. Both girls were in school together. This one got married, soon out of school, because her parents found a boy too good to turn down, while the fruit vendor's daughter went on to premedical studies. "Although my grades were just as good," says Baji with some pride, as her friend nods her head in agreement. Baji, too, had wanted to be a doctor.

"Her husband must be a terrible cad," Lucymemsahib says, more in frustration than anything else.

"Oh no, Madam!" The girl rebukes Lucymemsahib gently, looking her in the eye for the only time during the whole conversation. "He is a very nice person, and a loving father. So handsome, too. He is always very kind to me, or at least was before all this happened. He brought all his salary home to me and never frittered it away in drink or cards as a lot of men do. It was I who used it as I saw fit, and he never ever shouted at me for anything, even when I did not have the dinner ready. He would say never mind,

I'm just happy to be home with you, I do not care for food. . . ." And with this admission, she bursts into another torrent of tears.

Time for Shots—or Not?

There is a lot of commotion all of a sudden. The children, finally all lined up for their shots, are in the yard, all shapes and sizes and colors and sounds. They are wonderful to behold, in their homemade caps and outfits, some oversize and some too tight, all knitted and handworked in mirrors and beads and colorful thread by mothers, grandmothers, and older sisters. Their eyes are shining, and their cheeks are dry and cracked as a result of the dry mountain winds; their noses are running, and their lips are spread out in smiles of innocence and unconcern. They reach out with eager fingers or cover their faces with their hands. One, who looks about three years old, stands on a little mound with her hands on her hips, her hair dry and spiky and orange-tinted, looking around with critical concentration.

These children are the future of this country, the joy and the pride and the treasure of their families. They are held firmly by their mothers or rest on the hip of an older sibling, usually a sister, for the boys that age are usually in school. The mothers, young women in or barely out of their teens, are chatting, trying to catch up on the happenings in the area. Who is getting married, who has had a child, whose husband/son/father/brother has found a job in the city. In Karachi, too! They earn a lot of money there, God was surely kind to them! All this is said not without a tinge of envy.

It looks like a festive occasion. Two little girls about eight years old, in colorful huge *shalwars* and wide frocks worked in intricate threads and patterns, their hair in many braids, are playing jump rope and singing.

"They should be in school," mutters Lucymemsahib under her breath.

There is no school for girls in the village.

"Why can't they just go to the school for boys, for God's sake! They are just little kids!" Lucymemsahib is losing patience.

A monkey-man, followed by a fruit-and-drinks vendor, wanders into the courtyard. The children run to them, clamoring for stuff, for the show to begin; they touch and tease the monkey, who, dressed in a red-and-green mirror-work skirt and a cap to match, nips at their legs and bares its teeth. The monkey-man is shooed off, but we cannot get rid of the vendor, who by great public demand quickly sets up shop: multicolored slimy drinks and roasted corncobs, smeared with lime juice and red pepper. Mouthwatering! I clamor for these, too.

The line breaks and re-forms, and the women are beginning to get impatient; they have to get home in time to prepare lunch and do the dishes. One has left a paralyzed father-in-law unattended. Another has washed laundry waiting to be spread out. Others are worried about being out unescorted for so long.

The vaccinators work in pairs. One prepares the shots and sets them aside. Another gives the injections, based on an evaluation of the vaccination history of each child that the same team did earlier in the week. At that time, the team went from house to house and put the vaccination history of each child on a card. The mothers could bring this card to the vaccination camp or to any provider to get their child vaccinated. The vaccinators give the required vaccination, check today's date, and write in the date for the next dose.

"Very smart, and efficient, too," says Lucymemsahib. "They waste no time here, and also the parents have a chance to be educated and ask questions."

"Yes," says the director, "it has to be done that way. Only one-to-one communication works, and that, too, oral communication. Public service announcements and advertisements and fliers are quite useless, or at least not worth the effort and money. Most of the women, who are their target audience for such campaigns, cannot read. I always wonder who thinks of this way of doing things," he says, to no one in particular.

The vaccinator who is giving the shots is extremely skillful. First she gives the intramuscular injection for diphtheria, pertussis, and tetanus, which is painful, in the arm or the buttock. When the child cries, she quickly squirts the polio drops into its wide-open mouth. The child, startled, stops crying. The vaccinators work fast, without interruptions. It is only when the mothers start asking questions that the girls get flustered.

"If this is supposed to be good for the baby, why did my sister's baby become sick after the shot? He had fever and refused to feed, even refused the breast! For days after," says a rotund lady holding her child close to her chest. There are audible tut-tuts all around. "My sister had to take them to the hakim, in the next village. She told me not to get this done for my child." Other women pitch in with similar stories as they wait for an explanation.

The girls try to reassure them. Don't listen to your sister or mother, they say; they do not know. But the women are not reassured. The first lady looks suspicious. Her sister not know? Why, her sister, Siani (the nickname means "wise one," or "know-it-all"), she is the smartest in the family! Anytime there is a wedding or other important occasion, Siani is the one to handle it! She points to the vaccinator who has spoken: "She says not to listen to Siani!" And the rotund lady pulls away her baby's exposed bottom, which had been presented for a shot. The other women also huddle away, wary, unconvinced, and anxious.

The vaccinators look helplessly at each other and finally at me. The line cannot move until this woman has been reassured that her baby will not get sick as a result of this shot. I explain to the mother that her baby will get sick—but only slightly—as a result of this shot, just as her sister's baby did and as all babies should. She looks at me as if I am a witch and hides her child's face from my view. But do not worry, I tell her, this small illness is a good sign; it means that your baby is healthy and the shot is doing its protective work in the body. And I go on to explain more about the way the immune system is stimulated as a result of these shots, and the benefit of this process.

The women gather round and nod their heads as they understand. The rotund lady who started all this says she will convince her sister to bring her child for the second shot—"for without the second one and the third, this is no good? Her child can still get sick?" she confirms again.

That's right. These vaccinations need to be given in this sequence and at regular intervals. There is a collective "ah" from the crowd. At last they understand this business of protective shots! Now why didn't somebody tell them all this, eh? If they had known, they would have gotten these shots for their older children as well. Is it too late for them now?

"If these are supposed to be protective, then how come my friend's child still had the measles after he had had his shots?" asks another concerned—and intelligent—mother from the back of the crowd.

And the women in the group, who were eagerly offering their children's arms and behinds, pull back again as one. Now I have to explain this phenomenon. I tell them that this will continue to happen to some children, but the disease will be mild, with fewer complications. Yes, says one, my brother's daughter died when she had the measles some years ago, and another could identify a child in the village who became blind. But then there were children who had measles and did not die—they recovered without any treatment and without any residual damage. They nod their heads on being enlightened, and once again they offer up their children.

The Smiling Disease

We are almost done when there is more commotion at the back. An irate mother has just arrived, wailing and screaming, dragging her twelve-year-old daughter by the arm. The girl was vaccinated last week in another area, and now her whole arm is swollen—"poisoned" is the word her mother uses. The girl has had a fever for the past week and has been totally unable to help around the house. The mother flings back her chador and begins beating her chest.

"This serves me right! This is just punishment for me!" she cries. "For not listening to my own husband and of listening to these . . . these," she points to the vaccinators, who are trembling and cringing visibly, "city memsahibs. He had told me, the good-for-nothing he is, but he certainly turned out to be right in this case, that these injections were no good. He had told me that these were injections for family planning and they will poison my daughter and make her sterile." But she, the mother, the stupid thing—and here she begins to beat herself afresh—she had been convinced by these treacherous memsahibs, who told her that this injection would prevent her daughter's newborn children from dying from the "smiling disease."

And she, the poor innocent, has been convinced because, unfortunate woman that she is, she had lost two boys—boys! said in a horrendous yowl —to the "smiling disease," and was left only with these three stupid girls. She had decided to give her daughter this injection only from fear of the "smiling disease." And see what has happened? She appeals to the women in the crowd, who nod their heads in understanding and obvious sympathy. To lose two sons and to be left with an unmarriageable daughter on your hands were misfortunes indeed!

This mother is not done. "Now this one," she says, giving a big shove to the skinny child who is whimpering into the soiled chador, trying to hide behind her mother's ample frame, "will certainly lose her arm and will not be able to do any work, she will not have any children, and no one will want to marry her." And she, her poor, long-suffering mother, will have to take care of this invalid child even in her old age. For the rest of her life! Whereas if her sons had been alive, she, their mother, would have been cared for. . . . Daughters-in-law would have cooked and cleaned for her. . . . Oh God! She was certainly born under an unlucky star. . . . She wishes she had never been born. . . . She wishes she was dead, she is so tired of it all. She plops down on the ground, shedding copious tears and blowing her nose all over her chador.

I ask the girl, who seems more pained by the picture of her bleak future shared in so much detail with so many strangers than by her present physical condition, to show me her arm. It is swollen to three times its normal size, and is red hot and throbbing with reddish streaks all along its length— a classic textbook picture of lymphangitis of the arm, a complication of vaccination if done using unsterile needles or if infection is introduced by some other means, such as by scratching with dirty fingernails. The girl had been given an intramuscular injection of antitetanus vaccine, which protects mothers and newborns against tetanus, a common contributor to maternal and neonatal mortality in developing countries.

The local term for neonatal tetanus, which is almost 100 percent fatal, is the smiling disease.[4] It is so called because of its peculiar visible symptoms. Tetanus produces generalized spasms of the muscles, including facial and respiratory muscles. The facial spasm pulls the corners of the mouth outward, giving the dramatic and actually quite grotesque impression of a vivid smile. Spasms of respiratory muscles lead to respiratory failure, which is the usual cause of death.

Neonatal tetanus and postpartum tetanus in women are two of the most easily acquired infections in developing countries. Both the mother and the neonate get them at the same time, during delivery. Most of the deliveries take place at home, in unhygienic conditions or in animal sheds in rural areas, where there is more than an abundant supply of tetanus spores. The infection is introduced into the bloodstream when the umbilical cord is severed, usually with whatever sharp instrument is on hand—a rusted sickle or a blunt knife. Sometimes it is crushed with a stone. It is a miracle that under such conditions, any infants, or mothers, survive at all.

I explain to the mother the relatively benign nature of the problem with her daughter's arm, and that the girl will not lose her arm or become sterile. After praising the mother for taking the initiative to get her daughter vaccinated, I explain again the importance of this vaccination to the survival of the next generation as well as for the girls themselves. I then write a prescription for antibiotics to take care of the infected arm.

The mother wipes her face clean of tears and sweat with one end of her chador. She is beaming, her round, fair face like the sun after a cloudburst, and she congratulates herself on making this very radical decision to get her

---

4. World Health Organization, "Tetanus," http://www.who.int/immunization/topics/ tetanus/en/index.html.

adolescent daughter vaccinated, in spite of such opposition from her husband. She leaves the camp as if on the shoulders of her peers.

The session has ended well.

An Intricate Tapestry

The director is impressed by my detailed knowledge of the situations that can arise in a large-scale vaccination program. He is glad I was here today to sort out this mess. "Most of the time these issues create major hurdles for the vaccinators," he says.

"You mean this happens frequently?" asks Lucymemsahib, again looking surprised.

"Of course," he replies cheerfully. "What do you expect in a population such as ours? This kind of thing happens at almost every camp."

"Then what do you do when Dr. So and So is not here?" she asks again.

"Oh, nothing," he replies, again quite cheerfully. "I suppose the girls do the best they can. But between you and me," he says with a lowered voice, "this has major implications for the credibility of the program as well as of the vaccinators. Many women refuse to come back again to have their children vaccinated. That is a major reason for the poor coverage of the second round of vaccinations."

"Why don't these people just go to the doctors with this kind of a problem?" asks Lucymemsahib.

"Ah! Madam, you do not understand!" says the long-suffering director yet again. And I marvel at Lucymemsahib's capacity to make this remark. "There are simply no doctors available for this population. It is just to overcome the unavailability of trained manpower that this program has been established, and nonphysicians are being used to provide the services. It would take this mother two days to get to the city, with much running around, not to mention a significant investment of finances, to be able to find a doctor to treat this child. Money that she would have to borrow or steal. By that time, the child's condition would either have been resolved on its own or deteriorated." He sighs again.

"Why do you not have the medical officers from the health center of this area or from the Provincial Health Department accompany a vaccination team on their visit such as this?" I ask. The regulations stipulate that each service delivery outlet in the rural health system should have at least one medical officer, who is expected to provide exactly this kind of backup support to the rural health workers.

The director sighs again and looks at me. I expect him to say, Ah, Madam! Even you do not understand! But he merely shakes his head.

"Where should I begin?" he says with some exasperation. "It is a very complicated situation and has to do with the 'ownership' of the program and how it is monitored. This, as you know, is a vertical program with its own hierarchical system and its own personnel, who derive their rather lucrative salaries directly from the program funds and guard their turf most jealously. The EPI supervisors are not willing to have 'their program' taken over by Health Department physicians and thus appear redundant. Most of the medical officers, too, are reluctant to be involved in preventive health programs, preferring to work in the curative health system in the urban centers so as not to jeopardize their chances for postgraduate training."

"But the supervisors are not technically trained people. Their job is to administer the program, not to provide clinical support." Lucymemsahib delineates, correctly, the different areas of expertise involved.

"True," he replies. "But remember, the program was designed in Geneva or Washington, where everyone has access to a physician, so this is just assumed to be the case here as well. This is typical of the gap in understanding of the systems in developing countries, which has major implications for the successful implementation of programs."

"Can you not make this change since you are responsible for the implementation of the program?" Lucymemsahib wants to know, for it seems simple enough and logical, too.

"We are responsible only for implementation. After the program has been developed, we have no authority to change it; also, since it is a national program, it is too difficult to change it locally. Although most of the people involved with implementation feel that this is not appropriate for the circumstances in our country, by now it is too late, for there are deadlines to meet, deadlines tied to funds. Also there are too many vested interests."

"Maybe one way around this can be to make these basic clinical issues, which impact the program effectiveness, a part of the vaccinator's training curriculum. Why do you not do that?" We are looking for solutions to the problem.

"We cannot change the curriculum, either." The director is categorical about this. "That too is part of the overall program."

"Then surely you can do this as a refresher course?" Lucymemsahib is not going to give up. "The training program stipulates a refresher course of one week after the vaccinators have worked in the field for three months. Surely the purpose of that course is to deal with problems such as these?"

"The content of the refresher courses also comes with the prepared curriculum. That deals mostly with issues related to the cold chain," the poor man continues patiently. "An additional clinical curriculum would be impossible to teach in such a short time. It would not be possible at all, and besides by that time it is too late. These girls are gone. . . ."

"What do you mean 'gone'? Gone where?" Lucymemsahib looks at the girls as if expecting to see trained vaccinators vanishing in a puff of smoke.

"Either married off or gone to the Middle East." Of course. "And it is hard enough finding girls to replace them, even at this basic skill level. You know recruitment is a major problem in all the peripheral health programs." We know.

"But this is a ridiculous situation," says Lucymemsahib. "This has to stop. Why can't the government stop these technically trained people from leaving the country?" She asks the same question yet again, in the hope that someone will have an answer.

"Oh no. These people should not be stopped," the director responds immediately, as if alarmed—just as all senior government officers respond when confronted thus. "They have every right to improve their lives. And besides, if they are stopped from leaving, they will ask us for jobs, and the provincial government is in no position to absorb so much manpower. Why, as it is, we are behind on the payment of salaries for the people we already have." I wait for him to say what a "headache" the trained manpower creates for the government, but he doesn't.

What an unholy mess! And in every area! Recruitment, training, careers, job security, the social issues surrounding women, the needs of the population—all are intertwined in a rich and intricate tapestry, quite like the country. What will it take to unravel it and begin to make sense?

"Time, for one," he says, "and that is never available. We are always under pressure to come up with some 'scheme' or other, which someone is desperate to fund and someone else on the other side is desperate to have funded. These days anything will pass as long as it includes references to women, primary health care, and one or two things of a similar nature generally pertaining to human resource development. And this usually means training. For what and why and what to do with the trained people is never of concern. On paper these are 'visible' things. To be able to say that so many thousands have been trained is a feather in any politician's cap. That there are no jobs for these trained people, no career paths, no expansion or improvement in the recruitment pool, no thought given to what this will ultimately help achieve, or how this will integrate with the socioeconomic and cultural fabric of society. . . ." The director reiterates exactly what most of the other provincial managers have said.

"Well, now is your chance," I say to him. (Naively enough, as it turns out. For even as of this writing, in 2009, we are missing similar chances. Most donor-funded programs, including those funded by the U.S. government, are still concentrating on the training of health workers and their managers, and documenting these as success stories.) "You have the chance to include these issues in the future Social Action Program, which we have been assured is a 'very serious' attempt to sort out these very problems." The director looks at me as if from a great distance and again just shakes his head. He excuses himself; it is time for his prayers. "Maybe that's what all of us should be doing," says Lucymemsahib.

Twelve

Bank's World:
Witches' Oil and Lizards' Tails

Washington in the spring is one of the most beautiful cities—as it is on this balmy spring day. The crocuses are waving, the grass has been washed a lovely green by the recent rain, and at 12:30 p.m. the sun is smiling on the corner of Pennsylvania Avenue and 18th Street, NW, a stone's throw from the White House. On this corner, in Room 9002 of the Main Complex Building of the World Bank, a seminar is being presented by Bank staff on the Population Welfare Program in Pakistan. This group has been actively involved with the Social Action Program (SAP) for the past year, advising the Government of Pakistan on the design and implementation of a country-wide contraceptive delivery services system within the context of the overall SAP.

Jim—with his earnest expression and bush of white frizzy hair, which in better days might have made a great Afro but now looks like an ill-tended shrub from an avant-garde French garden—leads the pack. Pamela, a tall and broad woman of Asian heritage, in her serious pinstriped suit and neat little pageboy haircut, sits to Jim's left, just a tad behind him, looking alert and competent but as impassive as a sphinx. Christine, a little way off in a dark corner, already halfway through her sandwich, this being a bag lunch thing, is waiting for the show to roll so she can start her snooze. I have been with her in many lunchtime seminars, and her routine never varies. She sits in a quiet corner, finishes her lunch as soon as possible, curls up, and goes to sleep—her neck still, her chin resting on her chest, her glasses steady on her nose. Finally, presiding over the seminar is a senior official of the Bank's Population, Health, and Nutrition Department, who at this point has his rather ferocious-looking teeth sunk into a lettuce sandwich. This gentleman means business.

178

The presentation is fairly typical, and thus starts with a problem statement. We learn about the unrelenting problem of overpopulation in Pakistan for the past so many decades, which continues to undermine all economic development efforts. The annual population growth rate continues to be more than 3 percent, each year adding millions more mouths to feed, minds to educate, and bodies that need to be housed. The contraceptive prevalence rate is extremely low, and total fertility rates and lifetime fertility rates are unacceptably and extremely high, though all numbers are estimates. There is a large unmet need, 40 percent, for contraceptive services and devices.

We are also given the administrative background on the country's health and population delivery services. This time, we are told, the Government of Pakistan is really committed to developing a sound population policy with an effective delivery system reaching even the most remote rural areas. The erstwhile Population Welfare Division is now an independent ministry, the Ministry of Population Welfare, with its own minister and a dedicated bureaucratic structure. The government has further reinforced its commitment by funding the program directly from the federal budget, as opposed to other health programs, which have to seek implementation monies through the provincial governments.

Next we are given an overview of the SAP's contribution to the program. The development of a realistic Population Welfare Program, with a practical implementation strategy, is an important component of the SAP. That is why a special program for delivering contraceptive services has been developed with the World Bank's direct technical assistance. It is this program, designed by these experts, that is being presented here today. Everyone listens politely—well, kind of, for there is one's lunch to tackle. People ask tiny, quiet questions to show they are still there, amid the rustling of brown paper bags and modest little bites.

"What is the authority of the secretary, Ministry of Population Welfare?"

"He is a very powerful decisionmaker in the federal government," says Jim. "Fortunately, he thinks like us, so there was no problem bringing him on board."

"Are the provinces involved in the programmatic decisions, or are the decisions made at the federal level?" A very good question, because this is a major issue at the provincial level.

"Oh, yes, the provinces are involved. They are involved in training the manpower or, let me say, the womanpower needed for the program. Training programs are really huge and are totally the responsibility of the provincial governments," Jim says.

A deliciously tanned young woman, lean and mean, with a flowing blond mane—which brings to mind the term "Lithuanian Lioness," the male version of which was reserved for a tennis star of the 1980s—wants to know if there are any women involved in this program.

"Oh, yes. Of course, women are involved. How can women not be involved in a contraceptive health program? All the service delivery personnel will be women. They are being trained even as we speak," Jim answers, going on to add expansively, "even the prime minister of the country is a woman." (One year into the SAP, Nawaz Sharif's government was dismissed on corruption charges, and Benazir Bhutto replaced him as prime minister.) This should appease anyone worried about the involvement of women. The Lioness goes back to her bottled water, satisfied.

The man on my right is eating a sandwich that makes my mouth water. The smell is so overpowering—lots of mustard and onions. Brave man. We nod our woozy heads as we listen, trying to look intelligent in spite of our hypoglycemic states. My good friend Christine continues to snooze, and Pamela has neither blinked nor moved. One wonders if she is breathing. Jim is talking and explaining, warming to his subject—he projects slides on the opposite wall, showing horrifying statistics transformed into jaunty, colorful graphs.

We now come to issues of financing, and this is the most serious business of the day—our bread and butter. We are, after all, a bank; this is our business; we are all knowledgeable about the ins and outs of the process. Many complicated and highly technical notions are thrown around, and the group gets terribly involved. There is loud and animated conversation, with people cutting in on each other and updating each other on this step versus that one for this disbursement of funds. Half-eaten sandwiches are forgotten, and bottles of Perrier sit unconsumed. There is a discussion of base financing, line-item budgets, statements of expenditures, and the way the vouchers will be submitted—different processes of voucher submission are lobbed back and forth, each new and improved. There is something about a new office in Islamabad, a multidonor support unit, which will review each voucher so there will be no question of the misuse of funds. Each subsequent tranche will be released on the reconciliation of the previous one. (Despite the multidonor support unit, and well into the SAP's second phase, reconciliations remained problematic, and the donors' default action was to simply continue giving money.)[1]

1. Nancy Birdsall, Adeel Malik, and Milan Vaishnav, "Poverty and the Social Sectors: The World Bank in Pakistan, 1990–2003, Prepared for World Bank's Operations

Jim brings the discussion to an end a good thirty minutes later. "Excuse me, I'm afraid I have to curtail this," he says, "we are running out of time." The participants look flushed and pink, as after an invigorating game of tennis.

A bald man with a goatee, who looks like someone's widowed uncle, talks the loudest and longest about everything to do with population issues in Pakistan. I look at him in wonder. Just a few weeks ago, I was in a meeting with him at a briefing for another Bank expert who was planning to leave for Pakistan the next day concerning a nutrition project and wanted to find out all there was to know about its health and population sectors in a forty-five-minute meeting. Someone's widowed uncle was to get a ride home with the expert, who was his neighbor. During the quasi-social chitchat at that meeting, he told me that he had joined the Bank as a transportation expert twenty years ago and had later "branched out" into population issues and has been working in Africa for the past year. He was interested in getting involved in Pakistan as well.

The formal presentation is over, and the floor is open for questions. Right on cue, Christine stirs, and even before fully awake begins: "Correct me if I'm wrong, but to me it seems, since there is a large unmet need, the major policy issue seems to be delivery of services. . . ."

Absolutely. This gives rise to another round of jabbering. The unmet contraceptive needs in Latin America are dragged in for a cameo appearance, for a Latin America expert is in the audience. Then there is another question, now from the most senior expert, our gentleman of the ferocious teeth. Flashing them in a big indulgent smile, he is interested in the monitoring of the program. "Is anyone in India going to monitor this, or will this be our responsibility?" he asks loud and clear, with the confidence born of his high position and the authority that goes with it.

"Oh yes, yes, . . . the program will be monitored, locally, and by us eventually, . . ." is the reply from the team of experts. "There is the management support unit, no?"

More jabbering. The program monitoring in Indonesia and the management support unit in Jakarta? No one bothers to inform the senior expert that we are talking of population welfare and contraceptive delivery services in Pakistan. India and Pakistan have certainly gone through the same colonial experience, and were born of the same cataclysmic event, but they are now separate countries, and have been for the past fifty years. To this

Evaluation Department," Center for Global Development, Washington, D.C., June 1, 2005, and revised August 29, 2005, 26.

dear man—and to this group at large—it's all the same. Once you cross the ocean, what does it matter, eh? And what does it matter to us here in the hallowed halls of the Main Complex. India, Pakistan, Nepal, Indonesia, . . . they're all the same. Theoretical concepts, or interesting countries to visit. A way for us to earn a living, as good or bad as any other.

What is the new program plan proposed and funded by the World Bank's experts and adopted so eagerly by the Government of Pakistan? It is called the Area-Based Approach to Contraceptive Delivery. That is, contraceptives will be distributed to a whole area all at once! Jim looks triumphant as he announces this. It sounds to me like an air drop in response to some great emergency. I imagine it raining condoms and intrauterine devices in Chanesar Goth, in Kamoke, in Mithi—the grateful public scooping them up by the armfuls.

Maybe even this audience looks slightly skeptical over their sandwiches and Perrier, for our friend Jim, looking like Beethoven in the throes of creation, cries, "Hey, we are doing the best we can!" With an endearing earnestness, implying that this should be enough, he goes on, "Honestly speaking, we do not know much about it. We are learning as we go along. And anyway, we shall find out in a couple of years if we are right or wrong. . . . In the meantime, we've got to do something. . . ." He waves his hands wildly. "The problem is absolutely enormous. . . ."

I want to say that it will become more enormous, if you continue to do what you are doing.

The group breathes easily, and people go back to tackling the last remnants of their sandwiches, though some have moved on to dessert. They are satisfied. Jim and his team are off the hook. They are sincere and mean well; they are desperately trying to "do something." They are absolved.

But I am not satisfied with this response. Not at all, not me. By God, certainly not me. It is here, right here, when seeking absolution, that the Bank experts lose me. It is only now that I am mad. If I had a cerebral aneurysm, it would have burst. If I had a peptic ulcer, it would have popped. If I had been pregnant, my membranes would have ruptured, sending me into violent and instantaneous labor. That's how mad I am.

How can you say something like that and expect to be taken seriously?

You call yourself an expert, you go halfway around the world at enormous financial cost to the country you are sent out to help. (World Bank experts do not come cheap. All the costs of their technical input, including premium air travel, five-star hotel accommodations, and any other related expenses, are part of the loan to the developing country.) You give expert advice to national governments on a sensitive and crucial technical issue that has far-reaching economic consequences. You know that your advice will be taken seriously, and you know very well that it is half-baked. You know you are "learning" as you go along. However, the people in the country you are assisting do not know that you are only learning—at their expense—because you are sold as an expert.

You convince the government to spend this huge amount of money—a loan, which will be a burden for next three generations—to do what you, the expert, are telling them to do. And we are not even calculating the opportunity costs! You ask the country to deploy its already-meager human and financial resources for a certain number of years on this project, when here, before this gathering of your peers, you are saying that you do not know what you are doing! That you are learning as you go along! Learning? If you are learning, what are you doing strutting all over the world as an "expert," touting some harebrained scheme doomed to failure? You are basically selling witches' oil and lizard tails. You are just like those experts who can be found on every sidewalk in every developing country in the world, selling potions and creams for ailments both known and unknown to customers who have no other choice and nowhere else to go.

All I can say, in the words of my dear departed grandmother, may her soul rest in peace, is "Hai! Hai!" with many sad shakes of the head.

What is more worrying is that you in your arrogance have not even taken the trouble to learn what has happened so far. You think all that is needed in overcrowded Chanesar Goth—without water, without sanitation, without hope—is condoms hanging from every tree branch, pills scattered like pebbles in the streets for these ignoramuses. Walk down the streets of Chenasargoth one day, and you will see children playing water balloons with your colorful, free-of-charge, donor-funded condoms. Turn a narrow corner, and you will see a maternal health clinic overflowing with purdah-clad ladies who have come to get first- and second-trimester abortions for pregnancies resulting from contraceptive failures, or women who are looking for the "injection" that they have heard can prevent pregnancies. They will tell you that this is their third visit and thank the stars that at least today the clinic is open—whether the injection is available remains to be seen. Go into the storeroom of the clinic, and you will find shelves stocked with intrauterine devices, pills, and condoms sitting and rotting.

Do you really think these people need to run scavenging for dropped contraceptives?

Go into the house of a small shopkeeper, a taxi driver, an unskilled laborer, or a teacher in a primary school—those who struggle with dead-end, low-paying, but still-sought-after jobs—and each will tell you how many babies they have lost in infancy to tetanus (the smiling disease), to childhood infections like diphtheria and polio, and to meningitis, called "neck-break fever," which breaks the child's neck, the mother's heart, the father's back, and the family's fortunes, all in one stroke. They will point out their one or two surviving children, puny little girls, undernourished and uncared for, who rather than a source of solace become an added burden. Are condoms their only hope for getting out of this whirlpool of poverty, sickness, and death?

You will meet the old crone, the much-maligned mother-in-law, who will point an accusatory finger at her old-for-her-years daughter-in-law, reprimanding her for not producing a healthy grandson. What good is a daughter-in-law if she cannot produce an offspring who lives? Even a cow or a goat can do that!

The daughter-in-law, now pregnant for the fifth time, hopes that this time the midwife knows what she is doing and does not let the labor go on for so long—or that her husband can find enough money to take her to a private doctor and not the government hospital. After their last experience with the government hospital, she is afraid of going there; . . . two of her infants, twins, both boys, died in that hospital. They were born alright, though after two days of labor—but they became yellow, and the hospital's special machine that takes care of this condition was not working, and no one could be found who knew how to work it. She hopes that the electricity will not fail, as she was told had happened by the doctor who came the next day, or that the government doctor, if not too busy with his private practice, will be able to get to her baby in case he is needed. She thinks of her "boys," who would have been a year old, lying there slowly dying in front of her eyes. Her breathing slows to match their dying breaths. She knows she is weak after five pregnancies in five years, but if she doesn't have a son soon. . . . She casts an anxious glance at her mother-in-law.

Her husband is a good man. He works hard, hauling loads for the market, but there are too many mouths to feed. Aside from the two of them and the girls—well, OK, they don't count—there are the parents-in-law and his younger siblings. The poor man needs help; he is not too well himself, and with that terrible cough, some say he may have tuberculosis; a son or maybe two, that's four extra hands, . . . and what will happen if they grow old without a son? She shudders at the thought and decides to take a special offering to the local saint this Thursday night, and she begins to make plans to beg, borrow, or steal the money for the offering.

Programmatically, what has happened in Pakistan so far is no secret. All its population policies and programs of the past forty years have been well documented. Experts from the universities of Michigan, Berkeley, Johns Hopkins, London—serious academics with sound professional credentials —have analyzed and described again and again what has worked and what has not, and why. There are ample recommendations for what should be done in the future, and how. Even the World Bank has commissioned numerous reports that have evaluated the collective experience of the past one hundred and fifty years of contraceptive health programs in developing countries, including Pakistan. How can one be called an expert and not know this? How can one proudly unveil this Area-Based Approach to Contraceptive Delivery and not know that a similar strategy called the Inundation Strategy was the gospel of the day in Pakistan during the early 1970s? And the results of that are before us.

To me, I suppose, given my clinical background, statements like these sound especially bizarre, bordering on the unethical, coming from "experts" employed by a highly regarded professional organization with enormous credibility. Would experts in any other organization say anything like this and be able to get away with it?

Suppose you were an expert in designing, say, carburetors, instead of social-sector and development programs. You go to Ford Motor Company and say, yes, me and my team members, snoozy Christine and stoic Pamela, will design your carburetors for the 1998 models. We'll be honest: We don't know much. We'll learn as we go along.

You can imagine Mr. Ford's response!

But this is just hypothetical. We all know that you would not even go to them with such a proposal.

Or say you are sick. You need an appendectomy. You go to an institution known the world over for having experts in appendectomies. Your important-looking, high-sounding surgeon—who charges an arm and a leg for his expert services, travels first class, and sleeps in fancy hotels at your expense—reassures you before surgery:

> Sure, I'll do this surgery for you. You just need your appendix out. I don't know much about it, but I'll do my best. . . . Hey, I'll learn as I go along. And we'll always be able to tell some weeks later whether it works or not.

And this is exactly how I feel as this dream team tells us how they are going to help Pakistan this time. Exactly the same. And the mess made will be similar, too. The only difference will be that you can take your half-baked, well-meaning, honest surgeon who is desirous of doing "at least something" to court. There is an oversight and regulatory system to which the surgeon is answerable, and it will protect you, the consumer. There is accountability in medicine, but what about social-sector development? Who regulates your work? Who protects your consumers?

We all know that the situation is desperate. "Something" needs to be done. But does this something have to be a repeat of the failed somethings of yesteryear? Why this blind and foolish urgency? Why this unethical practice?

For the sake of development, of course!

For one brief, nightmarish moment, I wonder if such development planning is going on in other sectors as well. What about transportation, energy, roads, dams, hydroelectric power, forestry, agriculture, and fisheries? In all 175 developing countries of the poor world—in Bolivia, Brazil, Mexico, Peru, Benin, Botswana, Egypt, Ghana, Gambia, Burkina Faso, India, Sri Lanka, the Philippines, Laos?

The whole becomes messier than the sum of its parts. All for development's sake.

Ah, development! Development! You elusive and seductive mistress, what crimes are committed in thy name!

Thirteen

Packed, Sealed, and Delivered: Our Project Is Finished— in More Ways Than One

Today is our final meeting with the federal Social Action Program (SAP) adviser in Islamabad, where we are to present our recommendations. Lucy-memsahib and I have decided to have a seven o'clock breakfast meeting to put together our reports; we have arrived only the night before, she from Quetta in Balochistan and I from Lahore. I feel that in spite of all odds, we have identified definite areas that can be improved in the delivery of health services. I am keeping my fingers crossed, hoping for some miracle. After all is said and done, things do boil down to faith.

Over breakfast at Nadia in the hotel, as I go over our report, I see Lucy-memsahib weave in and out of the tables as she walks toward me. She is wearing a flowery, billowy magenta-print skirt, and an embroidered blouse of ivory silk. A flowing *dupatta* of ivory chiffon slung around her neck completes the elegant ensemble. Her hair, dyed a vibrant brown, is in a fashionable perm all fluffed up around her face—very flattering. She wears gold hoop earrings and colorful glass bangles on her wrists, which tinkle and jangle merrily when she waves, happily acknowledging me. As she sinks delicately into the chair next to me and picks up her napkin—breathing "Am I very late?"—I see that her fingernails, long and tapered, are painted a deep red.

"This place is changed," she says, looking around.

Is it? It is Nadia, early in the morning. There is the same crowd of foreign experts and government officials and hangers-on and sulky waiters. And there is the same clang and clatter of catering to the business of the day

187

through a smoky haze. The early morning spring sunshine streams in through an east window. Everything is the same. It is she who has changed.

"So, how was Lahore?" she asks nonchalantly, dipping into the fruit salad.

"How was Quetta?" I ask, trying to control a vague sense of disorientation.

"It was beautiful!" she exclaims, tossing her hair. "I had the most wonderful time of my life. Balochi men are so handsome, in a dark and brooding kind of way. It's a pity many of them do not speak any English. On the other hand, maybe its good that they don't. . . ." She winks knowingly at me.

"What about Punjabi men?" I cannot help asking, and a bit sourly, remembering the time she went off with the handsome, though not so brooding, chief of the Women's Division, leaving me eating their dust.

"Oh, they are OK, too," she says, taking me seriously, "only too loud and too sure of themselves." She waves a hand at the waiter, saying "aur chai," and "meherbani," as he pours the tea for her with a deferential tilt of his dark head and a hopeful demeanor. She beams at him, thrilled at having mastered some critical words of the language. He smiles encouragingly at her.

"Did you know that the director of provincial health services for Balochistan had gone to McGill, way back when?" She leans toward me as she shares this bit of information. "He was there for six weeks, attending a course on project planning and administration. I was a graduate student in nursing at the same time, and at McGill, too. Though we didn't get to meet. . . . What a pity. . . ."

She looks for a while into the distance and then continues. "He is such a wonderful host. Do you know he organized a picnic for me at that place near Quetta, the place where your . . . uh . . . where Mr. Jinnah. . . ."

"Ziarat," I tell her. Ziarat, where Mohammed Ali Jinnah went to recuperate from the pulmonary tuberculosis that eventually claimed him, is a famous and favorite tourist attraction—a serene place with dry and moderate temperatures and a forest of elegant junipers.

"Yes! That's it. What a beautiful place! So calm and quiet. And the most beautiful trees in the world. . . . Of course, I didn't get to see much of Balochistan, except Quetta. I was told it wasn't safe, what with the political unrest and all that. I didn't want to take any chances."

"But . . . your report, . . ." I start to ask, panic joining my disorientation.

"Oh, that." She waves a hand, as if shooing a fly. "That I got done the first day I was there." She explains between spoonfuls: "The very next morning after my arrival in Quetta, I learned that the provincial departments were preparing the Family Health Project. Because all projects are similar anyway, they were nice enough to invite me to share all their data and their observations and other stuff. There is really no need to reinvent the wheel now, is there? So, lucky for me; otherwise, I would have had a lot of problems."

She takes a generous bite of her Spanish omelet. "With work out of the way, I was able to concentrate on other things. Do you know I was able to get the most gorgeous mirror-work cushion covers from there, and for only four hundred rupees a pair? That is, what, a mere fifteen dollars! My God! I cannot believe my luck. These are museum pieces! I tell you I haven't seen anything like them either in Lahore or in Zainab Market in Karachi. Though I am told that this place in Islamabad, what's it called, the one near United Bakery, has some good stuff." She waves the waiter over for more tea.

"Oh, you do not know?" she says, looking at my face, for I am sure I look as if I know nothing, because that is exactly how I feel.

"Never mind," says Lucymemsahib consolingly. "I know where it is. I can take you with me, if you are interested. I am sure it is bound to be a bit touristy and so a bit pricey. . . . But who cares?" And pushing away her plate, she leans back languidly in her chair, fixing the folds of her *dupatta* on her shoulder and giving space to the enthusiastic waiter, who has been hovering around for just such a chance, to pour her another cup of tea.

"About today's meeting, the report," I begin a bit gingerly, for I am still not quite used to the colorful metamorphosis of our Lucymemsahib. The pupa has certainly turned into a butterfly, and it is fluttering its colorful wings too fast for me. I have hardly begun before Lucymemsahib interrupts me with a friendly pat on the arm.

"Oh, don't worry a thing about it," she says, "I have the whole thing right here." She taps her bag, which has the diskette. "And I had a printed copy sent two days ago to the federal SAP adviser's office. He has seen it already." He has just finished talking on the phone with Lucymemsahib, and she has already made all the amendments he has asked for.

"So it's packed, sealed, and delivered. You are all done," she says with another pat on my arm. "After all, it is their project." She delicately wipes the corners of her mouth with her napkin and continues, as if explaining a difficult point to a preschooler: "You and I will be out of here and on with our lives. He does not think that the idea of setting up an admission test for the entrants is a good idea. They will only cheat to get through and get false certificates, and this is going to waste a lot of time for the project. And all the administrative hassles at the provincial level are going to take forever to sort out. They want to get right into training so that these young women can go out into the field to provide the much-needed health services rather than be bogged down. You know, there are immense problems out there where these women should be. The notion of their being untrainable is totally ridiculous. I have never met anyone in my life who was untrainable, and I tell you I have certainly met my share of morons."

She goes on to tell me about all the amendments made to the report, in keeping with her, and the SAP adviser's, thinking. She was able to get in the recommendation about giving mobile phones to all women who are posted out of the city, she tells me with great pride. This should make them feel safe. I look at the draft report in my hand. It looks pathetic in its redundancy. But the point of the whole thing was not for the SAP adviser to write the recommendations, I tell her, whether this is "his project" or not. I am about to voice my protest at not being consulted before the changes were made, but she is getting ready to leave the table, picking up her keys and sunglasses, and the waiter is pulling back her chair, all smiles and deference, while she murmurs "shukria . . . shukria." (The man speaks perfect English, for God's sake; how else would he get this job!) She has to get her things from her room and make a phone call home to Canada, and so it is left at that.

Leaving Nadia, in the lobby right by the elevators, we run into a middle-aged, neat-looking blond woman in a little black skirt and a short, fire-engine-red coat. Lucymemsahib greets this person as if they were bosom buddies, and the two ladies chat merrily on, going over the agenda of the meeting of the day. The meeting where we are headed! Lucymemsahib is merrily telling the other one about the seriousness of the Government of Pakistan, the cuteness factor of some official or other, and how he had offered to arrange a bottle of red wine for her—no mean feat in this Islamic Republic, where alcohol is officially prohibited.

"But there was all kinds of alcohol at the party last night," comments the new lady.

"Shhhh!" Lucymemsahib puts a finger to her lips, looking over the new lady's shoulder at a tall potted plant and smiling indulgently.

This blond woman is Sallymemsahib, the new chief of the Overseas Development Assistance (ODA) Program, who has just arrived in Islamabad. She and Lucymemsahib met at a party last night, and Lucymemsahib had, on learning that the lady was staying at the same hotel (everyone stays at the same hotel), invited her to this meeting with the federal SAP adviser. This will help the new lady get integrated.

"You need to know some key people," Lucymemsahib tells Sallymemsahib, lowering her voice just a tad to give her some names that I cannot hear. "And by the way, this is Dr. So-and-So." Lucymemsahib at last thinks of pointing a red-tipped finger in my general direction, by way of introduction.

Sallymemsahib nods briefly, without making eye contact or showing any other acknowledgment, and mutters, "Very good, very good," as Lucymemsahib tells her that I have been helping her, Lucymemsahib, translate the "environment." And, I suppose, being useful to the memsahib? They walk ahead, arm in arm, talking very knowledgeably about the problems of women health workers in Dera Ismail Khan, "which is such a primitive place. I tell you. . . ." And they talk about the ethnic violence in Balochistan and its effect on the national infant mortality rates and the systemic problems that tie the hands of such wonderfully committed officers in the. . . . Sallymemsahib will really like working with them; they are so courteous, so helpful.

I give up trying to catch up with them. The native, having done her bit, has ceased to exist until the next time the memsahibs need her.

This pattern continues in the SAP adviser's office. The meeting is a mere formality. Everything has already been amended and worded according to the dictates of the SAP adviser; he is, after all, in a better position to know what the International Aid Consortium wants, and it is his job to provide it. And he certainly does not want any "hassles" at this stage. As everyone we meet seems to stress, the Consortium "wants to lend" and the Government of Pakistan "wants to borrow." This is the point that had disturbed me initially: A realistic program would qualify as a "hassle," so let's just get on with it.

The meeting is in full swing. The SAP adviser, bald, thick-necked, and jowly, is his charming self. He is busy thanking Lucymemsahib profusely on behalf of the Government of Pakistan for helping out in this very critical project, which is going to be of great benefit to millions of poor rural women. He is especially grateful that she was able to come at such short notice and at such personal inconvenience, for he knows that Pakistan is not a very comfortable country, especially when you come from North America. He hopes she can come again, maybe to evaluate the project in a year's time?

Most certainly. Lucymemsahib would be happy to help. She has fallen in love with the country. In fact, she is coming back next month. The brand new chief of the ODA Program, Sallymemsahib, has asked her to help with certain things, for starters to help her get oriented to the system and the country. She is going to "translate the environment"; this is, after all, the chief's first visit overseas, and given Lucymemsahib's experience and knowledge of the country, who could be more suited to the job?

"Wonderful, wonderful." The federal SAP adviser beams broadly at both ladies.

Tea and the goodies that go with it have been laid out, and we eat delicious chicken patties and drink out of fancy cups, though they are not Wedgwood and in fact are slightly grimy. Lucymemsahib fusses and preens and plays with her *dupatta,* which she has learned to carry on her shoulders with amazing expertise and grace. Sallymemsahib sits on the edge of her chair, listening to the SAP adviser with rapt attention.

He, the SAP adviser, is so pleased to make the acquaintance of Sallymemsahib. So this is her first assignment outside the United Kingdom? Where is she from again? Ah! Scotland. He has himself been to London many times, but never got a chance to go to Scotland. Beautiful place, he has heard, from a girlfriend during his college days in England when he was studying for his master's in Asian studies at the University of London's School of Oriental and African Studies. Heh, heh. There is much delicate laughter all round at this point. After a brief pause, the SAP adviser continues. He is sure that Sallymemsahib will like it here. Islamabad is a nice, quiet town—and so clean compared with the rest of the country, which is like a garbage heap. At this, all shake their heads regretfully and drink quietly and somberly for some minutes, as if taking care of that garbage was not the responsibility of senior government officials but of someone else entirely.

He will do all in his power to make Sallymemsahib's stay as pleasant as possible, personally as well as officially, for the Department of Planning and Development has always had a close working relationship with ODA, a wonderful organization. A pity we had left the Commonwealth, what a wonderful institution; so many needy students have benefited from its generosity. What does he mean? You know, the Commonwealth scholarships; . . . in his immediate family alone, there have been four recipients, and that is not counting the first or second cousins. Would Sallymemsahib perhaps like more tea, a fresh cup? See we have another thing in common, we are all tea drinkers, ha ha. . . .

The SAP adviser rings for the assistant. Fresh tea! The ever-suffering fellow keeps his eyes deferentially to the ground as he carries out the teapot on a tarnished silver tray.

Because I do not exist, I spread out my wings and float up to the ceiling above my three companions, my hair fanning out around. My *dupatta* hangs down, almost sweeping the tops of their heads. One brushes it out of her eyes. Another ducks out of its way as I swat him deliberately on his bald, greasy head.

Up above the sofa and the oversized desk and the ornate chairs I go, looking down on the dusty cabinets and the top shelves of the bookcases, where a comb with broken teeth and a copy of the Holy Quran, wrapped in its cover of red velvet, sit side by side. A little brown spider is diligently at work repairing the glistening threads of his intricate web, where he already has two flies all tangled up. He asks for a strand of my hair to tie them more securely, and I give it. For what can one do?

Meanwhile, my companions are chatting merrily away, nibbling on chicken patties and luscious lemon tarts from the famous United Bakery, busily solving the problems of this poor country.

"Lord, what fools these (foreign) mortals be."

The spider does not need me anymore, and after circling around a few times, I melt out of the walls into the dim corridor of the P Building. It is full of *shalwar-kameez*-clad assistants, and assistants to assistants, going around in circles. One bears a warm teapot and chicken patties on a silver tray—I pick a couple from my vantage spot—and another one holds a dog-eared file open to page 153, with much-crossed-out writing in ink. He peeks into the door, waiting for the great man to finish his important meeting with the memsahibs and sign the stuff. Others just stand around, alternately picking their noses or scratching their groins discreetly from behind the overhang of their crumpled *kameezes*. They look sad and resigned, and wait.

Suddenly there is a rumbling, a mighty thundering, a wild clattering. Pigeons flutter out of their coves on the ledge, cackling crows flap off the banyan tree, breathless peons run noisily up the stairs. Cars screech to a halt, and their doors open and close with determined thunks, thunks, and gusts of hot air. . . . One harried-looking fellow comes up panting, shouting "World Bank, World Bank!" The echo is taken up by the corridor, by the dust and all four walls, by the floor, all the way down. It curves up from below and booms over the roof and into the stagnant air of the sterile city, settling over the Civil Secretariat like a mushroom cloud. The Margalla Hills form a solemn backdrop for this production.

Inside the Civil Secretariat, doors bang and telephones ring. Orders are shouted. File drawers are closed, cupboard doors are opened. Cuffs and collars, such as they are, are straightened, papers are tidied up, hair is slicked down, and all spring to attention and take up their positions as the members of a new World Bank team march in, clasping bursting briefcases. High heels clicking sharply, dressed in natty pinstriped suits and well-tailored skirts, and with exquisite tans, they come, they come, the experts from the World Bank, agendas in hand. . . .

. I float down the stairs, touching the stained, gray, unhappy walls with all my love—there seems to be no hope for them—and glide out the door into the mellow sunshine. There are flowers everywhere, for it is spring in Punjab, and flowers have burst forth from each nook and cranny, anywhere there is a spoonful of mud, a little moisture and some sunshine, this is all they need. There are the sun-colored marigolds, dahlias in every shade of red, from the palest pink to deep as blood, serene little daisies, poppies, pansies, snapdragons, roses. All, in the words of the English poet Wordsworth,

> . . . fluttering and dancing in the breeze. . .
> Ten thousand saw I at a glance,
> Tossing their heads in sprightly dance. . . .

And my heart also "with pleasure fills" to see this sight. And to see the rows upon rows upon rows of that princess of all the spring flowers: the sweet pea. Pink, purple, lilac, lavender. Magenta, maroon. Ivory, baby-blue, gray. Perched on their stalks of pale green, delicate tendrils curving sensuously and lovingly around the cane stalks that valiantly hold them up while the nightingale sings, the grass shines a brilliant green, and honeybees buzz from flower to flower drunk on the sweet nectar. And this is just during the day. The moon hasn't even come out yet! Wait until you see it rise full and glorious; then your faith will truly be revived. In the words of my favorite poet,

> Jalwagah-e-visaal ki sham'en
> Voh bujha bhi chuke agar, to kya?
> Chaand ko gul karen to ham janen.
>
> (What if they put the candles out
> That light love's throne-room? let them put out
> The moon, then we shall know their power.)[1]

> —Faiz Ahmad Faiz

I flag down a taxi and make my way home to my children.

---

1. This translation is from Faiz Ahmed Faiz, *Poems by Faiz,* translated by V. G. Kierman (Lahore: UNESCO, 1971) p. 191 (originally published in 1971 by George Allen & Unwin Ltd.), part of UNESCO Collection of Representative Works, Pakistan Series.

Epilogue:
The Beat Goes On . . .

In March 1998, as the midterm evaluations of the Social Action Program (SAP) were documenting its disappointing results, the World Bank announced the continuation of its International Development Association's support for the program by extending a credit to the Government of Pakistan. This credit, which financed the SAP's costs on the basis of strategies agreed to between the Bank and the Government of Pakistan, was the main support for the government's provincial SAP projects.

The World Bank's decision was based on the determination that the SAP had made a substantial impact, including higher school enrollment for girls, particularly in rural areas; increased immunization for children; and increased family planning. Other substantial achievements of the SAP were noted as follows:

- There had been an increase in the total expenditures for social-sector programs, from 1.8 to 2.1 percent of the annual budget.
- Funds were being released in a more timely fashion.
- There was now a greater awareness of the importance of the social sectors.

The World Bank determined that continued support for Pakistan's SAP would allow the government to build on these initial positive results and further increase school enrollments and literacy rates, provide basic health services for rural areas, reduce mortality, and increase access to safe water supplies and sanitation.

In early 1999, the Pakistani newspaper *Dawn* reported that "the World Bank has assured the government that the Bank will provide $500 million to Pakistan during the current financial year. Officials [of the Bank] said that as soon as the IMF's Executive Board meets . . . and approves the $1.6 billion . . . program, $500 million will be extended to Pakistan by the World Bank." The paper went on to say that "the World Bank mission assured the minister of their support for this project . . . [and] that the project was very important to the World Bank Country Assistance Strategy for Pakistan."[1]

A few months later, *Dawn* reported that the World Bank would provide $400 million under a separate technical assistance program (called the Human Resource Development Program) to the Government of Punjab for improving health facilities in the province. The provincial health minister, who disclosed this information at a joint press conference with the health secretary, said that "the provincial government has chalked out a comprehensive plan to rectify the present health system with a view to provide better medical facilities to the masses."[2]

In 2001, the World Bank gave $350 million for the Structural Adjustment Credit Project and then added $90 million in 2003 for the Structural Adjustment Credit to Sindh and the North-West Frontier Province (NWFP), and for Community Infrastructure and the National Housing Authority Strengthening Credit to the NWFP, for "subnational activities to complement the Social Action Program."

The SAP ended in 2003.

In 2003, the World Bank gave $37 million exclusively for the Pakistani health sector to help control HIV/AIDS; $9.25 million of this amount was a grant. This project ended in 2009. Also in 2003, bilateral assistance to the nation's social sector included $250 million from the United States and £200 million from the United Kingdom.

In 2004, the Pakistan Public Sector Capacity Building Project received $55 million from the World Bank; the Bank also loaned Pakistan $300 million for the First Poverty Reduction Support Credit. The project's objective was to build a safety net for poor people, including education and health. It was to help the federal government make policy and institutional reforms and improve governance.

In 2006, the World Bank extended $350 million to Pakistan under the Second Poverty Reduction Support Credit, of which 23 percent was for health.

---

1. As reported in the Internet edition of *Dawn*, January 7, 1999.
2. As reported in the Internet edition of *Dawn*, April 9, 1999.

In 2007, the Bank approved a $451 million package of assistance to improve education in Punjab and Sindh, enhance irrigation in Punjab, implement reforms in education and health in the NWFP, and eradicate polio ($21.4 million) in the country. In announcing this package of assistance, the Bank's country director noted that "Pakistan has in recent years made good progress towards improving human development indicators and reducing poverty and vulnerability."[3]

In 2009, the U.S. government approved the Enhanced Partnership with Pakistan Act (the Kerry-Lugar-Berman Bill), which allocates $7.5 billion to Islamabad over five years for the development of social services.

And so the beat goes on. . . .

3. World Bank, Press Release 2007/436/SAR, 2007.

Index

Accelerated Health Program, 125
Aga Khan Medical College, 92
AIDS/HIV, 68, 91, 196
Allama Iqbal Open University (AIOU)
  Bureau of University Extensions and
  Special Programs, 45–55
Alma-Ata Declaration, 35–36, 66, 78
Armed Forces Nursing Service, 35
Asian Development Bank, 9n18, 22n3,
  29, 74, 103, 104, 119, 120

Balochistan Province, development in,
  17
Baqai Medical College, 92
Bengal (India), women's literacy rates in,
  160
Bhutto, Benazir, 25
Bhutto, Zulfikar Ali, 113, 132
Bihar (India), women's literacy rates in,
  160
Birdsall, Nancy, 2, 7–8
birth attendants. *See* traditional birth
  attendants (TBAs)
birth control. *See* contraceptive training
  and services

Canada, Pakistani workers in, 92
Canadian International Development
  Agency (CIDA): and midwives, 27;

and peripheral health workers, 29;
  representatives from, 14, 16, 18, 20;
  SAP support from, 11; training
  proposals for, 136
capacity building: as donor activity, 6;
  for health services delivery, 29–30;
  and social-sector indicators, 134
Center for Development and Population
  Activities, 97
Center for Global Development, 2
child health centers. *See* maternal and
  child health centers
children, vaccination of, 159–60
CIDA. *See* Canadian International
  Development Agency
College of Physicians & Surgeons
  Pakistan, 111, 112
community health workers, 27
Community Infrastructure program, 196
community medicine, 36
contraceptive training and services: area-
  based approach to, 182, 185; delivery
  of, 178–86; failure of, 65–66;
  intrauterine devices, 85, 86;
  Inundation Strategy, 64, 65, 185;
  pedagogic strategy for, 49–55; in
  project completion reports, 134–35;
  and regional training institutes,
  85–86; in Sindh SAP proposal, 128;

199

contraceptive training and services
(*continued*)
target-oriented approach to, 64;
women's involvement in, 65–66,
75–76, 135, 178–86
Control of Diarrheal Disease Program,
28, 91, 109, 147
Country Assistance Strategy of 1994
(World Bank), 17
Country Strategy Interim Report 1992
(World Bank), 16–17
curricula: at AIOU, 47; development of,
97, 129, 130–31; for family welfare
workers, 81, 86, 89; health education,
49–50; immunization programs,
175–76; medical, 85; nursing, 35, 36

Dawn (newspaper): on Pakistan's
motivation for SAP, 5; on SAP failure,
4; on World Bank support for SAP,
195–96
Demographic and Health Survey,
Pakistan, 134
Devolution Plan, Musharraf's, 61
diarrheal disease. *See* Control of
Diarrheal Disease Program
drug procurement professionals, 113–15
drug trafficking, 53

Easterly, William, 2
East India Company, 112
education: adult education in rural areas,
47–48; health education, 49–50; high
school matriculation certificates, 45,
46, 81. *See also* training
The End of Poverty (Sachs), 12
Enhanced Partnership with Pakistan Act
of 2009 (Kerry-Lugar-Berman Bill), 2,
6, 197
Expanded Program on Immunization
(EPI), 4, 28, 147, 159, 161–63, 175

Family Health Project: data on, 189; and
Pakistani workers in Middle East, 107;
and provincial health departments,

104, 117, 119, 121; purpose of, 103;
and traditional birth attendants, 106;
training through, 41
Family Planning Association, 131
family-planning programs. *See*
contraceptive training and services
family welfare centers, 74, 81, 87
family welfare workers (FWWs): criteria
for job category, 32; and PNC, 34–35;
in Population Welfare Program, 86,
87, 88; training of, 28, 66, 74, 81, 86,
125
Fatima Jinnah Medical College, 165
Federally Administered Tribal Areas, 53
fertility rates, 65, 179
First Poverty Reduction Support Credit,
196
Five-Year Plans in Pakistan, 4, 64, 66
French, Howard, 1
FWWs. *See* family welfare workers

Gandhi, Indira, 65
Gilani, Yousuf Raza, 91

Hasan, Arif, 8
Health Department, 27, 74, 158
Health Education Program, 49
health educators, 27
"health for all" slogan, 78
Health Manpower Development Project,
103
Health Ministry, 36, 62, 99–100
health services delivery systems. *See*
horizontal health services delivery
systems; vertical health services
delivery systems
Health System Improvement Program,
114
health visitors. *See* lady health visitors
health workers. *See* peripheral health
workers; *specific workers (e.g.,
traditional birth attendants)*
Hepatitis Control Program, Prime
Minister's, 91
heroin, 53

high school matriculation certificates, 45, 46, 81
HIV/AIDS, 68, 91, 196
horizontal health services delivery systems, 67–68, 75. *See also* vertical health services delivery systems
hospital overcrowding, 87
Human Resource Development Program, 196

illiteracy. *See* literacy rates
immunization programs, 154–77; and director of provincial health services, 157–61; evaluation teams for, 159, 160–61, 162; Expanded Program on Immunization (EPI), 4, 28, 147, 159, 161–63, 175; individual accounts of workers, 164–69; Peshawar, 155–57; "smiling disease," 172–74; vaccination camp in Mardan, 161–64
India, women's literacy rates in, 160
infant mortality rates, 135, 173, 191
Institute of Medical Sciences, Pakistan, 25
International Aid Consortium, 22, 22*n*3, 126, 134, 152, 191
International Development Association, 195
International Federation for Family Planning, 131
International Monetary Fund (IMF), 196
"intrahistoria," 10

Jinnah Postgraduate Medical Center, 94
Johns Hopkins University, 97, 130

Kardar, Shahid, 4, 5
Kerry-Lugar-Berman Bill. *See* Enhanced Partnership with Pakistan Act
King Edward Medical College, 105

lady health visitors: criteria for job category, 32; and PNC, 34–35; private practices of, 147; training of, 28, 46, 68, 85, 91, 131

Levine, Ruth, 2
Liaquat National Hospital, 44
literacy rates, 45, 108, 160

malaria and malaria control workers, 28, 68, 91, 113–14
male nurses, 43–44
Mardan, vaccination camp in, 161–64
maternal and child health centers, 91, 93–94, 100
maternal mortality rates, 77, 167, 173
medical technicians, 27, 91, 125
Middle East, Pakistani workers in: doctors, 92, 111, 113; peripheral health workers, 30, 41, 86, 88, 107–8, 137, 176
midwives, 27, 105. *See also* traditional birth attendants (TBAs)
Ministry of Women Development, 56–57
mortality rates, 77, 135, 167, 173, 191
Musharraf, Pervez, 22*n*2, 61

National Housing Authority Strengthening Credit, 196
National Impact Survey, 65
National Institutes of Health, 33, 34–35
New York Times on foreign development assistance, 1
Ninth Five-Year Plan in Pakistan, 4
nongovernmental organizations (NGOs), 128, 129, 131
No Objection Certificates for foreign travel, 40, 147
North-West Frontier Province (NWFP): immunization program in, 154–77; Structural Adjustment Credit Project in, 196
nurses, 27, 32, 33–44
Nursing Council. *See* Pakistan Nursing Council

Orangi Pilot Project, 8
Overseas Development Assistance (ODA) Program, 190, 191, 192

Pakistan Medical and Dental Council, 92

Pakistan Nursing Council (PNC), 13, 33–44; as certifying body, 32, 86, 91; curriculum of, 81; nurses, vanishing, 39–44; standards in, 39–40

Pakistan Paramedical Council, 28

Pakistan People's Party, 113

Pakistan Public Sector Capacity Building Project, 196

Pakistan Railways, 75

paramedics, 27–29

People's Open University, 45

peripheral health workers, 26–31, 45, 91. *See also specific workers (e.g., traditional birth attendants)*

Peshawar, immunization program in, 155–57

Planning and Development Department: and Overseas Development Assistance Program, 192; and Punjab SAP proposal, 142, 143–45, 149, 151, 152–53; and Sindh SAP proposal, 131–32, 138

Planning and Development Ministry, 14, 56, 64, 66, 121, 141

Planning Commission, 56, 60

PNC. *See* Pakistan Nursing Council

polio eradication, 197

population growth rates, 64–66, 179

Population Welfare Division (PWD), 64–80; population growth, 64–66; and regional training institutes, 28, 81; renaming of, 179; and vertical programs, 66–68; visiting chief of, 68–80

Population Welfare Ministry, 28, 179

Population Welfare Program: donor assistance for, 68; and family welfare workers, 86, 87, 88; and regional training institutes, 85, 96; and SAP, 74, 132, 178–79; training project of, 136; as vertical program, 66, 67

pregnancy prevention. *See* contraceptive training and services

Pressler Amendment of 1990, 74

Primary Health Care Conference of 1978, 36, 66

Primary Health Care Model, 26, 36, 66, 99–100

provincial health departments, 13, 99–121; director of provincial health services, 157–61; doctor's dilemma in, 110–12; drug procurement professionals, 113–15; and health workers, 106–9; medical profession, history of, 112–13; Provincial Directorate of Health Services, 99, 104; routine business of, 109–10; and vaccinations, 174

Public Sector Capacity Building Project, 196

Punjab Province: provincial health department in, 99, 100; regional training institutes in, 81, 82

Punjab Social Action Program Proposal, 142–53. *See also* Sindh Social Action Program (SAP) Proposal

PWD. *See* Population Welfare Division

regional training institutes (RTIs), 81–98

Royal College of Physicians, 112

Royal College of Surgeons, 112

rural areas: adult education in, 47–48; doctors in, 111; family welfare workers in, 81; health centers in, 3, 26, 66–67, 100, 124; health services delivery to, 11, 17, 27, 30, 99–100; peripheral health workers in, 29, 45; population policy for, 179; and provincial health directorates, 35; rural/urban disparities, 39

Sachs, Jeffrey, 12

Safe Motherhood Initiative, 105

SAP. *See* Punjab Social Action Program Proposal; Sindh Social Action Program Proposal; Social Action Program

Saudi Arabia, Pakistani workers in, 107. *See also* Middle East, Pakistani workers in

School of Public Health, 94, 96
Scott, Paul, x
Second Five-Year Plan in Pakistan, 64, 66
Second Poverty Reduction Support Credit, 196
sexual harassment, 94–95
Shah, N. M., 65
Sharif, Nawaz, 22, 22*n*2, 25
Sharif, Shahbaz, 25
Sindh Province: development in, 17; Education Department of, 124; Structural Adjustment Credit Project in, 196
Sindh Social Action Program (SAP) Proposal, 122–41; committee for, 122, 124; faulty programs, 134–41; program material for, 128–34; rehash of material in, 122–28. *See also* Punjab Social Action Program (SAP) proposal
"smiling disease," 172–74, 184
Social Action Program (SAP): achievements of, 195; author's involvement in, 10–12; background on, 3–4; Birdsall on, 7–8; communication within, 96; conclusion of, 196; and *Country Strategy Interim Report 1992,* 17; education services in, 45, 46; and EPI, 159; failure of, 4, 8–10; federal adviser to, 14, 16, 19–23; Federal Committee of, 11, 134, 145, 152, 153; final recommendations for, 187–94; human resource development of, 107; Pakistan's government proposal for, 10; and Population Welfare Program, 74, 178–79; and provincial health departments, 99, 102, 158–59; training under, 76, 85, 124, 177; and Women's Division, 57, 59; and women's education, 160; World Bank support for, 3–4, 11, 13, 178–86, 193–96. *See also* Punjab Social Action Program proposal; Sindh Social Action Program proposal

Staying On (Scott), x
Structural Adjustment Credit Project, 196

tetanus, neonatal, 172–74, 184
traditional birth attendants (TBAs): and Family Health Project, 106; program evaluation, 108–9; training of, 27, 76–77, 79, 105, 118, 119, 124–25, 137. *See also* midwives
training: regional training institutes (RTIs), 81–98; UNICEF and WHO training project proposals, 136; World Bank support for, 41, 42, 167. *See also* contraceptive training and services; *specific types of health personnel*
Tuberculosis and HIV/AIDS Program, 68
Tuberculosis Control Program workers, 28, 91

Unamuno, Miguel de, 10
UNDP. *See* United Nations Development Program
UNICEF: and EPI, 28, 161; and faulty programs, 134–41; and midwives, 27; and Punjab SAP proposal, 142, 144–45, 153; SAP support from, 11; and Sindh SAP proposal, 122–24, 129–30, 132–33, 137–39, 141; and traditional birth attendants, 27; training project proposals for, 136
United Kingdom: Department for International Development, 29, 30, 42, 105, 114; Pakistani doctors in, 113; social sector support for Pakistan from, 196
United Nations Decade of Women (1975–85), 56
United Nations Development Program (UNDP), 11, 123, 132–33, 141
United Nations Fund for Population Activities, 74
United States: aid to Pakistan from, 6, 196; government stipends in, 89; Pakistani workers in, 92, 111, 113; technical assistance from, 7, 91;

United States (*continued*)
vaccination education in, 160; visas
to, 19
United States Agency for International
Development (USAID): and
curriculum development, 97;
developing countries' dependence on,
ix; Health System Improvement
Program funding, 114; Pakistan
Mission of, 3; peripheral health worker
program funding from, 27, 29, 30, 42,
91, 105; PWD funding from, 74; and
Sindh SAP Proposal, 134
University of Hawaii, 27
urban areas: doctors in, 92; health
services delivery to, 27, 35, 36, 66,
99, 111; hospital overcrowding in,
87; midwives in, 27; rural/urban
disparities, 39; vaccinations in, 159
USAID. *See* United States Agency for
International Development

vaccines. *See* immunization programs
vasectomies, 79
vertical health services delivery systems,
66–68, 74–75, 110, 119, 159, 175.
See also horizontal health services
delivery systems
visas, 19

Water and Power Development Authority,
75
WHO. *See* World Health Organization
Wolfensohn, James, 1
women: and contraceptive services,
65–66, 75–76, 135, 178–86; education
and literacy of, 160; in immunization

programs, 154–77; as peripheral
health workers, 26–31, 45, 91; social
standing of, 135; "women in
development" mantra, x, 56. *See also
specific types of health workers (e.g.,
lady health visitors)*
Women in Development (WID), 14–16,
18
Women's Division, 13, 56–63
World Bank: assistance packages,
196–97; changes in, 1; Country
Assistance Strategy of 1994, 17;
Country Assistance Strategy for
Pakistan, 196; *Country Strategy
Interim Report 1992,* 16–17;
developing countries' dependence on,
ix; Overseas Development Assistance,
110–11; and peripheral health workers,
29; and Population Welfare Program,
178–79; PWD funding from, 74;
representatives from, 20–21, 23, 34;
SAP support from, 3–4, 11, 13, 178–86,
193–96; Sindh SAP Proposal, 134;
training support from, 41, 42, 167;
women in development funding
from, 56
World Food Program, 28
World Health Organization (WHO): and
EPI workers, 28; and midwives, 27;
and nurses, 39; and paramedics,
27–29; and provincial health departments, 105; and traditional birth
attendants, 27, 119; training project
proposals for, 136

Zimbabwe, contraceptive training in,
54–55